Teaching and Learning with ICT in the Primary School

...antly
vhich
ms of
rning
d the

have
based
imilar
with
ways
rning

:thods
ichers
her to

ersity.
inator
joint
editor of the Routledge series *Learning to Teach in the Secondary School.*
John Meadows is Senior Lecturer in Primary Education at South Bank
University. He has been involved in ICT projects such as Computer Pals
Across the World and the NCET Communique Project. Both authors are
members of TeachNet UK and MirandaNet.

Teaching and Learning with ICT in the Primary School

Edited by
Marilyn Leask and John Meadows

London and New York

First published 2000
by RoutledgeFalmer
11 New Fetter Lane, London EC4P 4EE

Simultaneously published in the USA and Canada
by RoutledgeFalmer
29 West 35th Street, New York, NY 10001

RoutledgeFalmer is an imprint of the Taylor & Francis Group

Typeset in Goudy by Florence Production, Stoodleigh, Devon
Printed and bound in Great Britain by St Edmundsbury Press,
Bury St Edmunds, Suffolk

British Library Cataloguing in Publication Data
A catalogue record for this book is available
from the British Library.

Library of Congress Cataloging in Publication Data
Teaching and learning with ICT in the primary school /
    [edited by] Marilyn Leask and John Meadows.
        p. cm.
    Includes bibliographical references and index.
    ISBN 0–415–21504–8 (hbk.). – ISBN 0–415–21505–6 (pbk.)
    1. Education, Elementary–Great Britain–Computer-assisted
instruction. 2. Internet (Computer network) in education–Great
Britain. 3. Telecommunication in education–Great Britain.
I. Leask, Marilyn, 1950– . II. Meadows, John.
LB1028.5.T382 2000
372.133'4'0941–dc21   99–40326
                                                          CIP

ISBN 0–415–21504–8 (hbk)
ISBN 0–415–21505–6 (pbk)

Contents

Illustrations

Figures

Tables

Activities

Contributors

Ray Barker was Director of the National Literacy Association Docklands Learning Acceleration Project. He is now Managing Director of Advantage Learning Systems UK Ltd.

Lyn Dawes taught Science in secondary schools before re-training to teach in the primary sector. As Science Co-ordinator at a middle school, she carried out action research with staff from the University of East Anglia and the Open University to evaluate the quality of children's talk whilst working in groups at the computer (Spoken Language and New Technology (SLANT) Project). This research developed into the Talk, Reasoning and Computers (TRAC) Project and continues in the Raising Achievement Through Thinking with Language Skills (RATTLS) Project. She is now a Research Student at De Montfort University, studying the introduction of ICT into schools, with a particular interest in the professional development of teachers.

Glen Franklin taught in Tower Hamlets and Greenwich before becoming Assistant Director of the National Literacy Association Docklands Learning Acceleration Project. She is now Literacy Consultant for the London Borough of Tower Hamlets.

Hamish Fraser taught for ten years in inner city London schools. He taught for five years in Lambeth where he was co-ordinator of maths in a primary school. He has considerable experience of ICT developed through his work as a teacher and in his present role as lecturer in maths and ICT in De Montfort University, Bedford.

Gordon James has been involved in primary education for the past twenty-six years, as a classroom teacher in both South Wales and Suffolk and for six years as an advisory teacher for science and technology. Since working as science and ICT co-ordinator at Wickham Market Primary School he has become deeply involved with the integration of computer-based communications into the primary curriculum.

Darren Leafe has worked in both the primary and the secondary sector and has been involved in a number of national and international curriculum projects using ICT. His interests include the effective use of new technologies in education and he is currently responsible for all content development at NETLinc, Lincolnshire's response to the UK Government's National Grid for Learning (NGfL) initiative.

Marilyn Leask is principal lecturer in education at De Montfort University. She has been involved in a number of national and international projects exploring the potential of ICT to enhance teaching and learning and to support teachers' professional development. She is chair of TeacherNet UK (*http://www.teachernetuk.org.uk*) and is director of the Learning School project in the European School Net initiative (*http://www.eun.org*). The website for the secondary text (*Learning to Teach with ICT in the Secondary School*, Routledge) accompanying this text is on *http://www.ioe.ac.uk/lie/ict/*.

Avril Loveless is a senior lecturer in IT in Education at the University of Brighton. She has been a primary teacher and advisory teacher for IT in primary schools. Her particular areas of interest are pedagogy and IT and the creative use of IT in the visual arts.

John Meadows was a primary school teacher in inner London schools for thirteen years before becoming an advisory teacher for primary science. Although he is currently teaching primary science to trainee teachers at South Bank University's Education Department, most of his research and publications are on the theme of ICT in Education. He has been working with the internet for over ten years, developing projects and networks with schools and universities.

Neil Mercer helped establish the Centre for Language and Communications at the Open University, where he has carried out applied educational research and developed courses on language and literacy for teachers and other audiences.

Ken Millar has taught in Tower Hamlets primary schools for fourteen years, covering both key stages and holding a job as ICT co-ordinator in school. He is currently early years co-ordinator at Hermitage Primary School, where he also uses ICT to promote links between the school and others in Europe, through a Comenius funded project.

Jane Mitra is an experienced teacher, Deputy Director of the Nuffield Primary Design and Technology Project, Home–School Co-ordinator for Parents Information Network and Academic Consultant for the Learning School project.

Norbert Pachler works at the Institute of Education, University of London, as Lecturer in Languages in Education with responsibility for the

Secondary PGCE in Modern Foreign Languages and the MA in Modern Languages in Education. His research interests include modern foreign languages teaching and learning, comparative education as well as the application of new technologies in teaching and learning. He has published in these fields.

John Potter is currently Senior Lecturer in Primary ICT at the University of East London, teaching on both the PGCE and Masters programmes. Before that, he worked for two years as an IT advisor in the London Borough of Newham. He has substantial primary teaching experience in inner London schools, having taught for ten years across both key stages, mainly at Harbinger Primary School on the Isle of Dogs.

John Sampson is Co-ordinator for Initial Teacher Education at De Montfort University. He has a particular interest in primary school history and is a member of the Ginn History Team. Previously he taught in inner London primary schools and spent two years as Inner London Education Authority's Primary Advisory Teacher for History.

Terry Taylor is a visual artist who has a commitment to the development of art education. He uses photography and digital technology as tools in his work and is very experienced in working as an artist in residence in schools and galleries.

Rupert Wegerif is a research fellow in the Centre for Language and Communications at the Open University. His main research interests are the use of computers to support discussion, collaborative learning with CMC and the role of reason in education. He is co-editor with Peter Scrimshaw of the collection of articles 'Computers and talk in the primary classroom' (Multilingual Matters, Clevedon).

Preface

The 'C' in ICT (Information and Communication Technology) stands for communications. Linking computers through telecommunications networks allows teachers and pupils around the world to send text and pictures to each other with ease. Through computers connected to the internet, you and your pupils can communicate with pupils, teachers, subject experts and people from all walks of life in a way never before possible. Even where the resources are not obtainable in schools, teachers are using resources available through the local communities; for example, in homes, public libraries and local companies, to gain access to international electronic educational networks. So the networked computer-based technology now available is different in its application in the classroom to the lone computer, which in many classrooms has been an underused resource for years. In this text, we introduce you to a range of ways that teachers are using ICT to support and extend the teaching and learning opportunities in their classrooms.

In writing this book, we are very aware that practice in teaching and learning in UK schools could change radically if the teaching profession grasped the opportunities available through the use of the internet and other forms of communication technology; for example, digital cameras, digital video cameras, scanners, video conferencing, voice-operated software and read-back options on software. But we are also aware that there is political pressure on teachers to move swiftly to more internet and web-based work in schools. Teachers around the world are feeling this pressure as governments produce statements about how their teaching force is to work with this sort of technology. In the UK this is demonstrated through the National Grid for Learning[1] and the Virtual Teacher Centre. Similar European initiatives can be accessed through the European SchoolNet site[2] and Commonwealth initiatives through the CENSE site.[3]

It is not possible for us, in a book this size, to cover all aspects of ICT. We do not cover every curriculum area in the same detail – we hope that the book will give teachers ideas which they can adapt and apply in their own situation. Nor do we cover special educational needs in depth. However, this is covered in the companion text, *Learning to Teach with ICT in the Secondary School*. There are many controversies over the use of ICT in schools. The intention of this book is to share ideas. Teachers wishing to enter professional debates about the use of ICT in schools are invited to join the online professional communities which are introduced in Chapter 1.

We believe that there is convincing evidence that the opportunities now available can significantly enhance pupil learning in, for example, the areas of knowledge and skill acquisition as well as concept and attitude development.

However, teachers will need to work and learn together to establish high-quality and new professional practice. Schools need to provide technical support so that equipment can be relied upon, and a school intranet so that teachers can, by downloading key web-based materials they need to have available for lessons, be sure that resources found on the web can be available at the time they want them for their classes. If teachers have always to plan an alternative lesson when they are using technology in case it does not work, then progress in using the technology will be slow.

Schools where staff are mutually supportive of each other's developing knowledge and skills are more likely to be successful in tackling these challenges than those where knowledge about computing is seen to be the province of a select few. It has to be acknowledged that some people feel the need to exert power over others by denigrating their lack of knowledge and where this situation exists, development in the school will be weak.

In this book we introduce ideas which have been tried and tested in innovative schools around the UK and abroad. The school in which you find yourself may not be able to offer you some of the opportunities which you read about here. However, you may find that working through networks of colleagues, some of whom you may find on the internet, provides you with opportunities to extend your skills and knowledge in the area of ICT.

We hope you enjoy reading this book and we thank our colleagues who have contributed their ideas thus making this book possible.

Marilyn Leask and John Meadows
January 2000

Notes

1   The National Grid for Learning (*http://www.ngfl.gov.uk/*) encompasses a range of developments by the government. The Virtual Teacher Centre website is one example and is found on *http://vtc.ngfl.gov.uk*

2   The European SchoolNet can be found on *http://www.eun.org*. The 'partner networks' button you will find on the front page will lead you to a map of Europe surrounded by symbols for the networks from each country *http://www.en.eun.org/countries/countries.html*

3   The Commonwealth site (*http://www.col.org*) is developing a Commonwealth Electronic Network for Schools and Education which can be found on *http://www.col.org/cense*

Acknowledgements

We should like to take this opportunity to thank all the teachers and other colleagues with whom we have worked who have shared their ideas, successes and difficulties in using ICT in classrooms with us over the years. These teachers, a number of whom have provided contributions to this book, are pioneers in the area of using information and communications technologies in primary education. Without their imagination and innovative practice, this book could never have been written.

In particular, we thank our colleagues in the TeacherNetUK (*http:// www.teachernetuk.org.uk*) and MirandaNet (*http://www.mirandanet.com*) online communities. Many of the contributors are members of these communities. We invite readers to join us online to carry on debates about the use of ICT in education and to develop new ideas. Members are invited to contribute to the process of lobbying government and industry to develop policies and products which support the teaching and learning process using ICT.

We also thank the companies who through their commitment to education have supported some of the activities and development of TeacherNet and MirandaNet. In particular we thank Oracle Corporation, Sun Microsystems, Cisco Systems and Xemplar.

We should also like to thank our families for their support and the team of staff at Routledge, Anna Clarkson, Jude Bowen, Lyn Maddox who have worked on the production of this book.

Marilyn Leask and John Meadows
January 2000

A Note to Readers

A website has been set up to enable readers to access the websites listed in each chapter. This can be found on

http://www.dmu.ac.uk/Faculties/HSS/SEDU/primaryict.html

Inevitably some of the sites which we reference may cease to be operational during the lifetime of this book but we felt the gains in including website addresses (Uniform Resource Locators or URLs) outweighed the disadvantages.

Chapter I

Why use ICT?

John Meadows and Marilyn Leask

Introduction

This chapter looks at a variety of answers to the question raised in the title: Why use ICT? There are many reasons why ICT is important in everyday life, since computers and associated technologies are increasingly necessary in all businesses and commercial concerns. But it does not logically follow that computers should also be used in primary schools. In some countries in Europe, in Germany for example, few computers are used in education before the secondary phase. Yet we could not identify a lack of industry skills following from this. So why should teachers and children in British primary schools spend time learning skills which may be out of date by the time they need to use them for work? Can it be said that learning with ICT in the primary school helps to develop in children the sorts of transferable skills, such as problem-solving and communication, which will be useful to them in the future?

In this book we do not claim to cover all aspects of ICT in the primary school,[1] instead we focus particularly on areas of practice in classrooms where the communicative potential of ICT is still to be developed. We consider the reasons for using ICT from a number of perspectives, including educational, as well as political, professional and personal ones. We include a case study of an online community of teachers who use ICT extensively both in their own schools and in a wider international context – these are the MirandaNet scholars. We examine the reasons why these teachers are motivated towards using ICT.

The notion of an audience for children's writing is explored as a major reason for using the communicative power of ICT. Children as creative users of ICT is an important issue which is also considered briefly. Other issues raised in this chapter include literacy and ICT, numeracy and ICT, although these areas are explored in more detail in later chapters. Some of the tools associated with using ICT are also introduced briefly, with the intention of developing many of them further in later chapters.

Objectives

By the end of this chapter you should have:

• an understanding of the recent background to ICT in schools, business and society;
• an awareness of some of the factors which motivate teachers towards the use of ICT;
• recognition of the reasons why schools must take on board new technologies;
• an awareness of some of the contentious issues surrounding ICT in schools.

Background

Information and Communication Technology is a relatively new subject area for schools. Until recently, primary schools used IT (Information Technology), both as a subject in its own right and as a tool to support other curriculum areas. In recent times, the UK government, through the four Education Departments in England, Wales, Scotland and Northern Ireland, has expressed great interest in the Information Superhighway[2] and the National Grid for Learning.[3]

Funding offered to schools, both for the purchase of hardware and software and for training purposes, has followed consultation papers. So the push towards ICT comes partly from government, but it is also arising from the interests of teachers and pupils, from the needs of computer companies and educational internet service providers and from a general awareness in society of the influence and importance of new technologies.

Evidence still indicates that the majority of teachers use ICT only occasionally and often under a sense of obligation rather than conviction of its value as an educational medium (Goldstein 1995–96).

Since the launch of the Superhighways for Education challenge, the government has made sensible plans to create the infrastructure of the National Grid for Learning, provide the resources and train the teachers. This grand strategy is based on research into good practice (DfEE 1997a and b; BECTA 1998). Senior management teams now must grasp the initiative and make the most of these serious opportunities to enrich teaching and learning because the launch of the National Grid for Learning presents a significant challenge to the traditional role of teachers.

The media suggests that the internet, and especially the world wide web, is a solution to all the needs of Education. However, there are many ways in which ICT can impact on the teaching and learning process. The extent of the impact of communication technologies depends on teachers changing their practice in classrooms. Some teachers are of course resistant to change, but one can sympathise with them since so much of the change in Education can be regarded as retrograde in the wider context. Teachers who have experienced the vagaries of Conservative and Labour Governments, of local and national initiatives, can be perhaps forgiven for a certain amount of cynicism when faced with ever more changes. But it does begin to seem that the internet is bringing a new way of life to many people at many different levels in both work and leisure, as well as in the educational sectors of society.

Reasons for using ICT

There are a number of categories of reasons why ICT is an important teaching and learning tool, we have divided these into five groups:

- Political
- Personal/professional
- Professional/pupils' needs
- Professional/curriculum
- Professional/educational theory.

Political reasons

The government wants all pupils to have the necessary skills, hence their teachers need to know and understand the importance of ICT. British primary schools have been fortunate to be supported by government funds to purchase computers, although many enlightened Local Education Authorities (LEAs) have also supported schools through hardware and software provision. Current priorities in Education include the development by pupils of basic skills, not only in literacy and numeracy, but also in the more transferable skills, which industry and government advisors suggest are needed by all in the modern information society. It is now suggested that Britain is, or should be, a 'Learning Society', one in which all adults expect to need retraining and updating on a regular basis and the notion of 'lifelong learning' is common and accepted. These skills include the use of ICT as well as problem-solving and communication. Close co-operation is now expected between education and the business world, with partnerships offering mutual benefits to all who share in these joint enterprises.

British Government Education Departments are pushing teachers towards a training in ICT (see Appendix, p. 249), with the result that 'by 2002 serving teachers should feel confident, and be competent to teach, using ICT within the curriculum' (DfEE 1997a).

Even when in opposition, the Labour Party expressed its interest in ICT by commissioning the Stevenson Report, which examined the state of ICT in British schools and made extensive recommendations for future initiatives.

The Stevenson Report discussed the context of ICT in schools as follows:

> ICT in schools works in different ways.
> We suggest that in addressing its effects it is important to recognise that ICT may be used for a wide range of purposes:
>
> - to administer schools;
> - to train students in skills which they will need in further education and ongoing learning throughout the rest of their lives and for their future jobs, e.g. word processing, computer programming, etc.;
> - to provide access to information and communication outside the classroom walls, e.g. video conferencing with students in other countries, using the internet, etc.;
> - to support teacher development, e.g. through external networks;
> - to support and potentially transform the learning/teaching process in many and diverse ways.[4]

Personal/professional reasons

Many teachers use ICT in their own personal lives, as do many other adults in our society. Teachers may do their personal accounts using spreadsheets, they may write letters and articles using word processing, they may enjoy computer games, or surfing art or antique collections on the Web. But there are also professional reasons linked to personal ones which may affect educators. The need for professional development may be a reason for further use of ICT, especially if this is connected to promotion. Professional development through ICT as well as about ICT is now becoming more common, as Inservice trainers linked to the National Grid for Learning are urged to provide some of their training courses through ICT, e.g. using interactive CD-ROM technology. Many traditional training courses provided by higher education are also turning to ICT for cheaper and more efficient delivery, so teachers are again given the opportunity to achieve personal and professional goals through the implementation of ICT.

Many teachers also join professional organisations linked to education, partly as a personal interest and partly for professional reasons. Subject groups like the Association for Science Education (ASE) have well developed websites providing information, publications, advice and news to the community of science educators. Although much of this service is also provided through traditional paper methods, it is becoming common to use the website, not only for information, but also as a means of interacting, e.g. when booking attendance at the annual conference. Many educational organisations now use ICT regularly to supplement the paper-based communications. One example in the research field is the British Educational Research Association (BERA).[5]

Other groups which run websites for teachers, as either charitable trusts or limited companies, are MirandaNet and TeacherNetUK.[6] Figure 1.1 illustrates the variety of websites available for a range of educational purposes: resources, information, networking and ecommerce (sales through the web) provided by government, industry and independent teacher networks.

Professional/pupils' needs

Changes in the curriculum are expected these days by teachers. Reviews of the National Curriculum in England and Wales, as well as curriculum in other parts of the UK, are fairly frequent and these are often linked to the implementation of new technologies. One of the pledges of the current Labour government is to provide an email address to all pupils over the age of nine years. In this climate of change, all teachers have a duty to keep abreast of developments which are affecting their pupils.

ICT in the pupil's home

Many pupils also live in homes which are rich in ICT, using computers, CD-ROMs and the internet regularly with help from parents and siblings. Again, teachers need to be aware of such developments in order to help these pupils learn better. There are also pupils in our schools who come from less affluent or less richly resourced backgrounds. Teachers need to be aware of these possibilities and to provide opportunities for all pupils to make the best use of the technology available in both school and home. Further ideas about home and school issues can be found in Chapters 11 and 14.

Professional/curriculum

As new curriculum revisions arrive in British education, they are often announced through ICT media like the internet, and many of the resources associated with curriculum change and content are also provided through websites. This means that the documents need to be translated through a program called Adobe Acrobat, freely available on the internet. So documents like the QCA[7] schemes of work in ICT and Science are available through the Standards site.[8] Ofsted reports on schools can also be found on websites[9] in this same format. Many trainee teachers and those looking for jobs find this information about schools extremely valuable when preparing for job hunts and interviews.

Other curriculum resources and information are available on websites, including the texts of all the National Curriculum documents. The National Grid for Learning and the Virtual Teacher Centre (is this a centre for the virtual teacher, or a virtual centre for teachers?) are obvious starting points

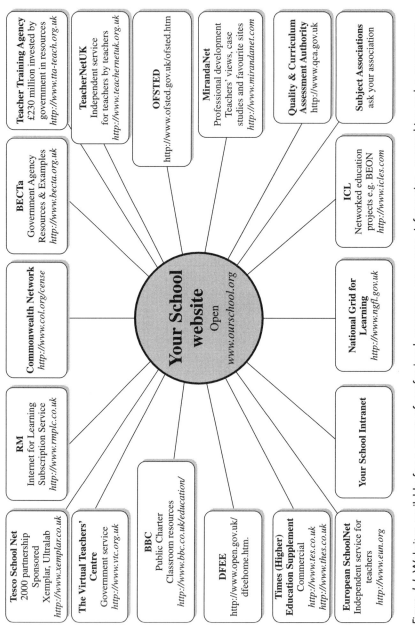

Teacher Training Agency
£230 million invested by government in resources
http://www.tta-teach.org.uk

TeacherNetUK
Independent service for teachers by teachers
http://www.teachernetuk.org.uk

OFSTED
http://www.ofsted.gov.uk/ofsted.htm

MirandaNet
Professional development
Teachers' views, case studies and favourite sites
http://www.mirandanet.com

Quality & Curriculum Assessment Authority
http://www.qca.gov.uk

Subject Associations
ask your association

BECTa
Government Agency
Resources & Examples
http://www.becta.org.uk

Commonwealth Network
http://www.col.org/cense

RM
Internet for Learning Subscription Service
http://www.rmplc.co.uk

Tesco School Net
2000 partnership
Sponsored
Xemplar, Ultralab
http://www.xemplar.co.uk

The Virtual Teachers' Centre
Government service
http://www.vtc.org.uk

BBC
Public Charter
Classroom resources
http://www.bbc.co.uk/education/

DFEE
http://www.open.gov.uk/dfeehome.htm.

Times (Higher) Education Supplement
Commercial
http://www.tes.co.uk
http://www.thes.co.uk

European SchoolNet
Independent service for teachers
http://www.eun.org

Your School Intranet

National Grid for Learning
http://www.ngfl.gov.uk

ICL
Networked education projects e.g. BEON
http://www.icles.com

Your School website
Open
www.ourschool.org

Figure 1.1 Websites available for a range of professional purposes: resources, information, networking and e-commerce provided by government, industry and independent teacher networks

Source: adapted from Preston in Leask and Pachler 1999

for teachers wanting to explore the online information. All the websites mentioned in this text can be found through the text website (see the Note to Readers, page xvi). Further details are provided throughout the following chapters.

Activity 1.1 The National Grid for Learning

Look up the DfEE[10] site and find information about the National Grid for Learning, its origins and development, schools involvement, issues about computers and the internet, issues about training for teachers and its funding. Make sure you can download documents using Adobe Acrobat, the translating software for some graphic-heavy or larger sized internet documents. Adobe Acrobat reader is free and can be downloaded from many government sites. Once it is installed on your computer hard drive, it will automatically translate the downloaded documents and present them in a clear and printable format.

Professional/pedagogic theories

What is the pedagogic justification for investing huge sums in the provision of ICT resources in schools? If the teaching profession cannot answer this question by demonstrating enhanced pupil learning outcomes, then governments cannot be expected to provide the resources to support the work outlined in this book.

In this section, we introduce different theories of learning and we suggest you compare the characteristics of learners described with the characteristics of the pupils for whom you have responsibility, asking yourself the following question as you read this text: In what contexts might my pupils learn more effectively using ICT? Some teachers when identifying learning objectives for any work they are planning for the classroom use the CASK model, that is, they identify the ways in which the work planned is developing pupils' Concepts, Attitudes, Skills and Knowledge in the area under study.

Pedagogical justifications for using ICT across subject areas

Effective teaching takes account of the different learning styles of pupils. For this reason, teachers usually present and explain material in different ways – this enables them to communicate with pupils who, in any group, will have a range of preferred learning styles. Riding and Pearson (1994) and Riding et al. (1993) report on research which shows that learners' preferred styles fall within a continuum.

The two basic dimensions of cognitive style may be summarised as follows:

1 The *Holistic-Analytic style* – whether an individual tends to process information in whole or in part;
2 The *Verbal-Imagery style* – whether an individual is inclined to represent information during thinking verbally or in mental images.

(Riding et al. 1993: 269)

What seems to be emerging from the evidence collected from teachers in the projects in which we are working is that the opportunities provided through ICT; for example, CD-ROM work and internet work, allow learners to approach material from any or a combination of these perspectives. This means that to some extent learners can tailor the path of their own learning through their choice of the way of working with the medium. Take for example the pupils' work on the Bones multimedia presentation which is reported in Chapter 9. Pupils, working in groups, are able to take different roles and approach the task from a variety of angles. Of course ICT does not have to be used for this to happen but in this section we are just concerned with ICT and learning.

It is possible, therefore, that in a carefully constructed learning environment, pupils may indeed learn better and faster where a variety of technologies are used, that is, ones presenting ideas using images and words which allow pupils some degree of individuality in their approach to the task.

Later in this book Dawes *et al.* (Chapter 3) point out the importance of using the communicative potential of ICT to develop thinking, reasoning and talk skills both for primary and secondary pupils. Meadows (Chapter 6) stresses the importance of communication using ICT in the study of science in the primary school. He goes on to discuss constructivist learning theories in relation to learning with ICT. He takes the example of curriculum projects conducted through the internet.

A useful overview of theories of cognition is provided by Pachler (1999: 3–18). For example, Pachler cites the work of Howard Gardner (in MacGilchrist *et al.* 1997: 23–4) who suggests that

learners are potentially able to develop at least seven types of intelligence:

1 linguistic: the intelligence of words
2 logical-mathematical: the intelligence of numbers and reasoning
3 spatial: the intelligence of pictures and images
4 musical: the intelligence of tone, rhythm, and timbre
5 bodily-kinaesthetic: the intelligence of the whole body and the hands

6   interpersonal: the intelligence of social understanding
7   intrapersonal: the intelligence of self-knowledge.

(Pachler 1999: 9)

He goes on to make the point that there are an increasing number of ICT applications; for example, web-based materials, which cater for these different 'types of intelligence' thus allowing the teacher more easily to provide differentiated work for different types of learners. He cites Reid as identifying four particular forms of learning:

1   visual learning (for example, reading and studying charts)
2   auditory learning (for example, listening to lectures and audio tapes)
3   kinaesthetic learning (involving physical responses)
4   tactile learning (hands-on learning, as in building models)

(1987 in Ellis 1994: 506)

and the work of Willing (see Table 1.1).

It is not the intention to explore these issues in depth here. We simply make the point that teacher understanding of the pedagogical applications of ICT is crucial to successful learning in an ICT rich context. In many of the ICT applications above, the teacher's role in diagnosing the pupil's

Table 1.1   General learning styles according to Willing 1987 (source: in Ellis 1994: 506)

	General learning style	Main characteristics
1	Concrete learning style	Direct means of processing information; people-oriented; spontaneous; imaginative; emotional; dislikes routinised learning; prefers kinaesthetic modality.
2	Analytical learning style	Focuses on specific problems and proceeds by means of hypothetical-deductive reasoning; object-orientated; independent; dislikes failure; prefers logical, didactic presentation.
3	Communicative learning style	Fairly independent; highly adaptable and flexible; responsive to facts that do not fit; prefers social learning and a communicative approach; enjoys taking decisions.
4	Authority-oriented learning style	Reliant on other people; needs teacher's directions and explanations; likes a structured learning environment; intolerant of facts that do not fit; prefers a sequential progression; dislikes discovery learning.

needs and providing the appropriate learning environment to allow that learner to excel is critical. Cox (1999) reports on the positive motivating effect ICT often has on pupils. This is another factor for teachers to consider in the integration of ICT into their work in classrooms with pupils.

Case study: teacher motivation for ICT – the MirandaNet experience

> MirandaNet is for a community of innovators in education and industry who are at the cutting edge of teaching and learning. We recognise that Information and Communications Technology is central to the management of change.
>
> (From *http://www.mirandnet.com/index.htm*)

Preston (in Leask and Pachler 1999) describes MirandaNet as operating on four levels which indicate the facilities that can be provided by online professional communities:

- On level one are online study groups where teachers discuss subjects that interest them, often led by a group moderator and resulting in a digest.
- Level two refers to email and conferencing for the whole group where newsletters and notices keep members up to date with events. Posting regular messages into the personal email box, which require a response, is an important feature of effective communication in the early days. Teachers will get into the habit of looking if there is a need. This kind of facility is provided by a list server which the ICT co-ordinator can set up with the service provider.
- Level three is a publications area which offers a variety of formats for teachers and trainers to publish their own work: articles and papers, flyers for books, recommended sites, case history studies, personal profiles.
- The fourth level provides a realistic method by which teachers can advance their professional development. Face-to-face workshops, conferences and seminars are an essential aspect of professional development, although frequency is reduced for reasons of cost and time. Many teachers are discouraged to leave the school for professional development because a supply teacher has to be paid. Also many teachers are parents and cannot commit to evening training.

Fellows' personal learning outcomes depend on ownership of powerful hardware and industrially compatible software, which are essential to professional self-esteem. Maintenance and upgrading are issues which schools must address.

Fellows report that a major advantage of having their own machine is that they are clearer in predicting their own training needs. Also time does not need to be wasted on skills training. Administration becomes more efficient and easier to share and in one case minute taking was transformed into action plans from staff meetings. Teachers can do their administration anywhere. Staff reports and action plans are more easily circulated and collaborative writing is more feasible.

Online has proved to have many advantages in the life of the school: teachers and pupils who are ill can link in from home; beginning teachers can consult their tutors, homework tasks can involve parents and school refusers can be encouraged to keep in touch; links with LEAs are improved.

Below is what some experienced ICT users say about why they prefer to use ICT.

Gordon James, a MirandaNet Fellow, from Wickham Market Primary School in Suffolk has defined an ideal online learning environment for teachers based on his extensive knowledge of other sites and his work developing a homework site for BT (see Chapter 11). The features he recommends are:

- A place to search for and subscribe to suitable exchange projects.
- A place to post your own project briefs.
- Information and advice on funding projects.
- Support with management services such as group mailing lists on request.
- A forum for teachers and other educationalists to discuss their work and share ideas.
- An electronic newsletter.
- An electronic library of research papers for those wishing to delve deeper, case histories and profiles.
- Graphical conferencing interfaces like First Class with an offline reader that saves telephone costs.
- More funding information service from major bodies.
- A set of ready made projects from 'expert institutions'.
- Help and advice in project design and management.
- Free Web pages and Web building tools, and advice on using them.
                    (Preston in Leask and Packler 1999: 220–21)

Other Miranda Fellows participated in an online discussion about their own motivation towards the use of ICT. There were many issues raised, some of which are outlined here.

Having thought about this question for several minutes, I have come to the conclusion that it is the freedom and flexibility that motivates me to use new technologies. The fact that I can use ICT in the way that I want to use it, provides a strong stimulus for me and this can also apply to pupils when they have the choice. Another factor is, that it has now become a part of my everyday life – just like a car. Keeping up with the latest developments and making use of them is another factor for me – the list is endless.

(Rukhsana)

And here is what is known as a 'thread' – a series of linked conversations, each message picking up a point from a previous one and adding to it with an example from their own experience. The thread concerned the theme of creativity with ICT.

. . . I also enjoy the challenge of creating things on computers.

David

I think David hits an important element for me when he talks about the creativity of using computers. I am far happier writing and planning with a computer than with trad. paper and lead. For a start I always feel – well if it's not right, re writing it is no major hassle. Spreadsheets and databases allow you to be far more creative and imaginative with the data you possess.

Ben

I agree with Ben about creativity when using computers. I find it much easier to organise my writing on a screen these days. Also playing around with the layout and presentation helps to organise my thinking. Collaborative writing with kids and colleagues is much easier too when two or more of you are able to sit around a screen and make changes.

Geoff

So membership of this online community provides an extra reason for using ICT, because it helps teachers to maintain this sense of belonging and sharing, which can sometimes be lacking within a small school environment.

The long-term benefits Fellows identified were:

- on-line links preventing professional isolation;
- international focus on good classroom practice;
- peer mentoring gains;
- peer support advantages.

Further information about motivation of teachers can be found on the website of CAL99,[11] where a poster is presented on the subject.

Activity 1.2 Teacher motivation

What motivates teachers towards using new technologies? It may be that there are certain teachers who are predisposed to taking risks and trying out new ideas. It may be a technical fix which turns on some teachers – a feeling of being in control of something new and innovative. On the other hand, some teachers may be motivated by the idea that pupils themselves seem more keen to use the new technologies and that this helps them in their learning. It would be interesting to explore this point further, to see if there are factors in motivating teachers, and also to explore how those teachers who do use new technologies can motivate others within their schools.

What motivates YOU towards the use of ICT?

Some issues in using ICT

Writing and audience

Children themselves gain a lot from co-operative writing projects when they use the communication power of the internet, in terms of their confidence and motivation, as the audience is genuine. One of the major criticisms one hears from Ofsted about children's writing is that it too often has only one contrived audience – the teacher! A real audience, interested in communication and replying, is much more motivating and encourages children to put a lot more effort into drafting and redrafting their writing so that they remove spelling and grammatical errors. Since the writing has to be in a form that can be sent through computers, children also improve their skills with word processors through participation in this sort of communication project. Yet another Ofsted criticism is that children often use word processors only when they have written out their work in a book first – this does seem an awful waste of their time.

Computers in classrooms or computers in suites?

However, the advent of the new communication technologies does have implications for the ways in which computers are used in schools, especially in primary schools. It does not seem sensible for every classroom to have one computer – how can any teacher integrate just one computer into the work of the whole class? Surely our primary classrooms need to have at least four or five computers (if not yet one per child!). Then a group of children can spend enough time using ICT so that they actually develop some skills and understanding from the hardware. Yet the costs of this approach would be excessive in most primary schools. One common solution is to set up a computer suite, or a special computer room. This decision needs to be examined carefully, recognising the advantages and drawbacks. Some teachers are nervous about taking whole or even half classes into such as specialist environment, in which their own weaknesses may be exposed. For further discussion of this issue, see Chapter 8.

Access to phone lines in the classroom

The telecommunication part of computer use also needs some examination. With the new internet access, teachers and children will need more time to browse the networks in order to find the right resources for their own needs. This will mean they will need more access to telephone lines in classrooms, rather than having to use the head's or secretary's telephone line. Teachers will need to lobby the school governors and parents to persuade them that such changes are needed. And not just ordinary copper telephone lines, but preferably the broadband type, ISDN, which costs more to start with but actually saves money by being a lot faster. Schools are now investing in the networking of their computer equipment, so that all classes can get access to the internet and the school's internal intranet.

Parents and computers

In fact, it is perhaps the parents who will be our closest allies in the development of schools online. Many parents are now buying computer systems for educational purposes – many are aware of the enormous potential of the Information Superhighway – most are keen to help their children cope with the changing world so that they gain the skills and flexible approach to new technologies they will need in their own working lives. Estimates of homes with computers in the UK vary from 22 per cent to 50 per cent, depending on the area and whether there are school-aged children in the family. In many of these families, the age of the home computer is less than those found in schools and the specification is better. These issues about parents and schools are followed up in later chapters.

Costs and cutting them

What will it cost? Telephone charges are often thought to be the big problem with telecommunication, especially the idea of browsing online. This can be a problem, but schools are usually very conscious of these costs and find ways to reduce them. It is worthwhile training the children to be aware of the economic aspects of telecommunication from an early age. Some practice at browsing through CD-ROMs will help children to understand how to use such technologies efficiently. Increasingly, the service provided which links people and their computers to the internet is free, because the service provider relies on advertising to earn income. This free service is more problematic in education, though, since we may not want to give children access to some of the products advertised.

Time

The problem of time is also capable of resolution, if you can find some children to help – most schools which are successful with telecommunication rely on the children themselves to carry out many of the tasks, leaving the teacher to concentrate on teaching, rather than being the technical expert. In the case of web design, it is less likely that children can play an active role, since the website is a public face of the school and needs to reflect the school ethos, rather than the interests of individual children. The time it takes to prepare and then update a website can be daunting for many teachers, so one answer to this is recruiting volunteers to help. There are perhaps children in the school with parents or siblings who have the necessary skills and even the interest to support the school in this.

Activity 1.3 Exploring school websites

Go to a site such as Yahoo for the UK (*http://www.yahoo.co.uk*), to search for schools which have their own websites. Examine some primary school web pages in projects such as Brixton Connections.[12]

How can you find the home pages of other primary schools? What do you think schools should display on their web pages? What seems to make a good school website? (Additional school sites are listed at the end of Chapter 3.)

Literacy Hour

The use of communication technologies obviously concerns language, since that is the traditional medium for communication. But we now communicate through pictures and moving images just as much as through words. The notion of graphical literacy is one which is beginning to be researched, in order to find out whether teachers need to adapt their teaching materials and practices to the new skills of the pupils. There are many opportunities to support the literacy through the use of ICT. If schools are really spending an hour a day on literacy, there is a real danger that less motivated or under-achieving pupils will become resistant to this regime, especially if it focuses attention on their mistakes, rather than their achievements. The audience available through wise use of the internet has been shown, in many case studies, to have a powerful motivating effect on children of all types. See Chapter 2 for further consideration of the use of ICT in the Literacy Hour and generally for reading and writing, and Chapter 3 for more on talking and listening with ICT.

Numeracy and the Net

A recent (1997/8) survey by John Meadows of 100+ primary schools in London suggests that teachers know very little about how numeracy can be supported through the internet. Maths used to be the main application for computers in the early days, but now the internet is seen by many teachers as a resource for maths learning, as much as for languages and geography, science, etc. There are certainly plenty of mathematical data available on the networks, but most are too complex for primary school pupils. One way in which numeracy can be approached is through communications projects rather than through data gathering *per se*. Numeracy can of course be supported through a variety of other curriculum areas, some of which can be very motivating for the pupils. Examples of these projects in the past have included:

- Virtual Sports Day, where children decide upon a range of sporting events, like running races, or high and long jumping, collect data from them and post it to their partners.
- A survey of the prices and type of fruit exported from New Zealand, then converting the prices into one's own currency, in order to compare costs in the two countries.

Other areas like science can provide maths contexts too, especially when environmental data are collected and compared. Chapters 5 and 6 provide further ideas about ICT in maths and science.

Video and audio conferencing

Chapter 11 describes one school's experiences with video and audio conferencing. Further examples are available through the websites mentioned in Activity 1.4.

Independent learning systems

In this book we do not deal with the use of independent learning systems (ILS) in schools. ILS systems are computer-based systems; for example for maths or English, which are designed to allow pupils to work relatively independently on individualised programmes. BECTA[13] produces guidance

> **Activity 1.4 Video conferencing and schools**
>
> Look up BECTA information on video conferencing in schools at
> *http://www.becta.org.uk/info-sheets/videoconf.html* especially three case
> studies from Whitby, North Yorkshire, involving primary schools
> *http://www.becta.org.uk/resources/desktopvc/videoconf/*
>
> What lessons could you learn from these experiences?
> Do you think video conferencing is likely to be a popular tool in
> education in the future?

in this area which covers outcomes of research into the effectiveness of
ILS, lists of ILS products and the companies which produce them as well
as views from users.

Ray Barker used ILS successfully with primary pupils on the Docklands
Literacy Project (Chapter 2). He defines ILS as: 'An independent learning
system containing comprehensive curriculum coverage within a managed
learning process ie a child is assessed by the software at the start of the
programme and is fitted into a highly structured programme at an appropriate level. He/she is then given appropriate work and driven through the
programme by positive reinforcement looped back to the teaching of important issues if he/she is seen to be failing. The system will also provide the
child and the teacher with feedback and results.' From his experience, he
suggests that the implementation of any ILS system needs to be decided as
a whole school issue and not be the responsibility of any one staff member.

Summary

There are, then, a number of reasons why schools need to use ICT:

1   The communication aspects and the ways in which a constructivist
    theory of education can be supported through ICT.
2   The skills which children gain by being able to control the applica-
    tions used in ICT.
3   The confidence children gain by communicating through and control-
    ling their environment.
4   The needs for communication skills in their future careers, both in
    school and in the workplace.
5   Access to information on the World Wide Web, although this is still
    a problem, since much of the information is in an adult form.
6   The creative power of ICT, especially in the making of web pages,
    using text and graphics, as well as more advanced facilities.

7   Communication technologies such as audio and video conferencing,
    enabling children to communicate their ideas across national and local
    boundaries.

Notes

1   Special Educational Needs is not dealt with specifically in this text. Franklin
    and Litchfield in Chapter 7 in the accompanying text *Learning to Teach with
    ICT in the Secondary School* (Leask and Pachler (1999), London, Routledge)
    give considerable detail in this area.
2   The website for BECTA (British Educational Communication Technology
    Agency) has extensive resources for teachers including research from the
    Education Departments' Superhighways Initiative EDSI: *http://www.becta.org.uk/
    projects/edsi/index.html*
3   The National Grid for Learning is a website, *http://www.ngfl.gov.uk/ngfl*, but is
    also an idea which links teachers and schools with resources and with industry
    and professional development.
4   The Stevenson Report was set up by the British Labour Party to report on the
    provision of ICT in schools. It relied on statistics from the Kinsey Report.
    Further details of the Stevenson and Kinsey reports can be found on the
    Ultralab website *http://rubble.ultralab.anglia.ac.uk/stevenson/McKinsey.html* and
    http://rubble.ultralab.anglia.ac.uk/stevenson/ICTUKIndex.html
5   The BERA website helps to keep members in contact, gives information
    and advice, provides links to other educational research organisations and
    holds archives of abstracts of papers and posters delivered at conferences.
    http://www.bera.ac.uk
6   *http://www.miranda.com*
    http://www.teachernetuk.ac.uk
    These two groups provide a variety of different services to teachers, in co-oper-
    ation with industry partners and at times funding from organisations like the
    European Union.
7   The Qualifications and Curriculum Authority (QCA) can be found on
    http://www.qca.gov.uk
8   *http://www.standards.gov.uk*
    This government education site is devoted to issues about teacher training and
    the standards of teaching expected before trainees can be awarded qualified
    teacher status.
9   *http://www.ofsted.gov.uk*
    The Ofsted website contains a searchable database containing the reports made
    by Ofsted inspectors on schools.
10 The website for the Department for Education and Employment is at
    http://www.dfee.gov.uk and provides links to many other educational resources
    and websites. The National Grid for Learning site is at *http://www.ngfl.gov.uk*
11 *http://www.elsevier.nl:80/homepage/sag/cal99/*
    Abstracts of papers and posters can be found on this publisher's website.
12 Brixton Connections was a project supported by the business community in
    South London to train teachers and classroom assistants in the use of the
    internet. Many of the schools have set up their own websites, publishing a
    variety of materials across the curriculum *http://www.brixton-connections.org.uk*
13 Guidance on independent learning systems is available from: *http://www.
    ncet.org.uk/info-sheets/ils.html*

References and further reading

BECTA (1998) *Connecting Schools, Networking People*, Coventry: BECTA.

Cox, M. (1999) 'Motivating pupils through the use of ICT', in Leask, M. and Pachler, N. (eds), *Learning to Teach using ICT in the Secondary School*, London: Routledge.

Department for Education (1995) *Superhighways for Education*, London: DFE.

DfEE (1997a) Stevenson Report. The Independent ICT in Schools Communication. *Information and Communications Technology in the UK Schools: An Independent Inquiry*, 78–80 St John Street, London, EC1M 4HR.

DfEE (1997b) *Preparing for the Information Age Synoptic Report of the Education Departments' Superhighways Initiative http://www.becta.org.uk/projects/edsi/index.htm.*

Ellis, R. (1994) 'Individual learner differences,' in Ellis, R. (ed.), *The Study of Second Language Acquisition*, Oxford: Oxford University Press, pp. 471–527.

Goldstein, G. (1995–6) *Information Technology in English Schools: A Commentary on Inspection Findings*, London: NCET/OFSTED.

Leask, M. and Pachler, N. (1999) *Learning to Teach using ICT in the Secondary School*, London: Routledge.

Mailer, N. and Dickson, B. (1994) *The UK School Internet Primer*, London: Koeksuster Publications.

Pachler, N. (1999) 'Theories of learning and ICT', in Leask, M. and Pachler, N. (eds), *Learning to Teach using ICT in the Secondary School*, London: Routledge.

Riding, R.J. and Pearsons, F. (1994) 'The relationship between cognitive style and intelligence', *Educational Psychology*, **14**(4), 413–25.

Riding, R.J., Glass, A. and Douglas, G. (1993) 'Individual differences in thinking: cognitive and neurophysiological perspectives', *Educational Psychology*, **13**(3 and 4), 267–79.

The National Grid for Learning *http://www.ngfl.gov.uk/ngfl/*

Chapter 2

Reading and Writing with ICT

Ray Barker, Glen Franklin and John Meadows

Introduction

The opportunities for reading and writing with ICT are many and varied, which is why we are devoting a whole chapter to it. There are many other places in this book where reading and writing are used with ICT, in a variety of contexts and for many purposes. But here we focus on reading and writing skills themselves and how these skills can be enhanced through the use of ICT.

There are three case studies described in the chapter. The first is a project carried out in east London, with primary schools using portable (palmtop) computers as well as standard PCs with CD-ROM drives. The second study is of some second language work carried out in German schools where English was being taught through electronic mail links with English and American children. Many of the lessons learned in this have application in the teaching of English to British children, when communication through the internet is one of the teaching and learning methods. Finally, there is a set of ideas about how to use email texts creatively in a classroom. This case study arose from a project which collected and distributed stories written by children around the world.

Objectives

By the end of chapter you will have been:

- introduced to a variety of ways in which teachers have successfully used ICT to support the development of pupils' literacy;
- challenged to try some of these ideas out for yourself.

Case study 1: Integrating ICT into the curriculum – to develop literacy

Ray Barker and Glen Franklin, from the Docklands Learning Acceleration Project report on some of the work undertaken with pupils in the project. The context was the focus on literacy in England.

In September 1998, virtually all primary schools in England introduced a daily Literacy Hour – a strategy designed to raise standards of literacy and with a target of 80 per cent of 11 year-olds reaching Level 4 in Key Stage 2 SATS in 2002. It was interesting to note that although more and more technology was being installed in schools in order to provide new skills for the children of the new millennium, there was surprisingly little reference in the National Literacy Strategy (NLS) Framework (1998) to the use of ICT in the Literacy Hour, apart from a few passing references to word processing and CD-ROMs.

Why this omission?

One main reason was possibly that the introduction of something as radical as the Literacy Hour was bound to create management and resource issues for many teachers and schools. Adding a computer, with all its technical foibles, into the equation, might just have proven to be the final straw. However, to leave out ICT from such work would be to do a disservice to an amazingly motivating and versatile tool.

The National Literacy Association ran the Docklands Learning Acceleration Project which worked with six hundred 7 and 8 year-olds in school and at home. It proved that using multimedia and portable technology, as well as more traditional methods, could raise standards and expectations of children's literacy. The project encountered many of the problems which arise when introducing technology into the primary classroom:

- There isn't time
- No more money to replace the colour printer ink
- I'm technophobic
- How will I know that the children are not just playing about?
- It's not working.

and tackled them head on. Now some of the 'yes buts' are known and they are the same when anything new is being introduced. The project took account of these and developed a number of ways of using ICT to support literacy development.

Text and sentence level work – using writing frames and templates

Literacy Hour jargon is used in the following: Y4 means year 4, T2 means term 2, T13 means text level 13, S10 means sentence level 10, W17 means word level 17, etc. The structure of the Literacy Hour includes whole class interaction with the teacher focusing on a big book (or multimedia alternative), individual work and group work. There is a focus on different styles of texts, alternative arrangements of sentences, words (spelling, meanings, forms of words).

A Year 3 class had been exploring traditional stories in whole class Shared Reading and Writing. In their group work, using a letter template stored on a portable computer, the children wrote to a chosen character, responding to aspects of the text and giving reasons for their opinions (Objective Y3 T2 T2,7). The first drafts were printed out and edited with a writing partner. They used the thesaurus to change words such as 'pleased' and 'angry' to 'delighted' and 'fuming' (Y3 T2 W17). They discussed appropriate endings for particular sorts of letters – whether it would be more suitable to write a formal impersonal phrase (e.g., 'Yours sincerely') or to adopt a more friendly tone (e.g., 'With best wishes') if you were writing to the Big Bad Wolf. This work enabled the children to explore the use of first and third person pronouns as included in Y3 T2 S10. The final version was produced using Clip Art computer graphics.

Writing frames (structural templates) can be set up on portables and computers to provide generic activities which can be related to class books and can be developed from the Shared Reading or Writing session. They are easily used by children in their groups; they can use a spell check and thesaurus facility and so can work independently. The edited drafts provide an ideal focus for the Plenary session, where the intention would be to revise teaching points, rather than merely showing work. The emphasis would be on drawing out how the computer is a valuable tool to assist us in the editing process, rather than just showing the final draft.

Tried and tested picture books can be a resource at all levels. For example, one Year 3 class looked at the story *Not Now Bernard* by Michael McKee (Y3 T2 T3, 8, 17). The class used a 'Wanted Report' writing frame to hunt the monster (see Figure 2.1). This required close observation of the text, but the children also had to invent some aspects needing informed guesses and some discussion; for example, how old they thought the monster was. They downloaded their first draft onto the computer graphic and edited this with a writing partner, using a talking word processor which enabled them to hear what they had written.

Other activities associated with this book included:

- writing in character as an Agony Aunt;
- giving advice to Bernard about his relationship with his parents;
- completing a sequel and retelling the story from the monster's point of view;
- a child with learning difficulties used the teacher's typed text of *Not Now Bernard* and employed the computer's search and replace facility to change character and setting. This gave him a solid scaffolding for his work and he was thrilled with his results (see Figure 2.2).

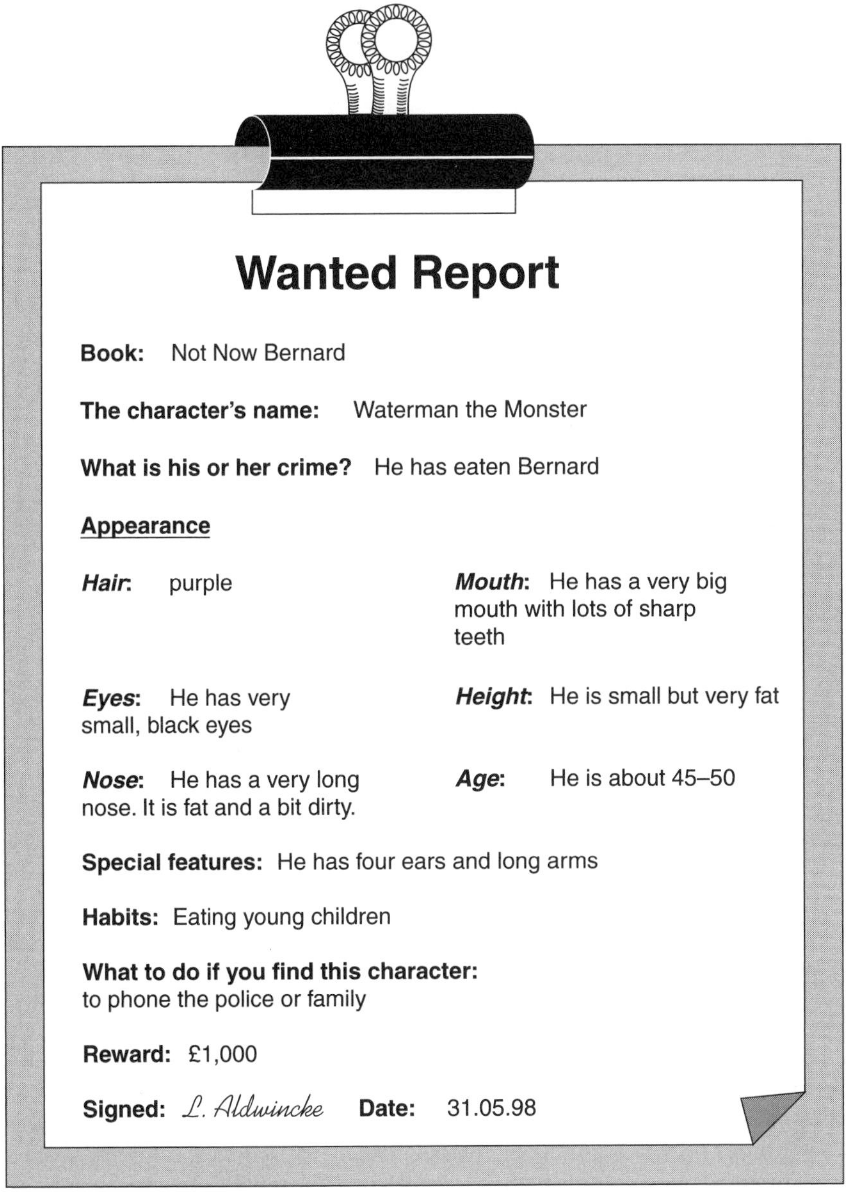

Wanted Report

Book: Not Now Bernard

The character's name: Waterman the Monster

What is his or her crime?   He has eaten Bernard

Appearance

Hair: purple

Mouth: He has a very big mouth with lots of sharp teeth

Eyes: He has very small, black eyes

Height: He is small but very fat

Nose: He has a very long nose. It is fat and a bit dirty.

Age: He is about 45–50

Special features: He has four ears and long arms

Habits: Eating young children

What to do if you find this character:
to phone the police or family

Reward: £1,000

Signed: *L. Aldwincke*   **Date:**   31.05.98

Figure 2.1 Not Now Bernard – wanted report

Hello Dad said Darren.

Not now Darren said his dad.

Hello Mum said Darren.

Not now Darren said his mum.

There's a dragon at the door and it wants to burn me up said Darren.

Not now Darren said his mum.

Darren went to the door.

Hello dragon he said.

The dragon burnt Darren up till there was nothing left.

Then the dragon went into the house.

Figure 2.2 Not Now Darren by Darren

Opportunities for this kind of work occur at all ages and stages; for example, Y5 T3 T3 focuses on retelling from a different point of view or perspective.

Children are encouraged, throughout the Literacy Framework for teaching, to 'record their feelings, reflections and predictions about a book' (Y5 T1 T13). These activities, which encourage a response to text, can all too easily become unimaginative 'book reviews'. One can use database packages for computers and portables; for example, to compare books by the same author (Y2 T3 T2), to explore recurring themes in books from other cultures (Y4 T3 T2) and to compare and contrast points of view and reactions to stories (Y5 T3 T7), enabling children to become experts in their own right on some area of an author or a subject. Others in the class can ask them to recommend a book or tell them where the best place is to find one. Children are more in control of their learning and so make the management of the independent group work much easier for the teacher to handle.

A Year 4 class explored text level objectives Y4 T1 T1, 2 (e.g., covering feelings and moods of characters) following a Shared Reading of the first chapters of *The Bears on Hemlock Mountain*, by Alice Dalgleish. Using a writing frame, they explored the character and text, predicting what they thought would happen. They were completely wrong! This made them keen to go back and complete their book review to put the record straight.

A non-fiction example: using spreadsheets and CD-ROMs

A Year 4 class began their topic on Ancient Greeks by appraising the content of the non-fiction books in their class for their usefulness (Y4 T2 T15) in finding out about Greek schools. Again the introduction for the week was the Shared Reading session and the work grew naturally out of this. In groups, the children recorded their facts on a spreadsheet, paraphrasing the information in note form. They then compared the facts they had found in their extract with another, more complicated article from different source. Having completed their findings, the children printed out their spreadsheet and decided which of the two information sources had been the more useful in providing the information they needed for their topic work.

Another group researching the Roman invasions, took the technology one step further. The children posed themselves two questions: 'Were the countries further away from Rome occupied for less time than those nearer?' 'Why did the Romans stay so much longer in some countries?'

The children used a variety of CD-ROMs, maps and books to complete a database, then used this information to plot two graphs, in order to answer their questions. On their portable computers, they posed a series of questions for their classmates to answer. Questioning skills are central to children working independently. How do they know what they are looking for? How do they know how much information will be needed? The computer had now become a complete resource, holding all the information needed in one format or another, to answer the questions.

Word level work: using a multimedia spelling package

Much of the word level work in group work in the classroom was given to the children in the form of worksheets – picking out a particular phonic pattern perhaps, looking at the particularities of word building: do you drop an 'e' when you add 'ing'? However, many worksheets merely ask children to write in letters and they soon get wise to this. Pictures are not all they seem. A child, writing in the final consonant sounds of 'pin' and 'can', thought the pictures were of a nail and of cat food. But she still wrote the correct answer.

Using a multimedia spelling package can give the child access to sound as well as text, so that they can click on the word and hear it any number of times. This encourages phonemic awareness and teaches phoneme/grapheme correspondence. They can click on the separate onsets and rimes. They can click on pictures and be told what they really are. Most packages ensure that children actually place the letters in a particular order, thus promoting a multi-sensory approach to spelling. Children can also find their scores and often print out the words they could not spell. The teacher too has a record of exactly what the child is doing. The disadvantage is that the important link with handwriting is missing.

On the pocket book computers used in some schools, there is a simple but effective program called Spell. Basically a spell checker, it also has an anagram and crossword facility. This enables children to investigate word patterns for themselves, generating words for spelling logs and class word banks; for example, at Y1 T2 W3. There can be positive results from children using the spell and thesaurus facilities collaboratively, since these programs are easier to use than traditional dictionaries. If children have spelt a word incorrectly, a series of phonetically similar words is presented to them; for example, did they want to write 'cut, cup, cap, cat'? They have to read, discriminate and choose. Children become more aware of their own spelling errors, beginning to spot patterns in the mistakes they make: 'I forgot to double the p again', rather than just 'I got it wrong'.

Why use computers?

All the above activities can be done using pencil and paper. But is ICT the most effective tool for the task? Does ICT:

- ease and support the task in hand?
- enable the learner?
- ensure that learning outcomes can be achieved?
- ensure the quality and value of the task?

If it doesn't, don't use it.

We have found that using ICT in the Literacy Hour can:

- provide a change in approach to tried and tested ideas;
- offer structure and support for less able children;

- extend those at the top end;
- give new insight into vocabulary and word level work;
- show children a more positive approach to drafting and editing, one that is less tedious and enables them to focus on content;
- motivate and encourage a fresh response to the skills of reading and writing.

Activity 2.1 Using ICT to develop literacy skills

Test some of the ideas listed above with children whom you teach. Consider how well your experiment went and whether this teaching approach was a more effective way of achieving learning outcomes than your normal approaches. If you can, work with colleagues testing out these ideas and consider what is most appropriate in the context in which you work.

Case study 2: second language learning – an example from an English as a foreign language research project

In the next two studies, John Meadows draws on the research into a number of educational projects to examine how international email projects and telecommunications can support pupil language learning.

One of the most obvious reasons for doing projects in school using international email or telecommunication is to gain real audiences for foreign language teaching and learning. Although many projects exist which deal with the teaching of foreign languages through telecommunication (Hovstad 1993; Wells 1993), few have reported on the effectiveness of the medium for improving specific aspects of language learning. It is unlikely that many primary schools will be teaching foreign languages to their pupils through telecommunication, but it is possible that during internet-based projects, children in primary schools in Britain may be communicating with other children in Europe who are learning English as a foreign language. So much of the research is applicable in several contexts.

Background

Ranebo (1990) described telecommunication systems and their educational uses, including foreign language learning. He stressed the importance of a real audience for pupils' written texts, as well as the opportunities such networks provide for co-operative work on an international level, leading to improved cultural understanding and the gaining of skills necessary for the modern information society. The notion of a real audience is one which motivates children writing in their home language as well as those working in a foreign language. Tella's work in this area (1991) led to some tentative conclusions about the effectiveness of email for foreign language teaching and learning. He stressed the importance of email for developing the communicative functions of language as well as its role as a precursor to the notion of a 'virtual school'. The development of the technology in teaching can, he considered, lead to concepts of the Global Classroom, and can encourage pupils to develop the skills necessary for success in an information society. But he also analysed some of the difficulties that can arise, such as: finding suitable partners for Finnish schools; problems about maintaining contacts over long periods; the fears of teachers about using new technologies; changes that may be needed in working methods in classrooms; the ways in which new technologies can lead to learner autonomy.

Tella found that teachers dealt with incoming texts in rather traditional ways, but that teachers' creativity and initiative increased during projects. He also found that language and culture studies became intermixed, with social aspects of working co-operatively in their own classrooms being very important. Teachers in the project reported that forty-five minute timetabled sessions were problematic, as more time was needed if telecommunication was to be successful. In this study, student teachers and teachers worked much more co-operatively in this type of language lesson, which broke new ground. Student teachers may have had more advanced IT skills than teachers; for example, in sorting out directories and hard-disk operating. There are several ideas later in this chapter suggesting ways of dealing with incoming email texts in a more creative fashion.

Milligan (1991) reported on an Anglo-Dutch telecommunication project which had limited success and suggested that the main problems were in finding suitable contacts for the international exchanges and then in maintaining these contacts over a longer period. Although there were benefits in helping pupils to change their stereotypical ideas about life in other countries and writing for a real audience helped to stimulate creativity and motivate research, some schools within the project had major problems which could not be resolved in the short timescale. It did seem that developing international links through telecommunication required a large commitment in time and energy.

Implications from research

A project in which German pupils communicated in English with partners in the UK and USA was evaluated jointly by British and German researchers, who found that all the teachers in this sample agreed that pupils gain a lot by working in groups in their classrooms for this sort of language work. For example:

- 'They work better in groups, at least in twos.'
- 'Group work is done very thoroughly with a lot of discussion on content, mistakes, etc.'
- 'They seem to clear up their ideas together before producing texts.'

In most primary schools in Britain, one would expect that pupils would work together in pairs or slightly larger groups when using computers for writing. It may also be more practical for them to co-operate when reading texts which arrive by email, although teachers do have the option of printing out such texts for individual reading. The importance of grouping children for work on ICT tasks is highlighted by Underwood in her chapter in Monteith's (1998) book *IT for Enhancing Learning*. She concludes that same sex pairs and groups work better in this context than children working alone or in mixed sex groups.

One of the key questions in the Anglo-German research was the following: 'What do you think pupils really learn through electronic mail?' The use of email in English could be seen to have a number of possible learning outcomes, so we were interested in finding out which of these seemed to be the most likely results of such use. Did the pupils; for example, increase their range of English vocabulary by being exposed to messages written by their peers in other countries, rather than the carefully graded vocabulary provided in text books, or did this less-planned series of new words confuse them? Did they seem to be keen on using exactly the right grammar when writing to their partners, or was this emphasis on correct grammar less important when communicating through a less formal medium like email? The eight teachers who were interviewed in this part of the research gave the responses reported in Table 2.1 to our predetermined categories.

Of course the sample is very small. Nevertheless, there is some agreement among the teachers of the benefits to be gained.

Overall, teachers considered most of the real learning took place in English vocabulary, communication functions, reading ability, text production, culture/lifestyle and motivation; some learning occurs in the area of co-operation, self-awareness and empathy, but much less in grammar or spelling.

In British primary schools, many of these aims for reading and writing are also important, especially when the development of the language is linked with purposes beyond the important acquisition of basic skills.

Table 2.1 Developing pupils' English language skills via emails

	Quite a lot	Some	Very little
English vocabulary	7	1	0
Grammar	0	5	3
Communication functions (e.g., greeting, explaining)	7	1	0
Reading ability	7	1	0
Spelling	0	6	2
Text production	7	0	1
Culture/lifestyle	7	1	0
Empathy	5		
Co-operation	5	2	1
Self-awareness	4	3	1
Motivation for EFL	7	1	0
Other aspects of learning?	0	2	0

Activity 2.2 Finding partners for literacy projects

There are a number of ways in which schools can find partners for projects. We suggest you take this opportunity to find out how to do this and to read some of the examples of work other teachers have done. The European SchoolNet site[1] offers a partner finding service which incorporates that offered by the UK-based Central Bureau for Educational Visits and Exchanges.[2] If you discover colleagues who have undertaken such projects, find out what went well and what in their view is the most effective way to organise such projects. Chapter 10 provides further advice on the organisation of projects.

Case study 3: using global stories in the classroom

Global Stories was an email based project organised by John Meadows which involved children in primary and secondary schools writing stories, some based on local myths and legends and then sending them to others through email. Participants were from several countries, including England and Scotland, the USA, Germany, France and Australia.

The development of the ideas below was carried out by teachers and the project came to a natural end. However, you will find teachers advertise for partners for such projects through a number of sites such as those mentioned at the end of Chapter 10 and through other professional networks. What follows is a series of ideas about how stories produced by children in other countries and shared through email can be used to develop pupils' literacy skills.

Example 1: Christmas stories from other cultures

Pupils are asked to write stories about how Christmas is celebrated in their country. Using stories sent from other countries teachers make a cartoon, which could be used to prepare a teaching unit dealing with Christmas.
  Teaching aims:

- creative text production (with the aid of the given vocabulary list);
- the fostering of independent thinking and cultural understanding.

The teacher first gives the cartoon on the worksheet to the pupils to take home, where they write their own version of the story. Later in class, pupils read out their versions of the story and a general discussion takes place. Only then are pupils given the original version of the story, in order to compare it with their own.

The box below contains an example of how one pupil involved in this project described a Christmas story from her home country. Using multimedia software[3] you could extend this by adding sound and graphics.

A Christmas custom from Argentina

In Argentina we celebrate the three wise men.
  The tradition is to put grass and water with a pair of shoes at the front door. All children go to sleep and when they wake up they find the grass and water gone and on top of their shoes they receive presents. The grass and water have gone as a symbol that the three wise men have come and their camels have eaten and drunk.

Gabriella: an 11 year-old pupil from a school in Cabramatta, Sydney, Australia

---

After comparing the original version of the story with their interpretation, the pupils take part in the following activities:

- The pupils interview each other about their experiences at Christmas, e.g.:
  – 'Is there anything special you do at Christmas?'

- 'Do you have a special meal at Christmas?', etc.
- Possible extensions or homework:
  - 'Describe how you celebrate Christmas.'
  - 'Rewrite Gabriella's story from the perspective of one of the characters involved in the story, e.g. imagine you are one of the three wise men and write the story as he would have experienced it.'

Example 2: St Catherine's Fair

The story of St Catherine's Fair which was supplied by children in France provided opportunities to achieve a number of different learning outcomes.
   Teaching aims:

- improvement of reading ability and understanding of text;
- understanding of other cultures.

Citizenship issues can be raised about the similarities and differences in customs and events like these across Europe. For example, why is Boxing Day so called? Does it refer to boxes containing presents given to friends you visit the day after Christmas? Or is it a reference to boxing tournaments at medieval fairs similar to the one featured here:

A story from pupils in France: Saint Catherine's Fair

Pupils in France described a festival of importance to them:
   'Every year, in Altkirch, there is a fair which delights all the neighbourhood of the town and opens the Christmas season. This feast is the >'St Catherine Fair'. It takes place on the nearest Thursday to St Catherine, towards November 25. This fair has been famous for centuries: street hawkers come from far away. Allier, Haute Saone, Doubs and some Swiss and German tourists come to visit us.< It is an important meeting of many people from the whole area, street hawkers, shopkeepers and inhabitants. No one can >drive through town because all the streets are so crowded by the numerous stalls. And we can see plenty of cars on the roads outside town.< The whole town looks completely different, strange. >We don't recognise the houses behind the stalls. As the cars can't enter the town, the persons and the children who either work or go to school there but don't live in Altkirch can't work or go to school on this day. How lucky!< Then some pupils can have a stall too: we do it to >raise money; most of us go for a walk in town, have a drink or eat a sandwich

continued

---

with their friends. The day itself begins very early in the morning: the lorries enter the town and their owners install at about 6.30 a.m. Many different things are sold at the fair: cattle, cars, tractors, toys, clothes for the winter, furniture, sweets, jewels, all sorts of bread, vegetables and fruit of autumn. There are also many snack-bars for all the people who eat at the fair.< It's difficult to walk <in the streets: there are so many people, especially in the afternoon. The weather is usually cold and cloudy. So the stalls propose some coffee, tea or mulled wine, a typical Alsatian drink.< At nightfall, >towards 6 p.m., the street hawkers start tidying things away. The fair comes to an end. The fair is over but the feast itself is not. In the evening, there is a 'Catherinettes' ball. They are the young women aged 25 who are still not married. They must transform a simple hat into a master-piece and they wear it to show their creation at this ball.< On the next day >the newspapers print the photos of the nicest and most original ones. Then the fair is really finished.< From now on, children think of Saint Nicholas we celebrate on December 6th.

Mme M., et ses eleves de 4me, un college d'Altkirch.'

Note: the symbols <> indicate where to break up the text in the classroom example accompanying this story.

Such stories can be used in a number of ways and to achieve a number of learning outcomes. For example, you might start by reading the story together, with a copy for each pupil, making sure the pupils understand the vocabulary. You may divide the class into groups, each with about four pupils, then give each group one version of the story, cut into smaller sections (see the symbols in the boxed text above). This re-ordering, or jigsaw procedure is based on the principle of slowing down the reading process so that the pupils have to read each part several times. The decisions about cutting up the text are important. Cuts need to be made in such a way that grammatically possible combinations are determined by the logic of the story's structure. The story could actually be put together in a variety of grammatically correct ways, but there would be only one correct version from a logical point of view; for example, the two short extracts from the skeleton of the story, 'At nightfall . . .' and 'On the next day . . .' could be grammatically interchanged, but would not make logical sense. So pupils need to really understand the contextual symbols or the logical structure of the text.

Example 3: role play to develop discussion and debate

A Chinese story provided by a participating pupil: 'An iron bar can be ground into a needle'

Li Bai was one of the greatest poets of the Tang Dynasty in China. When he was a child he was very naughty and didn't work hard at all. One day he went to the river bank where he saw an old lady with white hair. She was grinding an iron stick. Li Bai was really surprised, so he asked the old lady, 'What are you doing?' The old lady replied, 'Making a needle.' Li Bai was even more surprised, he said, 'Making a needle? It is impossible!' The old lady said, 'Nothing is impossible. An iron stick can turn into a needle if you work hard on it.'

Li Bai understood something from that. One should work hard at whatever you want to do and finally you will succeed. From that day on Li Bai studied very hard and made progress every day. At last he became a very famous poet.

Contributed by Irene, Year 6 pupil in Sheffield
(Irene came from Shanghai, China; she was a pupil in the UK whilst her parents were at a UK University.)

Teaching aim:

- to develop discussion about attitudes and values.

The teachers involved in this exercise approached the use of this story from a number of different angles. For example, this short but very impressive story can be seen from a modern, industrial perspective. Pupils can identify the moral of the story and then compare it with situations within their own lives. One could possibly transfer the moral into a modern context – imagine a situation with a similar moral and then act out the story.

Stories from other countries can raise interesting questions and give relevant contexts for discussions. This example could be used to talk about old Chinese traditions and to compare these with the modern Chinese traditions and with those of the pupils' own country. The class established email contact with others in the project who had read the story and this was a starting point for a whole series of email discussions focused around values, attitudes and cultural similarities and differences.

Example 4: 'Swobble' cloze procedure text

In this example, any words from the stories can be substituted by 'swobble', with accurate endings of course, so that correct grammatical structures and vocabulary can be reinforced. The pupils then have to try to decipher the original words or even to substitute other words which will allow the story to make sense. For children who have difficulties with thinking of synonyms or substitute words, a computer with a thesaurus might be useful (see Glen Franklin and Ray Barker's work on the Docklands literacy project earlier in this chapter).

> ### Swobble' cloze procedure
>
> #### 'An iron bar can be ground into a needle'
>
> Li Bai was one of the greatest swobbles of the Tang Dynasty in China. When he was a child he was very swobble and didn't work hard at all. One day he went to the swobble where he saw an old lady with white hair. She was swobbling an iron stick. Li Bai was really surprised, so he asked the old lady, 'What are you doing?' The old lady swobbled, 'Making a needle.' Li Bai was even more surprised, he said, 'Making a needle? It is swobble!' The old lady said, 'Nothing is impossible. An iron stick can turn into a needle if you swobble hard on it.'
>
> Li Bai swobbled something from that. One should work hard at whatever you want to do and swobble you will succeed. From that day on Li Bai swobbled very hard and made swobble every day. At last he became a very swobble poet.

Example 5: understanding the meaning of texts

Using stories from different cultural contexts, the pupils are given statements concerning any of the texts and then have to decide whether these statements are right or wrong, according to the original story. This well-known technique does not have to be explained in detail. One way that this process might be simplified and less onerous for the teacher is if the pupils themselves make up some of the statements to test their peers, rather than the teacher doing this job. The pupils would then learn more about writing and understanding the meaning of the texts.

In examples 6, 7 and 8, the use of email and video conferencing with pupils in the countries concerned could provide an extra dimension to pupil learning. Projects using this technology take some time to establish so we recommend you develop partnerships with the intention of doing joint work in several areas over a long period (see the guidance in Chapter 10). In this way, you can gain an understanding of how to run projects effectively using email and the internet.

Example 6: posters and collages

Since Global Stories come from all parts of the world and deal with typical ways of living, legends, etc., they offer potential to teach first hand knowledge of the country. Posters and collages can enhance the ability of the pupils to discover and demonstrate the special quality of a story in terms of its cultural roots.

Groups receiving different stories

Groups of three pupils each receive a different story from one country or from different countries. No group knows the story of the other group (taking for granted that they already know the basic vocabulary). The pupils draw the outline of 'their country' on a large sheet of paper (or the back of a piece of wallpaper) and choose photos from travel brochures, make their own little drawings or use parts of the texts and stick them within the outline. In this way they can characterise the country and locate the story geographically. After that all the stories are read, the pupils find the stories which go with the posters and explain why they associate them in that way; for example, 'I think that poster goes with this story because. . . .'

Groups receive the same story

Each group is given the same story, makes a poster and explains why it has created the poster story in this way rather than in another (all this discussion should be taking place in English, of course). The posters can also be exchanged amongst the groups. The groups describe the posters and ask the 'makers' for explanations if they think anything is not clear. In both cases a real discussion amongst the pupils can arise because there is an information gap between the different groups.

Example 7: using games to develop knowledge of other countries

After dealing with several stories from the Global Stories collection, pupils can make dice games concerning the countries being dealt with. An outline map of the country is made and the country is filled in with pictures, photos and drawings. Then a games board is constructed on the map, where pupils can move according to the number on the dice. For each position, a card is made, referring to the story. The card has a question which must be answered correctly in order to move on. Every group can make a game like this. The games can be exchanged and played with dice and coloured figures, so knowledge about the country can be reinforced and the construction of questions and commands and general reading ability can be practised.

Example 8: making audio-tapes of 'radio plays' about the stories

Since the stories are relatively simple in structure and easy to understand, most do not need detailed explanation. A simple introduction of the new vocabulary suffices in order to allow the pupils to work independently and invent their own radio plays. Although generally fairly simple, the stories do have different grades of difficulty so teachers can differentiate between them and use them with pupils of different abilities. After that, the stories which go with the radio plays can be matched, which can be another reason for further discussions. Access to a digital video camera brings another dimension to this work.

Activity 2.3 Developing literacy using stories from other cultures

Investigate the availability of stories from different cultures through the European SchoolNet and Commonwealth Electronic Network.[4] Consider how such resources could be used in the context in which you teach. Test the ideas involved and evaluate their usefulness with the pupils whom you teach. If you consider this appropriate, look particularly for stories from cultures which match those of pupils in the class. Some pupils may of course not wish to have attention drawn to the fact that their cultural heritage may be different to that of other pupils in class.

Summary

In this chapter, we have provided a wide variety of examples of how ICT provides opportunities to stimulate the improvement of pupils' literacy. Stimulus material from a huge range of cultures can be relatively easy obtained. In this respect, the Commonwealth Electronic Network and the Virtual Teacher Centre[5] supplement the networks of the various European countries which can be accessed through the European SchoolNet site.

Notes

1   The European SchoolNet site is on *http://www.eun.org*
2   Central Bureau for Educational Visits and Exchanges is on *http://www.en.eun. org/menu/projects/windows.html*
3   Multimedia software such as Hyperstudio is used by many teachers. It is available through *http://www.tagdev.co.uk/hs/hs.html*
    More examples are provided at the end of Chapter 9.
4   The Commonwealth Electronic Network is on *http://www.col.org/cense*
5   Virtual Teacher Centre *http://www.vtc.org.uk*

References and further reading

Hovstad, U. (1993) 'Sans passeport: learning French in Norwegian schools', in Davies, G. and Samways, B. (eds), *Teleteaching*, Elsevier Science Publishers BV (North-Holland and London) IFIP, pp. 421–27.

Meadows, J. (1992) 'International collaborations in teacher education: a constructivist approach', *Journal of Information Technology for Teacher Education*, **1**(1), 113–25.

Meadows, J. (1993) 'Telecommunications across the school curriculum', in Davies, G. and Samways, B. (eds), *Teleteaching*, Elsevier Science Publishers BV (North-Holland and London) IFIP, pp. 427–36.

Meadows, J. (1994) 'Mind your language: how effective is electronic mail for foreign language teaching?', *Campus Journal*, Spring (5), 11 (British Telecommunications Plc).

Milligan, J. (1991) *The Shell Anglo-Dutch Project*, Coventry: National Council for Educational Technology.

Monteith, M. (1998) *IT for Enhancing Learning*, Oxford: Intellect Books.

Ranebo, S. (1990) 'New communication technologies in learning', Colloquy on *La Télématique, une chance pour l'éducation et la communication interculturelles*, Luxembourg: Commission Des Communautés Européenes.

Tella, S. (1991) *Introducing International Communications Networks and Electronic Mail into Foreign Language Classrooms*, University of Helsinki, Finland.

Wells, R. (1993) 'The use of computer-mediated communication in distance education: progress, problem and trends', in Davies, G. and Samways, B. (eds), *Teleteaching*, Elsevier Science Publishers BV (North-Holland) IFIP, pp. 79–88.

Chapter 3

Extending Talking and Reasoning Skills Using ICT

Lyn Dawes, Neil Mercer and Rupert Wegerif

Introduction

As discussed in the Preface, the C for 'communications' in the acronym ICT (Information and Communications Technology) refers to what could prove to be the most important and influential use of computers in education: sharing information and jointly constructing knowledge. New opportunities for communication have been made possible by links between computers. This chapter considers the questions: how effective is the communication pupils achieve as they talk with others in your classroom, and at a distance? What can teachers do to encourage genuine collaboration between those working on joint tasks at the computer, either face to face or over electronic networks? Examples of classroom work provided in this chapter can be used to encourage effective group talk for children working at the computer.

Objectives

This chapter should enable you to:

- become more aware of the value of communication and collaboration;
- understand the concepts of literacy and network literacy;
- consider the developing talk skills of your class;
- look at some classroom applications of ICT;
- organise children into effective groups;
- consider your children's awareness of the educational aims for their discussion at the computer;
- understand the value of exploratory talk;
- look at some ways of teaching and recognising exploratory talk;
- consider important aspects of software design;
- recognise that your involvement in the structuring of the computer-based task is essential for effective use of ICT;
- understand the link between reasoning in talk and in writing.

Communication and collaboration

In primary schools it is common practice to ask children to work together at the computer. A crucial requirement for the success of such joint work is that pupils are able to communicate competently with one another. Without such collaboration, the potential of ICT to support learning is diminished.

Linking computers together into networks which allow constant and instant information transfer is not enough to achieve effective communication. Communication happens between people, and is not about uploading and downloading bytes of information – it is about reaching a shared understanding. But achieving such a shared understanding is not something that can be taken for granted. Being able to communicate effectively and reach a shared understanding with others is a skill which has to be learned, and which can be taught. Networked computers are a valuable medium for communication, but the crucial issue is how people use that medium to construct joint meanings.

Human communication allows people to share experience in ways which are denied to other species, and which have given us striking advantages in the struggle for survival. Useful knowledge can be conveyed, in detail and with considerable accuracy, not only between contemporaries but also between generations. Because we can talk to each other we can jointly recall and reconstruct events in a way that is more accurate than relying on individual experiences and memories, and draw shared meaning from them. People can consider their own potential decisions in the light of the opinions of others: such critical, rational examination of choice can make eventual choices more successful. And of course communication is also essential for sustaining the social, emotional aspects of human relations.

Diversity and variation between people is extremely important, and each of us may have some special skill or talent. But this individuality depends on the support of a culture. Despite the conventional tendency to celebrate the achievements of famous individuals, no one can justly claim that they 'did it all themselves'. It is in societies where collaboration ensures that knowledge is communally owned that individuals are enabled to excel. As rewarding as solo performance may be, there is something equally satisfying about being part of a group whose members successfully collaborate to perform, create, or achieve any joint purpose. Teaching pupils to collaborate is helping them to participate fully in the society they live in. It also helps to ensure that they feel true members of a society in which their own aims and needs are achieved through negotiation and joint effort.

Defining literacy and network literacy

A crucial task for schools is to create literate people. The introduction of the 'Literacy Hour' into primary classrooms in 1998 indicated an anxiety in society about the lack of literacy and its consequences. Literacy may not be essential for participation in our culture, but its acquisition can make a huge difference to the quality of that participation and to people's opportunities for controlling their own lives and making a contribution to society.

Literacy is best thought of not as an end product in itself, but rather as a capacity for engaging with other people in the process of making meaning.

The fullest participation in literate activities takes place when members of a society move easily between spoken and written language, talking and writing about what they read and hear, and transferring relevant language skills from one mode to another. When literacy becomes integrated into the fabric of everyday life, it transforms the nature of a society. Literacy is not just the skill of decoding written symbols, it is a facility for interrelating knowledge, understanding and skills to construct meaning.

The ability to use a variety of media is part of this. The conception of literacy is evolving to accommodate new forms of communication. A fully literate person might now be expected to be fluent in the uses of electronic communication. This new dimension to literacy is called 'network literacy': 'Network literacy is the capacity to use computers to access resources, create resources and communicate with others' (DfEE 1997: 10).

So the development of network literacy will enable people to interact competently and confidently through electronic media. Schools can offer their pupils this special sort of literacy. In this chapter, we will incorporate network literacy into a broad conception of literacy as effective communication using a variety of different channels. We also argue that different modes of communication can work together to reinforce each other. We will suggest ways that teachers can integrate the development of children's network literacy with the teaching of speaking and listening as part of normal curriculum-based activity.

Developing talk: some classroom applications of ICT

ICT can be used to encourage communication within a classroom, within a school, with other schools locally and elsewhere in the world, or with libraries and museums and organisations supplying news and information. The way computers can allow children access to global communication is important, but another and just as vital function is the way they can support each child's communication with their classmates.

Most children arrive at school with speaking and listening as their first and most fluent means of communication. School pupils are taught largely through the medium of oral language. Developing their speaking and listening skills is a constant, often informal process. ICT provides your pupils with new opportunities to extend their oral language repertoire. Its motivating power can be harnessed to encourage pupils to discuss work, exchange relevant ideas, and construct joint understanding. ICT can provide a focus and stimulus for talk related to decision making.

In this section the focus is on some practical ideas which have been found to encourage effective discussion between groups of children. The quality of the talk that goes on around computers largely depends on how you, the teacher, organise the activity. Of the many factors involved, there are four which are particularly important:

- organising children into effective groups;
- do the children understand the educational aims for their discussion?
- software design;
- your involvement in the structuring of the computer-based task.

The next part of this chapter will look at these factors in more detail, with some examples of how you might implement the ideas in your classroom.

Organising children into effective groups

Before grouping children for any classroom activity, two questions must be answered:

1   What is the nature of the task that the group will undertake?
2   What is the purpose of grouping the children?

For example, the questions might be answered like this:

1   The task will be to design a fair test for a science investigation.
2   The purpose of group work is to allow children to share their knowledge and understanding of science concepts, and to encourage collaboration to improve the design of the investigation.

Please read Activity 3.1.

Comments on Activity 3.1

An entire chapter could easily be devoted to the issue of girls, boys and computers. Very briefly, research shows that boys tend to be more confident with computers than girls. Boys spend more time using computers at home, although their expertise may largely be in the area of playing shoot-'em-up type games. The assertive approach of home computer users (girls or boys) may further diminish the confidence of others. Girls are found to perform better when the context of the computer task engages their interest (that is, the program is not to do with such things as motorbikes, pirates,

Activity 3.1 Organising group work at the computer

Imagine that you have a class of thirty children and one computer. To ensure that the computer task is undertaken by all children within the time available they must be grouped in threes. The nature of the task is that groups will work through a computer program designed to encourage problem-solving.

In this context, how would you answer this question:

What is the educational purpose of grouping the children?

Next, consider the following attributes that children working together may bring to their group. Arrange them in order of priority for constituting your groups, keeping in mind the purpose of the group.

sociability with peers	ability to write fluently
girl or boy	willingness to co-operate
specific subject knowledge	enthusiasm
computer literacy	general knowledge
ability to listen carefully	imagination
'talkative'	confidence
friendships with peers	ability to read fluently

or soldiers). Unless pupils are made aware that they have equal status within the group, stereotypical gender roles may be acted out: boys may take control of the machine and the talk, girls may let them. Also, girls may be overly assertive particularly in the grouping of two girls with one boy. Your awareness of the problems that may arise will help to ensure that boys and girls work together as equals. (Suggestions for further reading on this extremely important issue to be found at the end of this chapter are Swann 1992; Wegerif and Scrimshaw 1997: Chapter 11.)

Friendship groups are very productive for some sorts of activities, but not for work involving decision making at the computer. Friends tend to agree too quickly rather than challenging one other to give reasons for the opinions they offer. They 'know each other's minds' in a way that short-circuits the need to explain things out loud to one another.

Mixed ability groups may be the most practical arrangement in order to ensure that any text on screen can be read.

If the purpose of the group is to encourage effective talk to take place, then it is essential that the pupils are made aware that this is an important aim. Put another way, the group must give as much priority to the quality of their talk as they do to working through the program.

Do the children understand the educational aims for their discussion?

Pupils in primary classrooms are often grouped together to support one another by talking about their work. The rules for such talk are rarely made explicit. Some groups may cohere and seem to share an understanding of how to talk together. Other groups may find it hard to do so.

Activity 3.2 What rules will encourage rational discussion?

Write a list of up to ten rules that you would think necessary for children to follow in order to ensure the sort of discussion you expect in your classroom.

Once you have completed your list, look at the 'Ground Rules for Talk' on page 45. What similarities and differences do you notice?

Exploratory talk

As teachers, we need to encourage a certain sort of talk when children are engaged in group work. In the early 1990s the Spoken Language And New Technology (SLANT) Project (Dawes 1992; Mercer 1995: Wegerif and Scrimshaw 1997) reported how children aged 7 to 11 years talked and worked together on computer-based tasks in twelve English primary schools. This confirmed that computer-based activities are effective for motivating interaction and stimulating talk. However, the research also discovered that children often found it difficult to work together in a group. They did not seem able to negotiate with one another, or share relevant information, or listen to and accept one another's ideas. Many pupils seemed to be competing with one another. Collaboration often meant that children accepted each other's ideas without considering any alternatives. Some pupils were likely to be excluded from decision making. Only very rarely did groups engage in the sort of rational, critical, constructive discussion that is the most appropriate and useful for educational activities and for participation as an educated person in many social and cultural activities.

The classroom researchers Barnes and Todd (1977, 1995) call this kind of talk 'exploratory talk'. A distinguishing feature of exploratory talk is that assertions and opinions are supported by reasons. Reasons are asked for and critically challenged, and all the members of the group are actively encouraged to join in this process. Discussion of alternatives takes place until joint agreement can be reached, with all relevant information being pooled, and all suggestions given consideration. Exploratory talk is a rational way of thinking aloud in a group. It is generated by a group ethos in which individuals can genuinely 'change their minds' (that is, negotiate ideas and accept other people's reasons) without fear of undue ridicule, dismissal, or contempt. Neither can individuals expect personal glory. By agreeing to be part of the group, each individual accepts that their contribution is meant to make the whole group more effective.

Encouraging exploratory talk

Following the SLANT project, the Talk, Reasoning And Computers (TRAC) project devised a programme of 'Talk Lessons' which, within a fairly short span of time, does two things. First, it increases pupils' awareness of the importance of effective communication for the work they do in groups. Second, it increases the amount of 'exploratory talk' they use while working together. The TRAC programme is led by the pupils' class teacher, who encourages children to base their talk on a set of agreed 'Ground Rules'.

Ground rules which encourage exploratory talk

- Any suggestions and ideas must be backed up by a reason.
- The group respects everyone's contribution.
- Challenges are welcomed, and they too must be backed up by a reason.
- All alternatives are discussed.
- The group shares all relevant information.
- Group members invite one another to speak.
- The group seeks to reach agreement.
- The group takes responsibility for all decisions made.

The outcomes of the TRAC programme show that after the 'Talk Lessons' the ability of children to reason aloud together improved (Mercer *et al.* 1999). The commitment of the teacher to raising children's awareness of their talk was a significant factor. Specially designed activities for pupils at computers can help them to learn, practise and consolidate the skills required to engage in educated discourse. Supported by a set of ground rules, group exploratory talk encourages individual expression, group support and rational debate – the sort of talk that plays an important cultural function in helping our society to cohere and allows the pursuit of such educated practices as scientific investigation, the law, the conducting of businesses and of elected government. Its qualities give it a special, close relationship with some 'educated' ways of being literate, such as when explanations have to be made explicit, evidence has to be discussed, or alternative points of view rationally considered.

It is important to recognise that computers in themselves do not teach, insist on or even recognise exploratory communication, though their use can encourage it and provide practice. Teaching children how to use language in an 'exploratory' way remains the responsibility of the teacher.

ICT can provide an excellent medium for 'exploratory' kinds of spoken and written communication. Some examples and starting points are included at the end of this chapter:

- decision-making programs: talk between class members;
- video conferencing: talk at a distance;
- email: written discussion between distant correspondents;
- online projects: written discussion and talk between class members.

Talk, reasoning and computers

One of the hypotheses of the TRAC project was that pupils who under-took the talk lessons programme would not only be demonstrably better at using language to collaborate, but would also become significantly better at reasoning. We based this on the Vygotskian view that the ways that children learn to use language in social interaction will shape the ways they use language internally, as a tool for thinking when they are working alone (Vygotsky 1978: 27). Groups of pupils who had been taught to use exploratory talk were compared with others who had not. The pupils' abilities to reason (in groups and individually) were tested using the reasoning problems of a well-known psychological test (Raven's Progressive Matrices 1995) before and after the talk lessons programme. Children in both the TRAC and control classes also used computer software specifically designed by the team to stimulate talk and engage them in curriculum-related activities, with built-in decision-making contexts, and talk prompts at key points.

The TRAC pupils were found to have an increased ability to solve the reasoning problems together. Analysing video recordings of them working together revealed that improved success with the problems was related to an increased use of exploratory talk. Pupils' ability to engage in joint reasoning seemed to help them work out the correct solutions to the puzzles using a method that had not been available to them previously: rational debate.

A further TRAC finding was that once the pupils had been taught and had assimilated the basic skills of exploratory talk in their groups, their individual reasoning scores also increased. This confirms the Vygotskian claim that the kind of reasoning an individual uses when working alone can be taught and learned through engaging in social interaction. Pupils communicating their reasons to one another, speaking and listening to the sort of critical engagement with ideas that is necessary to distinguish the sound reason from the opportune suggestion or thoughtless interjection, seemed to have begun to use exploratory talk to 'talk to themselves' too.

This has profound implications for ICT use in classrooms. Teachers can enlist ICT applications to encourage pupils to become aware of themselves as speakers and listeners, and to help them learn how and why to use this powerful way of using language. They can then employ it to engage in classroom conversations and conversations with others at a distance. The power it confers lies in children being able to control the skills of discussion and argument.

Activity 3.3 Recognising exploratory talk

This activity involves you looking at the transcripts (pp. 49–50) of pupils who were talking together whilst working at the computer. The aim of the activity is for you to evaluate the quality of their talk. In order to do so, bear in mind the important question:

Have the pupils understood what is meant by 'talk together'?

To answer this, look for the following features in the talk as you read through the transcripts:

- Do they give reasons?
- Do they ask each other for reasons?
- Are alternatives discussed?
- Do the pupils ask each other for information?
- Do they ask each other for opinions?
- Are all group members actively encouraged to speak?
- Does the whole group take responsibility for decisions?
- Is the talk 'on task'?

The context of the transcripts

In Transcripts A and B, two groups of three pupils aged 9 years are working on software depicting a science investigation based on the topic of friction (see Figure 3.1). The simulation shows a hammer which can be released with different forces to strike a puck.

The weight of the puck can be altered, and it can slide over three different surfaces. The software was designed by the TRAC team to encourage exploratory talk, and includes talk 'prompts' in its screen display. Both sets of pupils undertaking the task have been asked to talk together about it. In the transcripts, the pupils tackle the same three (of ten) introductory questions, which check their understanding of the concept of friction, choosing the answer A, B or C to the question. Inverted commas show where pupils are reading from the screen.

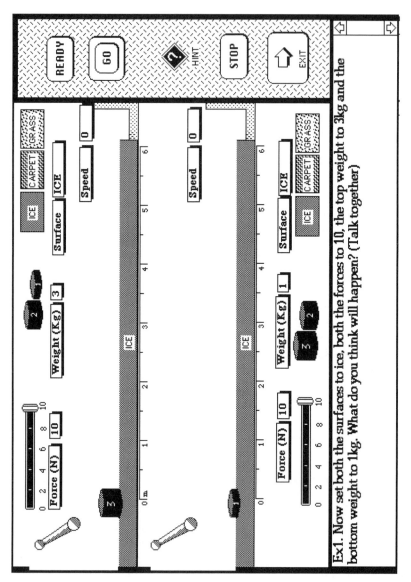

Ex1. Now set both the surfaces to ice, both the forces to 10, the top weight to 3kg and the bottom weight to 1kg. What do you think will happen? (Talk together)

Figure 3.1 The TRACKS software which is designed to encourage exploratory pupil talk

Transcript A: What do we know about friction?

Liam, Nicole and Peter (Year 5) answering questions 1, 2 and 3

ALL: 'You can reduce, have less friction, by heating the surfaces, pushing the surfaces over each other . . .'

NICOLE: '. . . changing the surfaces to make them slippery.' I think it's number, I think it's B.

PETER: B, yes number B!

LIAM: 'If you have 2 kg weight and a 4 kg weight, and you move them with the same speed on a slippery surface: . . . the 2 kg weight will stop after twice as much time, you need twice as much force to stop the 4 kg weight, the 2 kg weight will move twice as fast.' Number C?

NICOLE: Yes.

ALL: 'If you have a 2 kg iron weight on the floor, you can make it move furthest by hitting it with the force of five Newtons, hitting it with the force of ten Newtons, hitting it with the force of two Newtons'.

NICOLE: Ten. (Group goes on to next question.)

Transcript B: What do we know about friction?

Alan, Daniel and Sam (Year 5) answering questions 1, 2 and 3

SAM: 'You can reduce, have less friction, by heating the surfaces, pushing the surfaces over each other with more force, changing surfaces to make them more slippery.' Which one do you think?

DANIEL: Oh – what's the question – oh yes . . .

SAM: Which one do you think it is?

DANIEL: 'You can have less friction by changing it to be less slippery.' [sic]

ALAN: Yes, me too.

DANIEL: Suppose you have a metal thing, and you put some oil on it, it would be really slippery, wouldn't it?

SAM: Yes. So it's C then, yes?

DANIEL: Yes.

SAM: 'If you had 2 kg iron weight on the floor, you could make it move furthest by hitting with a force of five Newtons, ten Newtons . . .'

DANIEL: I don't actually know that one – let's take a guess?

SAM: What's a Newton – Oh I know what a Newton is.

ALAN: What's a kilogramme? What's two kg?

SAM: Well you know the big ones like that (*gestures*), well, two of them. What do you think?

DANIEL: A Newton couldn't do that – you need a lot of big ones to do that.

ALAN: So what do you think?

DANIEL: Ten.

SAM: Yes I think it's ten as well. Yes?

DANIEL: 'If you have a 2 kg weight moving at the same speed as a 4 kg weight on a slippery surface, the 2 kg weight would stop after: . . . twice as much time.' Yes it will, because that one will stop after a while, the other one is lighter so it'll go on longer, so that figures.

SAM: We've established it's not B, yes? It's not B?

ALAN: Yes.

SAM: Yes, now C and A? 'Two kilogramme weight will stop after twice as much time. A 2 kg weight will move twice as far.' So what this one's saying is that . . .

ALAN: It could be any of them we could choose because they mean the same sort of thing.

DANIEL: Yeah, I think it's C, because it moves faster.

SAM: Yes, I suppose so.

ALAN: So not A, C then, yes?

Comment

Both groups are 'on task', that is, all the pupils are engaged in the problem solving activities.

In Transcript A, the children do not ask each other for information, opinions or reasons, but state their own ideas without reference to one another. The questions are not discussed. These pupils are unlikely to feel that they have made group decisions. In Transcript B, the pupils encourage one another to speak by asking questions. Even though ideas might not be immediately forthcoming, this is a step towards genuine collaboration. Suggestions are discussed and information shared before the pupils come to a group agreement. This sort of talk is more likely to increase understanding of the science involved.

Transcript A is a recording of the control group, and Transcript B is a recording of pupils in the TRAC project after their Talk Lessons. It is not perfect exploratory talk: learning discussion skills takes a long time and a lot of practice, but it demonstrates that the Ground Rules have been understood and are being tried out, however tentatively. Effective talk engages the pupils with one another's ideas, and here the computer provides context and acts as a prompt and motivator.

These transcripts have been selected to demonstrate the 'before and after' effect of talk training, but they are typical of the talk collected by the project.

Activity 3.4 Recognising talk training

This activity involves you looking at a further example of the difference Talk Lessons can make – there are many more. The aim of the activity is simply for you to use your knowledge of the ground rules for exploratory talk to identify which group has undertaken Talk Lessons.

The context of the transcripts

Both of the groups in Transcripts C and D have been asked to talk together at the computer. The program they are working on (Figure 3.2) presents them with a moral dilemma. The story concerns two friends, Kate and Robert. Robert confides in Kate: he has stolen a box of chocolates from the shop. Kate knows that this is wrong, but there are extenuating circumstances – Robert's mother is in hospital, and it is her birthday. Kate has to decide whether to tell the secret.

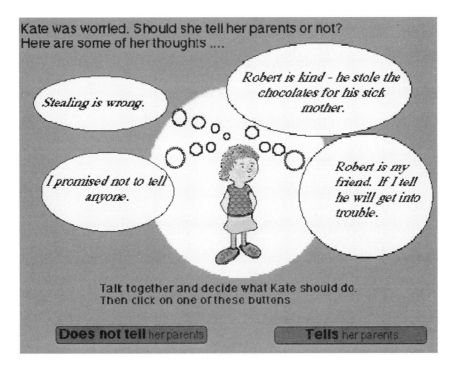

Figure 3.2 Kate's choice: an example of software stimulating exploratory talk around moral dilemmas

Transcript C: Kate's Choice

Laura, Olivia and Tim (Year 6)

LAURA: Wait. 'Kate was worried. Should she tell her parents or not?'
'Does . . .' no.
'Talk together and decide what Kate should do. Then click on' – one of those. Tells her parents I think.

OLIVIA: Do you think that?

TIM: Yes.

OLIVIA: I think that. 'Tells her parents.'

(*Clicks button.*)

Transcript D: Kate's Choice

Anna, Gavin and Zara (Year 6)

ANNA: Let Zara read this one now

ZARA: Well

GAVIN: Can you read all that?

ANNA: 'Kate . . .'

GAVIN: 'Kate was . . .'

ZARA: 'worried should she tell her parents or . . .'

GAVIN: '– not. Here are some of her thoughts'. Can you read that one? 'Stealing is wrong –'

ZARA: 'Stealing is wrong. I promised not to tell anyone –'

(*Children continue to read all information from the screen.*)

ANNA: What do you think?

ZARA: Tells her parents.

GAVIN: What do you think? You think, tell her parents? Why do you think she should tell her parents?

ZARA: 'Cos if she, she might get worried and that and it might – and she doesn't want to tell his parents, 'cos she wants to tell her parents so her parents can tell the boy's parents.

GAVIN: Would you?

ANNA: I'd tell the parents, because if –

GAVIN: Tell the parents is the right thing so I reckon, so we all go with tell the parents. You sure, tell the parents?

ANNA: Yes, tell the parents.

(*Clicks button*)

Comment

Again both groups are on task. Transcript D is taken from a class who had undertaken Talk Lessons. One useful indicator of exploratory talk is that the children spend much more time considering their decision.

Software design

The nature of the software used with pupils has an effect on the scope and range of their talk (Wegerif and Scrimshaw 1997: Chapter 13). So it is important to consider what features of the software or ICT will help or hinder the groups as they talk together. Some software may not be designed to support group talk, but it may have the potential to do so if the groups are well organised and the pupils have learned what 'talk together' really means. Some software will not support exploratory talk at all. Other software may be very helpful in providing contexts and situations which provoke and sustain talk, and may have screen prompts which remind or encourage the pupils to engage in rational discussion. Conferences and online discussion groups may well support educationally effective talk if the pupils are made aware that this is one aim of their work together.

Points to consider when choosing software

Some points to consider when choosing software with the aim of encouraging discussion and joint decision making are listed below. Software which is effective in supporting group talk has these characteristics:

- Evidence which can be used in reasoning about choices is clearly displayed on the screen. Pupils can then read it out, point to it, and refer to it in their talk.
- Choices are presented as part of a motivating 'story', so that the pupils are engaged with the characters and feel that the decisions they take 'matter' enough to deserve discussion. Choices may also be to do with undertaking a structured investigation, or solving problems by using logical deduction from information given.
- Problems are sufficiently complex (or 'real') to benefit from being analysed through reflection and discussion. Decisions which apparently have no consequence, or in which the consequence is unimportant, cannot engage pupils in rational discussion.
- Multiple choice options rather than typed input are preferable. Pupils can spend more time on futile searching of the keyboard to type in their response than they do talking, and the writing

continued

---

then becomes the focus of the activity. (Thus chat lines can only encourage effective discussion-at-a-distance once pupils' keyboard skills are developed to a level where typing becomes an 'invisible' activity.)

• Turn-taking is discouraged, that is, the task must not provide a series of unrelated sequential problems. This sort of software encourages other skills than talk.

Activity 3.5 Does your software support talk?

Consider an item of software that you have used, or seen in use, in a classroom by a group of children. Complete Table 3.1 to analyse the potential of the software to support exploratory talk.

Table 3.1 Analysing the potential of the software to support exploratory talk

	Yes	Partially	No
a) is useful evidence for rational decision making displayed on screen?			
b) are choices part of an involving narrative or investigation?			
c) are problems sufficiently complex, or do choices have 'important' consequences?			
d) are there multiple choice options to facilitate response?			
e) does the program discourage turn-taking?			

Note: Ticks in the 'Yes' column indicate that the software design can encourage and sustain discussion.

Your involvement in the structuring of the computer-based task

The entire curriculum provides a context for work undertaken at the computer. ICT can be thought of as a tool which facilitates discussion, research and presentation of work, once integrated into classroom practice. It is the teacher's framing and organisation of tasks with ICT that ensures the technology is used to good educational effect: 'School management and the personal competence and confidence of teachers are two vital elements in the effective use of ICT in teaching and learning' (BEON 1997: 17).

When the central aim of using ICT with children is to develop rational, educationally useful talk skills, pupils need to know this before they are asked to work together in a group. As described in this chapter, they can be encouraged to decide on and agree to a set of ground rules for talk. The ground rules can be displayed in the classroom, and pupils asked to remind one another of them before working together at the computer. The advantages of such rules can be a topic for discussion. Pupils can evaluate their own talk skills and decide whether increased awareness has been of value to them, not only in their computer groups but also in other curriculum areas and perhaps outside the classroom. The computer as a medium for communication is in this situation put to best use by the teacher's structuring of classroom activities.

The following are examples of the aims of three of the ten talking lessons undertaken by teachers and pupils in the SLANT and TRAC projects. The lesson plan for Lesson 1 is also included here. It demonstrates the shift in focus for the children towards considering their talk as a highly valuable resource, which they can work to develop. The activities are uncomplicated: it is the emphasis on talk aims that is the novelty.

The talk lessons and their aims

Lesson 1. Talk about talk

- To raise children's awareness of their talk;
- To introduce some words for describing ways of talking and to enable children to practise using them.

Lesson 2. Talking in groups

- To start children working together in their 'talk groups' and establish group cohesion;
- To help children practise 'taking turns' in talk.

Lesson 3. Ground rules for talk

- To encourage children to give and ask for reasons to support their opinions and suggestions;
- To decide on a class set of 'ground rules for talk'.

Lesson plan I. Talk about talk

(National Curriculum Key Stage 1 and 2. Speaking and Listening 1: Range a,b,c 2: Key Skills a,b)

Resources

Dictionaries, Thesaurus, Display materials, Sheets 1a, 1b, 1c (see Figures 3.3, 3.4, 3.5).

Aims

- To raise children's awareness of their talk;
- To introduce some words for describing ways of talking and enable children to practise using them.

Learning outcomes

By the end of this lesson, children will be able to:

- demonstrate an awareness of the value of talk;
- explain the meanings of some relevant words;
- display an example of collaborative work.

Whole class work

1 Introduce the new 'Talk' topic (2–3 minutes).
2 Explain to the children the aims for Lesson 1 (5 minutes).
3 Ask the children for their ideas about talk (15 minutes).

The following questions provide an initial structure for the class discussion. These are open-ended questions which should elicit a range of contributions based on personal experience and ideas.

BACKGROUND IDEAS

- Are you good at talking?
- Do you ever get asked to stop talking? Who asks this? When?
- Does anyone ever try to make you talk when you don't want to?
- Do you like using the telephone? Who do you talk to?
- Do you know anyone who is easy to talk to? Can you say why?

LEARNING TO TALK

- Has anyone got a baby at home? How do babies learn to talk?
- Who taught you how to talk?
- Do you learn how to talk in school?

USING TALK

- Are you asked to talk together in class? In which lessons?
- Can you think of any reasons why talking is a useful thing to be able to do?
- What 'jobs' can people get done by talking to each other?
- How would you communicate with other people if you couldn't talk?
- How many different languages can you speak?
- How many different languages have you heard of?

COMMUNICATING

- What happens when people talk but others don't listen?
- What are any differences between talking and writing?

Group work

1 Sorting Talk (15 minutes)

Provide each group of children with Worksheet (1a) 'A list of talk words' (Figure 3.3) and Worksheet (1b) 'Sorting talk' (Figure 3.4).

Ask the groups to talk together to put each word on Worksheet 1(a) into one of the boxes on Worksheet 1(b). Tell them that they should:

- use a dictionary to clarify any unfamiliar words;
- write the words in, once the group has agreed;
- find two new words to go in each box by using the thesaurus.

2 Speech Bubbles (15–25 minutes)

Provide each child with a copy of Worksheet (1c) 'Speech bubbles' (Figure 3.5).

Ask the group to:

- choose a word from the list on the sheet;
- in the first large box, draw a cartoon and speech bubble to show the word being used;
- write the word in the space above the cartoon;
- pass on the sheet to another member of the group until everyone has drawn a cartoon on the sheet.

Whole class work continued

1   Arrange for the children to share their completed work (5 minutes).
2   Organise a class discussion (10 minutes). Some suggestions for starter questions are:

brag	reply
chat	tell
chatter	softly
conversation	stammer
demand	argue
dialogue	splutter
enquire	threaten
explain	screech
gossip	answer
laugh	natter
loudly	ask
moan	croak
mumble	grumble
mutter	dispute
persuade	reason
scream	request
shout	explain
tell off	row
whisper	fiercely
yell	discuss

Figure 3.3 Worksheet (1a) A list of talk words

- Who did the most talking in your group?
- Did your group work well together?
- How can you share ideas in a group?
- How has talking together helped you think in this lesson?

3   Go over the lesson aims to check that the children feel that they have been achieved (5 minutes).

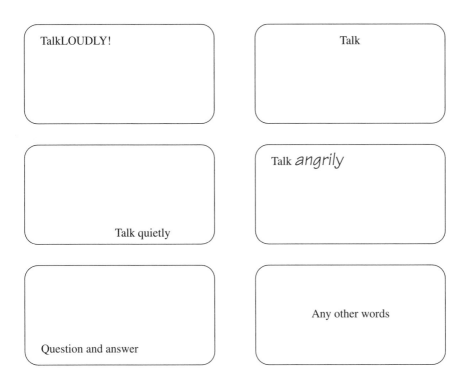

Figure 3.4 Worksheet (1b) Sorting talk

Follow up and extension work

DISPLAY

Ask each child to draw a life-sized 'talking head' with a large speech bubble, and put one of the talking words in it. The 'talking heads' can be mounted for display.

HOMEWORK

1   Children may ask parents/relatives to describe their experiences in class-rooms: when was talk allowed, encouraged, or discouraged.
2   Children can find out how old they were when they began to talk, and see if anyone remembers what they first said, or anything amusing they said as an infant.

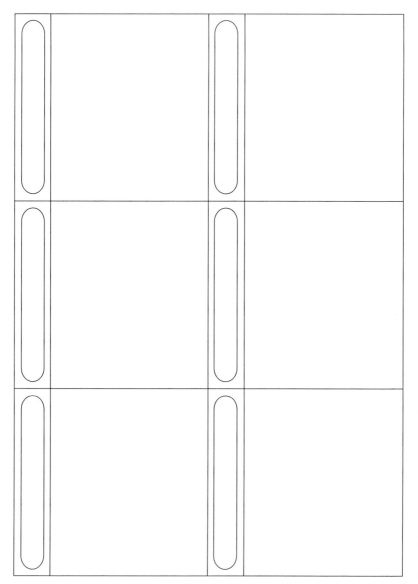

Figure 3.5 Worksheet (Ic) Speech bubbles

A path to full literacy and individual achievement

We can trace a progression in children's acquisition of literacy. Children usually arrive in classrooms with a functional vocabulary and range of talk repertoires. That is, they know how to take their audience into account when they talk. They are capable of dialogue, but are unlikely to be familiar with many of the various forms it can take. As teachers there are many activities we can organise in order to develop children's talk repertoires. As described in this chapter, one significant contribution is to encourage the development of reasoned spoken dialogue. This process can be supported by your use of classroom computers, and enriched by the opportunities ICT offers to engage with others at a distance in space and time. Through the rapid communication channels computers offer, the skills of exploratory talk can be transferred to written language. Children can 'talk' this way together via e-mail. Through the use of their new talk skills they can achieve genuine reasoning in their written contributions to networked debate. This enables more ready acquisition of network literacy.

The opportunity to talk or write with others who understand the value of such exchange of thoughts is invaluable. One striking advantage of exploratory talk is that the process of thinking aloud together in a rational manner allows individual children to progress towards thinking alone in the same way.

So, having internalised the 'dialogue' of reasoning about ideas, the child can use this as a personal resource when working alone. The ability to 'argue a case' clearly and effectively when speaking or writing is highly prized by the sort of society we live in, where literacy is integral. So children can take their place in such a society equipped with the means to make meaning, and enable others to make meaning.

Summary

Pupils using the internet and other ICT applications to communicate are not just speaking but being spoken to. Both things are likely to enhance their feeling of worth, and their perception of themselves as the centre of concentric circles of interesting and valuable societies – their class, their school, their community, their country, their continent – and to consider the worth of others in these terms.

Effective use of ICT in the classroom allows pupils to acquire the skills of network literacy – that is, to access electronic resources, to create resources themselves, and to communicate with others.

Networked computers can provide a wealth of information. They can also provide opportunities to practise the valuable skills of discussing ideas and suggestions, negotiating compromises, and reaching a group decision – that is, engaging in exploratory talk.

The quality of children's work with computers can be greatly improved if they are taught how to talk and listen to each other face to face. Technology can provide new opportunities but the essential skill of communication lies in knowing how to reach a shared understanding. This knowledge can empower children so that they are able to make the most of the opportunities for communication offered by technology. It is our responsibility as teachers to accept the challenge of preparing children to work collaboratively with the support of ICT. Without such preparation, the great potential of both the child and the technology may not be realised. Once learned, exploratory talk skills and the way of thinking they engender are invaluable in educational and social contexts – throughout life.

Acknowledgements

The research reported in this paper was funded by ESRC grant R000221868: Investigating Reasoning, Talk and the Role of Computers in the Primary Classroom.

We also gratefully acknowledge the co-operation of the schools of Milton Keynes who have supported our work.

Computer software

The programs 'Tracks' and 'Kate's Choice' were prepared for the TRAC project by Rupert Wegerif.

References and further reading

Barnes, D. and Todd, F. (1977) *Communication and Learning in Small Groups*, London: Routledge and Kegan Paul.
Barnes, D. and Todd, F. (1995) *Communication and Learning Revisited*, Portsmouth, NH: Heinemann.
BEON: Bristol Education On-line Network (1997) *Facing the Future*, Multimedia Communication Services, Bristol: ICL.
Dawes, L. (1992) 'Company at the keyboard', *CLAC Occasional Papers in Language and Communication*, no. 36.
DfEE (1997) *Connecting The Learning Society*, London: HMSO.
Grugeon, L., Hubbard, L., Smith, C. and Dawes, L. (1998) *Speaking and Listening in the Primary School*, London: Fulton Press.
   Spoken language is central to education. This book emphasises the importance of encouraging educationally effective talk.
Mercer, N. (1994) 'The quality of talk in children's joint activity at the computer', *Journal of Computer Assisted Learning*, **10**, pp. 24–32.
Mercer, N. (1995) *The Guided Construction of Knowledge: Talk Amongst Teachers and Learners*, Clevedon: Multilingual Matters.

Mercer, N., Wegerif, R. and Dawes, L. (1999) 'Children's talk and the development of reasoning in the classroom', *British Educational Research Journal*, **25**(1), 95–111.

Raven, J., Court, J. and Raven, J.C. (1995) *Manual for Raven's Progressive Matrices and Vocabulary Scales. Section 2: Coloured Progressive Matrices*, Oxford: Oxford Psychologists Press.

Swann, J. (1992) *Girls, Boys and Language*, Oxford: Blackwell.

By looking at classroom language, this book considers issues relating to the provision of equal opportunities for boys and girls in classrooms, and provides practical information for teachers trying to ensure this.

Vygotsky, L.S. (1978) *Mind in Society: The Development of Higher Psychological Processes*, London: Harvard University Press.

Wegerif, R. and Mercer, N. (1996) 'Computers and reasoning through talk in the classroom', *Language and Education*, **10**(1), 47–65.

Wegerif, R. and Scrimshaw, P. (1997) *Computers and Talk in the Primary Classroom*, Clevedon: Multilingual Matters.

An exploration of how computers are being used in Primary classrooms and how they could be used to better effect. A particular emphasis on spoken language.

Wegerif, R, Mercer, N. and Dawes, L. (1998) 'Software design to support discussion in the primary curriculum', *Journal of Computer Assisted Learning*, **14**, 199–211.

Useful sources

The following URLs provide useful sources of information and ideas from both government and school sources.

UK primary schools

Sutton on Sea Primary: *http://www.sutton.lincs.sch.uk*
Meldreth Manor School: *http://www.rmplc.co.uk/eduweb/sites/meldreth/help.html*
Lower Bentham Primary: *http://www.ednet.lancs.ac.uk/lowb/school.htm*

Teachers

National Union of Teachers: *http://www.teachers.org.uk*
The Online Netskills Interactive Course: *http://www.netskills.ac.uk/TONIC/*
Special Needs In Education: *http://www.becta.org.uk/senco/*

Links to lots of useful things, including schools

http://eyesoftime.com/teacher/ukpage.htm
Public Records Office: the Learning Curve Gallery: *http://www.pro.gov.uk/education/snapshots/default.htm*
Schools in Cyberspace: *http://www.strath.ac.uk/~cjbs17/Cyberspace/index.html*
Educational Resources (use 'listserv' link): *http://k12.cnidr.org:90/k12.html*

Government

Questions: *http://www.education-quest.com*
DfEE: *http://www.open.gov.uk/dfeehome.htm*
National Grid for Learning: *http://www.ngfl.gov.uk*
British Educational Communications and Technology Agency:
  http://www.becta.org.uk
Virtual Teachers' Centre: *http://www.vtc.org.uk*
Ofsted: *http://www.ofsted.gov.uk/ofsted.htm*
Teacher Training Agency: *http://www.teach-tta.gov.uk*
Standards: *http://www.standards.dfee.gov.uk*

Chapter 4

Creativity, Visual Literacy and ICT

Avril Loveless with Terry Taylor

It is my view that the production of powerful and meaningful art work is made possible through a long term development of ideas and their visual representation. It is the representation of meaning that is the key that elevates production to a position beyond the merely decorative. My experience as an image maker has led me to conclude that this is achieved by entering into a 'dialogue' with the work. By dialogue, I mean the dynamic and creative cognitive processes involved when encoding and decoding meaning in visual texts. The meanings encoded are not necessarily known completely before a piece is produced. A powerful piece of work simultaneously represents less and more than the artist intends. The meaning and its representation in a visual form resolve themselves through a working method – a dialogue where the maker produces and the work responds. This takes time and a continuation of intention and cannot be achieved by ad hoc projects based on mechanical processes.

(Terry Taylor, artist, 1998)

Introduction

Children can be creators and collaborators with ICT – not just consumers and collectors of information. This is a exciting thought for teachers involved in the significant developments in the use of ICT in education, in which, in the UK, the National Grid for Learning claims to connect learners to a physical network, a resource network and a human network (DfEE 1998). There is much discussion about the impact that ICT might have in primary schools, both to support the delivery of literacy and numeracy and to raise questions about the challenges that ICT presents to our understanding of the roles of learners and teachers. Easy access to information does not automatically lead to learning – no more than the availability of educational TV programmes transforms a couch potato into a scholar. As teachers, we need to explore, and be explicit about, the ways in which we can help children become good learners who use a wealth of resources to assist them in the construction of their own knowledge and understanding. We also need to think carefully about how we can encourage children to be active learners, using ICT to represent ways of knowing which have not been available to them with other technologies.

In an 'Information Society', meanings are communicated in a wide range of media – from the presentation of the weather forecast, to the packaging of a breakfast cereal or the conventions of the animated cartoon. Visual literacy plays a key role in our ability to decode and encode meanings, both to establish communication and to express our ideas to others. In helping children to develop literacies appropriate to our modern society, we need to provide them with informed choices about the media they select to explore and express their visual ideas. What might ICT contribute to the development of a visual literacy which is creative and collaborative? How might children's creative experiences in the visual arts be extended by the use of ICT? What role might teachers and schools play in children's learning and creativity, which will build upon the wider culture of children's creative use of ICT? This chapter will focus on two projects in which contemporary artists have worked with children and teachers using digital technology in the visual arts. Each project presents some of the challenging possibilities that can arise from the interaction between the use of ICT in the visual arts in the primary curriculum and the learners, teachers and artists involved in the creative process.

Objectives

By the end of this chapter you will have been introduced to:

• ways of using ICT in the classroom to stimulate visual literacy;
• examples of applications of ICT to the art curriculum;
• classroom management issues;
• case studies of innovative projects with children working directly with an artist.

Why use ICT in the art environment?

'Why bother at all with ICT in the visual arts in the primary classroom? Isn't there enough to do without having to deal with difficult equipment?'

'Doesn't the use of ICT come 'naturally' to young children? They know much more about ICT than their teachers and parents anyway.'

'Don't the children have enough experience of using ICT in creative ways outside the classroom? . . . They sit in their bedrooms playing with computers all the time these days.'

A busy teacher in a lively classroom working to implement a range of initiatives, from the Literacy Hour to the ICT development plan, might well argue that the use of digital technologies in the visual arts is inappropriate in a bursting curriculum using hard-pressed resources. The increasing number of children who have access to multimedia personal computers at home may be in a better position to use them in creative ways, arriving in the classroom with confidence and competence with these technologies which can then be used in other areas.

Notwithstanding the issues of 'haves' and 'have nots' on the effects of equity of access, these arguments are not based on evidence of children's actual use of digital technologies in their informal learning and culture. Some teachers and parents may be extraordinarily ignorant of the ways in which their children use computers, videos and games in their own time. They express concerns about the negative effects of games or inappropriate material found on the internet, yet have a very *laissez-faire* approach to children's experience in a world which is not understood or mediated by adults (Sanger *et al.* 1997). Even when children do have access to technology which enables them to make, save and display visual work – a feat not always possible if the hard disc space is limited or the printer is missing – they often find themselves producing visual images or animations which are incomplete and lack an audience for the presentation, development or exhibition of work (Sefton-Green and Buckingham 1998).

Teachers and artists working in school are in a position to provide a framework for children which gives them confidence and skills to extend the boundaries of their creative experience. They can offer opportunities to children to develop processes of visual literacy, practise techniques with different tools and resources and provide a range of audiences for developing and finished work – whether they be children in the same class or groups of people separated by space and time, communicating through electronic networks.

What unique contribution can ICT make to children's experience of the visual arts?

Digital data as a medium

There have been a number of discussions about the distinctive nature of 'digital data' as a medium in the visual arts and how it contrasts with other media, from paint and clay to textiles and photographic emulsions (Mitchell 1994; Loveless 1997). Computer graphics applications enable users to 'paint' or 'draw' on the screen, using a range of methods to input and manipulate the data – whether dragging a mouse pointer around the screen or using a digital camera or scanner to capture an image produced in other media. From the simulation of a brushstroke of red paint, to the use of a sophisticated filter to change the appearance of texture of an object, the visual effects on the screen are the result of different values being assigned to the pixels of the screen, altering their colour, intensity and the relationship between different elements on the screen. Such techniques are indeed 'making marks with mathematics' and we are still in the early days of understanding the distinctive expressive qualities of this medium (Loveless 1995).

Working with the medium

When first working with graphics packages, children often make marks by mimicking the techniques and processes of other tools, such as brushes, pens, spray cans and rollers, using the mouse or digital pen and tablet to simulate the movement around the canvas or paper. Such mark making can produce lively and interesting images, but it is often remarked that the traditional tools are less clumsy and much more responsive to touch, pressure and the texture of the paper. Graphics packages come into their own when they are used to manipulate and transform elements of images which may well have been initially constructed and created using different media and captured by a digital camera or scanner. Such techniques range from straightforward cutting, copying and pasting, to flipping, stretching, shearing, rotating or applying filters to alter the texture and depth of parts of images. This ability to take an image apart, reassemble it, manipulate it, substitute colours and textures, merge it with other images or use elements of it as starting points for new ideas, opens up a range of techniques and processes which were not easily available to children using traditional media.

Activity 4.1 Manipulating images

Children in Year 5 at Carden Junior School in Brighton took pictures with a digital camera. These were manipulated and combined to give images which promoted discussion from other children in the class. See Figures 4.1 and 4.2. What kinds of meanings and messages do you think the children were trying to convey?

Try this activity with children in your class. Discuss their intentions and experimentations with the image, as well as the techniques tried and practised.

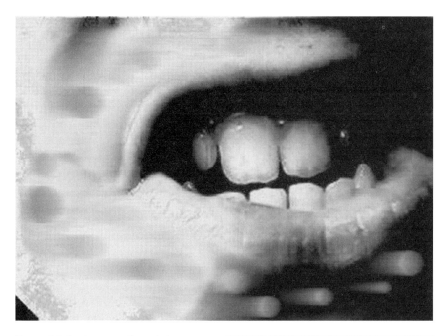

Figure 4.1 A close-up of teeth is manipulated with different effects

Figure 4.2 Manipulation of bottle and crouching girl images

Displaying images to an audience for exhibition or
collaboration

The visual images on the screen can be displayed in a number of ways. They can be shown on a computer screen, projected onto a large screen or printed out on a printer for a display on walls, boards, in books or folders. The images can be attached to email messages and sent to other people to be looked at in another place at another time, or incorporated with written text and sound to be part of a multimedia presentation, or web page. The form in which the image is to be displayed will influence the ways in which the audience views and interacts with the image and the choices that the children have to make about the appropriate ways in which to show and share work.

What contribution does ICT make to the development of visual literacy?

At the beginning of this chapter we quoted Terry's view of creative visual literacy being a long term, and tentative, development of dialogue between the artist and the work. This requires exploration, taking risks, engaging with new techniques and processes, taking time for evaluation and making the most of the unexpected. The characteristics of 'the digital' can be used to good effect in providing children with opportunities to develop this dialogue between 'maker and made'. The provisionality of ICT enables the children to explore visual ideas, try things out, erase, edit and re-work without the discouragement of 'spoiling' the work. Ideas can be saved, recalled and changed and there is always a choice to delete and overwrite previous ideas, or 'leave a trail' of different images saved to show how the ideas have developed from the starting point. Nothing need be final; images can be displayed and passed on to others to develop. The interactivity of ICT also supports this exploratory way of working, giving immediate feedback of the consequences of decisions and offering the chance to undo or change or extend the ideas and actions. The capacity and range of ICT enables the children to save complex images as digital information and to communicate and exhibit their ideas in a variety of forms across space and time.

Teaching and learning with ICT in the art curriculum

The use of ICT in teaching presents new challenges to teachers' understanding of subject knowledge in art, as well as IT, in order to underpin the children's experience with focused learning intentions in a meaningful context. The arrival of a new medium and new ways of working presents teachers with a challenge to think about how they will be incorporated and developed into the children's experience of the art curriculum. The National Curriculum for Art requires that pupils should: develop visual literacy to communicate ideas, feelings and meanings; be taught about the visual elements of pattern and texture, colour, line and tone, shape, form and space; be given opportunities to explore and use a range of media working on a variety of scales; be able to respond to and evaluate art, including their own and others' work (DfE 1995). ICT offers opportunities to develop all these areas in ways which contrast with other media and techniques and offer unique processes and experiences.

The role of the teacher

Having identified the ways in which ICT can be used to both support and extend children's learning in the art curriculum, teachers need to think carefully about how their teaching strategies and organisation will facilitate such learning. Organising the children's access to the resources to provide useful experiences demands careful planning and sensitive assessment of the children's achievements and needs. Selecting and refining appropriate teaching strategies requires thought, practice and evaluation:

- identifying starting points;
- explaining and demonstrating techniques;
- setting up peer group tutoring;
- asking challenging questions about the work as it develops;
- discussing the processes and finished work which the children produce.

The teacher also plays a role in giving the children access to wider audiences, whether that be leading a critical discussion with peers in the classroom at the end of the day, displaying work around the school, collaborating with children in other schools, or exhibiting work on the school website.

Case studies: artists in residence in primary schools

What do artists bring to this situation in which children and teachers are encountering new learning experiences? How do they support teacher development in the nature of art as a subject, in the technical skills required, in the ways of working as individuals and with others, in the opportunities to share and develop work with an audience and in the dynamic process of developing visual literacy as a 'dialogue between maker and made'?

The role of an artist in residence has the potential to be stimulating, encouraging and provoking – bringing new ways of looking and working which can be built upon by teachers, children and artists at the end of the project – a powerful learning experience for all. There is also the danger that the work that artists do, both in their own right and with the children, takes place outside the classroom and curriculum concerns of the school and does not touch the development of teachers or learners. It might be seen as threatening or irrelevant, leaving behind some work and experiences which gather dust over time and have little impact on any of the people involved.

The following case studies are accounts of work carried out in two projects by Terry Taylor, a contemporary artist who works with children exploring the development of visual literacy. In each project he worked with ICT to exploit its potential to allow children to construct visual images, develop them immediately and dynamically, display them in a number of forms to different audiences and develop the children's ideas over time. Each project illustrates the ways in which the interaction between the learners, teachers, artist and ICT provoked debate about the purpose and practicalities of such activities in the primary classroom. These discussions highlight ways forward to exciting developments in the use of ICT, in which children are able to use tools to help them express visual ideas in sophisticated ways and engage in ways of working which challenge the development of teachers' subject knowledge and pedagogical strategies.

Access: The Brighton Media Arts Project

The focus of the Access project was to support teacher development in the creative use of digital technologies in the visual arts. The fieldwork for the project took place in three primary schools in Brighton, working with teachers who had little experience of using ICT in their art work. The teachers were given three days to meet and work with Terry, the artist working on the project. They were given time to look at work that he had done with children previously, in which he used photography and ICT to help the children construct visual images, develop their ideas and present them to others. The teachers engaged in similar exercises themselves in which they used Polaroid and digital cameras to help them work together to construct and frame images which expressed some meaning – from 'how I would like to represent myself today' to 'how I feel about teaching'. They spent time discussing these images and then learning how to use various computer graphics packages to manipulate them further. They also looked at work being developed by practising artists using digital media and the internet. At the end of the period they discussed how they felt they might be able to incorporate similar work into their curriculum plans. In short, the days were used to present and discuss areas of work in which the teachers had not been engaged before, provide some technical training with the ICT resources and suggest ways forward in curriculum planning and classroom practice.

The model for the project was to use Terry's own work as a starting point, explore some of the ideas arising from the children's responses using traditional and familiar techniques of cut, paste and collage and then develop the children's ideas within the curriculum context using digital cameras and graphics software. The children were fascinated and drawn in by the prospect of meeting with a 'live' artist doing contemporary work. Much of the work they had done previously in looking at the work of other artists in their curriculum had focused on people who were dead, and who had produced their work in different contexts and societies – several children commented on this! Terry's work raised questions about notions of contrast and difference between the natural and the manufactured, using space and positioning in the images to create surprising, curious or seemingly impossible juxtapositions of elements of the image. Having discussed their responses to his photographs and asked questions of Terry, the children were asked to select and use cut-outs of pictures from magazines and comics, explore ways they might place images together to create effects of contrast, difference or opposites, and consider how the impact of the image was altered by the selection and placing of separate elements.

The sequence of images, produced by children in Year 4 in Glebe Middle School, Southwick, (Figures 4.3, 4.4 and 4.5) demonstrates how the children developed their ideas. They were exploring ways of placing images together to show differences in material and texture. The first image showed the use of a simple background to the picture of the keys. Later the children took a number of pictures of a drinking fountain and manipulated the original picture of the keys to change the orientation and colour. The final picture of 'Keys in Water' was the end result of several ideas.

The children's work developed from this starting point in different ways according to the curriculum context in which the activities had been planned. In one school; for example, the project took place in the middle of the theme 'Fashion and Fabric', in which the children created images which could be printed onto T-shirts and paraded at a Half-Term Fashion Show. In another school, the children explored ideas of 'Natural and Unnatural' to build up their images. The third school was focusing on language and poetry, and the teacher wished to incorporate words and images into a sequence of responses. This sequence started with words suggested by looking at Terry's pictures and used to stimulate the ideas for the paper collages. These words and collages were passed on to peers who then created poems in response to the words and pictures. These poems were, in turn, passed on to children who were asked to create a digital image, constructed and captured with a digital camera and manipulated and transformed using graphics software. Throughout the process, children worked as individuals and in pairs at different times, sometimes with the teacher and sometimes with Terry. The ongoing work was discussed with the whole class throughout the period of the project.

Figure 4.3 Keys

The work was therefore grounded in clear learning intentions relating to the medium term curriculum planning for art, English, D&T, IT and science. The underlying ideas which ICT would support were prepared by providing experiences for the children which set the scene for questioning, discussing and exploring visual ideas stimulated by Terry's work.

What contribution did ICT make to the development of visual literacy in these activities?

In each of the activities the children came to a point where they needed to construct their own images – looking at contrasts or responding to poetry or searching for examples of the natural and unnatural world. The ideas behind these themes were abstract and sometimes difficult for the children

Figure 4.4 (opposite above) Water

Figure 4.5 (opposite below) Keys in water

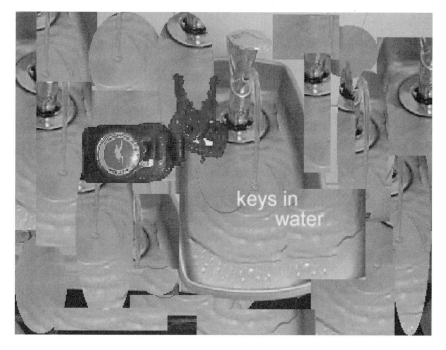

to express and they needed the opportunity to try out their ideas, discard those they did not like and develop those that came closer to that which they were trying to express. Using the digital camera they were able to 'frame' a picture which could be used to develop a more complex image. The children selected a range of possibilities – fragments of brick walls, close-ups of keys and flowers, parts of the body, vistas of the street near the school, a man reading a newspaper. When viewed on the computer screen, the children could make decisions about whether they had managed to capture some of their ideas in ways which could be worked upon, or whether they needed to go out to look for and construct another initial image. The capacity of ICT to store these images and the immediacy with which they could be displayed and considered were powerful starting points in the children's dialogue with their work.

Once these images had been downloaded, displayed on the screen and saved, the children were able to think about how they wished to manipulate and combine them to express their ideas and relate them to the themes they were exploring. They were able to discuss their suggestions with Terry, their teacher or with their peers, and think about which tools and techniques they might need. Indeed, in trying out new techniques, it often happened that unpredictable effects occurred, from colour substitution to producing a negative image, which the children then incorporated into the process. Again, the dialogue was supported by the ease with which the children could make changes and try things out, move back to look at the effects, save or discard, develop or start again. Uniquely, they were able to save the different stages of their ideas along the way. Some groups even returned to their early images some months later, developing them and taking them further than they could have imagined now they were more confident in the techniques and able to focus on visual ideas rather then technical tips (see for example the pupils' work in Figure 4.2).

The display of the work and the development of the children's ideas took different forms at different times. In the initial stages, the coloured, glued, 3D paper collages were photocopied in black and white and displayed on the walls of the classroom for discussion by the whole class and presentation to classroom visitors. As the digital images were captured and transformed, they were displayed on the screen where small groups of children could gather round to discuss and make suggestions. The final works were printed out on colour printers, either onto paper which was then mounted and incorporated into wall displays reflecting the story of the project, or onto transfer paper from which the images could be ironed on to T-shirts to be worn in the Year Group Fashion Show. The completed work was also used in presentation software which was then projected onto a screen for larger audiences of children, teachers and students to see and comment.

Learning outcomes

The key issues raised about the use of ICT in these activities were related to the ways in which it enabled the children to develop a 'dialogue' between themselves and the images they were making. The interactivity, provisionality and capacity of ICT gave the children the opportunities to look at, think about, refine and evaluate their work with immediate feedback and reassurance that mistakes would not frustrate their ideas. The digital medium provided access to techniques and effects which could not be produced easily, if at all, with more traditional processes and resources. The digital camera enabled the children and teachers to build upon work developed with photography in framing and capturing images from the immediate surroundings. The graphics software enabled the children to develop these images with their imagination, using the variety of tools and techniques to present their ideas in different forms.

The Bristol Internet Project

The activities in the Access Project could have been produced by using traditional photography, sophisticated developing and printing techniques and photocopies, but it explored ways in which children's visual literacy could be developed and supported by using ICT to provide immediacy to the process in the classroom environment. The Bristol Internet Project focused on other features of ICT which enable children to collaborate with others in their creative work. The ICT facilities were simple to use, but the processes in which the children were able to engage were powerful. Two artists, Kam Ghandi and Terry Taylor, worked in two schools in different parts of the city, which has a multicultural population, but in which communities may be isolated or confrontational. The children in the schools represented two different communities which would not have had much opportunity to meet and work together. One of the aims of the project was to use art and ICT to set up communication between the groups of Year 2 children who could work with each other over space and time to produce visual images.

In each school, the children talked with the artist about activities that they liked or would like to do – driving a racing car, flying like superman, playing basketball or sleeping and reading. They worked in pairs to construct images of themselves acting out these activities, thinking about how they would present themselves and instructing their friends on how to frame and capture that image using a digital camera. These images were downloaded and saved on a desktop computer to be manipulated in a simple graphics package. The children were asked to work on the initial image – changing colours or cutting out irrelevant backgrounds – to produce another image which focused clearly on the activity in question. Again, the features of ICT were used to support this creative process – constructing, developing and presenting visual ideas which conveyed meaning.

The next stage in the project took the presentation of these ideas a few steps forward. The children attached the saved image files to an email message, which they sent to their counterparts in the school in the other community, requesting that they look at the picture, think about what the activity might be, develop and complete the picture using a graphics package and send back their ideas with another email message. A boy who sent a picture of himself 'flying' over the camera, received his returned image in which he had been given Superman's clothes. Another boy who sent a cut-out of himself in a contorted position on the school wall bars, received a picture of himself jumping up to a basket ball hoop. A girl who wanted to be a waitress came back as an airhostess. The children at each end of the internet link were able to communicate with each other through text and visual images, think about what their partner was trying to say to them and respond by developing their visual ideas. They used straightforward graphics techniques to interpret and complete the pictures – from painting, drawing, cutting, pasting, to using the 'dropper' to pick up, and use, a subtle range of colours from the clothes of the child in the picture.

Certainly the project could have set up communication by sending photographs, drawings and letters through the post, but the ICT resources were used to make two particular and unique contributions to the collaboration. The first was associated with the ease, speed and informality of the communication over the internet, covering gaps in space, time and culture. The second was associated with the ways in which the children could alter and develop the piece itself, working with the digital medium to produce an image which was the result of more than one person's imagination, but leaving a trail of saved images which traced the development of ideas between those people.

The key issues raised about the use of ICT in these activities were related to both the unique facilities of the resources and the limitations imposed by ICT tools and techniques. The nature of the communication and exchange of ideas between the two groups of children was certainly facilitated by the technology, from the digital cameras to the email links. Questions were raised about the 'origin' and 'ownership' of the shared images and the shifting roles of 'authors' and 'audiences' in such an activity. Some of the children, however, were disappointed in the images that they received back from their 'collaborators'. They felt that using a mouse to control the tools for painting, selecting or cutting was clumsy and inaccurate, especially for young hands. They felt that they were capable of more careful work with real brushes, scissors and paste, which would do justice to the initial pictures which had been so carefully considered, composed and captured. The digital images could have been developed with a range of other media and the results then scanned and digitised in order to be sent back via email. ICT had certainly had an impact on the ways in which the children were able to capture, communicate and collaborate, which would not have been as immediate with traditional methods. It did not necessarily provide the most appropriate medium or techniques for these young children to express their ideas, but raised questions about the choices that could have been made.

Activity 4.2 Developing visual literacy in your classroom

Consider the ideas for the artwork undertaken in the two case studies. What new approaches would you like to try in your classroom? Look for ideas for arts projects on, for example, the European School Net,[1] or the British Council Montage[2] websites. Chapter 10 also lists partner finding websites.

Summary

Each of these projects demonstrated how artists could work with children and teachers to contribute their expertise and experience to the art curriculum. Their work focused on the meaningful ways that children could express and communicate their visual ideas to others. Within this context they drew upon a range of media, techniques and processes to support and extend the children's capabilities. They used the features of ICT to provide the children with a new medium with which to work, a range of techniques, an immediacy in the processes and the opportunity to explore, refine and express their visual ideas. ICT assisted the artists and teachers in setting up and maintaining a 'dialogue' between the children, their work and their audience.

Acknowledgements

Access: The Brighton Media Arts Project was a collaborative project funded and supported by the Arts Council of England, the University of Brighton, South East Arts and Lighthouse, the Brighton Media Centre. The schools participating in the project were Carden Junior School, Brighton, Peter Gladwin Primary School, Portslade and Glebe Middle School, Southwick.

The Bristol Internet Project was funded and supported by Artists in Education, Arts Council of England, Watershed Media Centre, Bristol and NUgates Internet Service Provider, Bristol. The schools participating in the project were Luckwell School and Millponds School, Bristol.

Notes

1   Projects can be found through the European School Net site on *http://www.
    eun.org*
2   The British Council Montage Projects can be found on *http://www.bc.org.au/
    montage*

References and further reading

DfE (1995) *Art in the National Curriculum*, London: HMSO.

DfEE (1998) 'Connecting the learning society: national grid for learning',
    Consultation Paper, London: Department for Education and Employment.

Loveless, A. (1995) *The Role of IT: Practical Issues for Primary Teachers*, London:
    Cassell.

Loveless, A. (1997) 'Working with images, developing ideas', in McFarlane, A.
    (ed.), *Information Technology and Authentic Learning: Realising the Potential of
    Computers in the Primary Classroom*, London: Routledge.

Mitchell, W.J. (1994) *The Reconfigured Eye: Visual Truth in the Post-photographic
    Era*, Cambridge, MA: MIT Press.

Sanger, J., Willson, J., Davies, B. and Whittaker, R. (1997) *Young Children, Videos
    and Computer Games: Issues for Teachers and Parents*, London: Falmer Press.

Sefton-Green, J. and Buckingham, D. (1998) 'Digital visions: children's "creative"
    uses of multimedia technologies', in Sefton-Green, J. (ed.) (1998) *Digital
    Diversions*, London: UCL Press.

Chapter 5

Mathematics and ICT

Hamish Fraser

Introduction

Mathematics as a subject has for many years embraced, at least at the level of 'principle', constructivist theory (see Chapter 6, p. 98, for a definition). The National Numeracy Strategy's (1999) emphasis on Mental Maths, and their clear definition of it as a process that involves children building up a network of understanding, further emphasises what has been clear for some time: good teaching of maths involves learners in a process that extends their understanding through making connections between their existing ideas, or more succinctly, by enabling them to construct and extend their framework of concepts and ideas.

Yet when using IT or ICT with children so much of the learning has not been toward these ends. Much of a class's work can be viewed as typifying pure behaviourist theory. In some cases, computer use has been too bound up with technical 'issues' and has thus become the preserve of one or two teachers who have an interest in the technology. Where this happens in a school, the ethos about ICT use which becomes established may mean that the way to produce evidence of ICT learning is to have the pupils repeatedly follow a clear list of instructions until the instructions become internalised. Successful pupil learning requires teachers to focus on objectives beyond the development of technical skills (Chapter 1 lists different areas of learning which may be stimulated by ICT).

What this chapter examines is not the technical aspects of using computers but the potential they have to promote learning. The discussion then moves into an examination of constructivist thought which provides a powerful explanation of how pupils learn. This is not to say that knowing how and when to turn the computer on and off is not an essential skill but to place it into its proper context.

Objectives

By the end of this chapter you will have been introduced to ideas about:

- communication and mathematics using ICT;
- creative approaches to data handling;
- Logo as a means for developing mathematical thinking.

Communication

It is vital that the use of computers for communication is placed into context. The internet is a powerful tool for communicating with websites and between schools. Other chapters in this book (for example 6, 10 and 13) provide guidance on the development and management of curriculum projects using the web, many of which are cross-curricular. John Meadows provides examples in the sections 'Fast food – maths, geography, IT' and 'Examples of cross-curricula projects using ICT in a variety of ways' below, which indicate the kinds of work which teachers are undertaking using cross-curriculum networks.

Fast food – maths, geography, IT

Children investigate conflicting views about proposals for new fast food restaurants in their locality, linking geography (school's locality and settlement) with maths (data handling) and IT (communicating and handling information).

They might design a questionnaire and computer database to gather and store local opinion, as well as undertaking field work in a local shopping centre.

They might then link with children in different countries, e.g., in the USA and compare food preferences and shopping styles (e.g., the Mall). International food chains and restaurants might be compared, e.g., the MacDonald chain, to see which local varieties of the regular meals are used and how these dishes are named.

It may be possible to link with developing countries and compare ways of preparing and cooking food and explore cultural similarities and differences regarding food.

Learning outcomes might include:

- designing a questionnaire to explore local people's views about fast food;
- setting up a database to record the information collected through the questionnaire;

continued

- visiting and gathering information about local foodstores and fast food outlets;
- understanding the differences between their own food preferences and those of others;
- learning of new ways of cooking and preparing food;
- comparing prices and other costs associated with fast food consumption.

Spreadsheets and databases are commonly used mathematical tools. Chapter 6 includes projects using spreadsheets for pupil work which link mathematics and science.

Examples of cross-curricula projects using ICT in a variety of ways

Project 1

UK participants were sought by a teacher in New Zealand for a project tracing the export of fruit from NZ. Children involved from other countries were asked to find out how much the fruit cost in their countries, e.g., Kiwi fruit, pears, apples. The work involved currency rates and conversions, and weights and measures.

This type of project also links schools to their local communities as children explore their local food shops for fruits and prices. The curriculum areas supported include maths and English, as well as science since the preservation of fruit during its long journey might also be investigated.

Project 2

UK participants were sought by a teacher in Australia for the Sports online project. Children in collaborating countries carried out a variety of field and track events and the results were sent through email or websites to others. The results were collated and made available. The maths involved included measuring length and time, data handling and averages, tabulating and graphing data, comparing and looking for patterns, etc.

As sport in English schools is in need of revival, with school playing fields disappearing and so much emphasis on basic academic skills,

continued

networks like this, linking physical exercise with ICT and writing and maths, can help put back some balance into the curriculum.

Project 3

UK participants were sought by a teacher in USA for a problem-solving maths project linked to design and make ideas and activities, e.g., design and make and evaluate a device to catch an egg from the height of 1 metre, without it breaking. Maths involved included measuring length, time perhaps, accuracy, recording data, presenting data, shape and size, etc.

Chapter 13 on networks provides advice to help teachers find partners for projects.

Communication can also be stimulated within the classroom by encouraging children to discuss maths issues and resolve them with the computer as the context for discussion is very powerful. Discussion is the basis of much mathematical development. Chapter 3 provided a detailed examination of how teachers can stimulate effective talk around computers: 'By trying to articulate their mathematical ideas children clarify their concepts and gain mastery of the language patterns of mathematics' (Haylock 1991: 47).

In this chapter we will examine the use of the computer to develop such situations. The activities selected lend themselves to the promotion of pupils working together to discuss mathematical issues. The effective use of the computer for learning requires this.

> If we believe that children are not passive receivers of knowledge, but are continually involved in constructing meaning, and that meaning may need to be negotiated, this demands a forum within which such negotiations and constructions can take place.
>
> (Orton and Frobisher 1996: 60)

As such the work around the computer becomes a forum in which meaning is constructed and children learn. The most basic communication, individuals in a group, in most situations is the most powerful. The computer can make links with many internet sites but the discussion of the issues raised by those who choose to visit them is the most important. The computer provides the 'forum' by which much maths is discussed and a platform for the 'construction of meaning'.

There are also a number of excellent web-based resources for maths teachers and an annotated list of recommended sites is included at the end of this chapter.

Data handling

There have been many software packages that enable children to handle data. An issue when handling data in school is often not one of software but one of a misunderstanding of the best means to develop an appreciation of data. With or without computer support good maths teaching dictates that any data collected for analysis are interpreted and questions are raised from it. This can be represented as a circular process as in Figure 5.1.

The computer must be used in the same way to display data and to prompt pupils to ask questions and make conclusions from it.

Using the computer to present data following the same process offers three benefits:

1   It enables data to be represented quickly (once entered) in a variety of adaptable forms and thus examined for meaning.
2   It enables children to experience and discuss wider forms of data presentations.
3   The technicalities of graph construction are demonstrated for children. Issues of scale and layout can be identified as data are produced by the computer for children to adopt in their own pencil and paper work.

Before examining these issues in greater depth we will look at the problems of using data outside of the cycle.

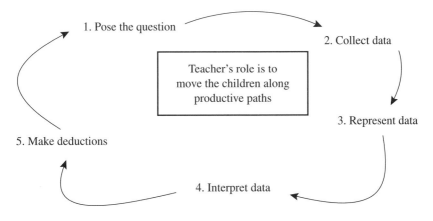

Figure 5.1 The data handling process
Source: adapted from Hopkins *et al.* 1996

Issues of a misuse of data (or the myth of the bar chart)

For the computer to be used effectively it must be used in conjunction with the principles of the data handling process (Figure 5.1), that is, that the process of working with data requires pupils to interpret data rather than just display data. The effective use of ICT does not allow this thorough investigation of data issues that are relevant to children to be ignored.

As identified in Harlen (1985), children can come to view creating a block graph as a means by which data problems are resolved. This is done without consideration of or experience of any other possibilities. This could simply be a product of the pupils' experience that each time data are collected it is always placed into a block graph.

A block graph is not the mystical means by which some data become clearer once entered into it. It is an appropriate means by which some data can be displayed. If it becomes the default means by which data are displayed, it is likely that data handling has become a linear process (Figure 5.2). This process is a limiting one. Using the computer to produce charts in these terms is also limiting.

If constructivist thought is to be applied to data collection, classes need to avoid this linear approach which can be typified as broadly behaviourist. Once the class has some vested interest in the data, their thoughts concerning collection are required and a discussion can be shaped. This process enables the issue of displaying the data to best show the information sought, to be discussed and experimented with. Such activities allow the development of greater experience with handling data and a greater understanding of the process. Once the data have been displayed and discussed, they are likely to raise more questions requiring further investigation.

This method of working is in clear keeping with a constructivist notion of maths teaching and can be further enhanced with the use of ICT. The basis of this enhancement will be outlined on examination of the three areas identified earlier.

Figure 5.2 Linear collections of data

Representing data quickly in a variety of forms

This chapter examines the strengths of ICT. The ability to enter data once and choose to display them in a variety of forms is an advantage, which needs to be managed. Once data are entered onto a spreadsheet the power to select the form in which they are displayed is an aid to interpretation and to raising issues for further enquiry.

Access to a range of graphs has further advantages:

1   The block graph is placed into a context that allows other means of data handling to be selected where appropriate.
2   The discussion of appropriateness is wholly mathematical and one that is valid of itself.
3   Interpretation of data is aided by seeing them in a variety of forms.

When analysing real data they tend to be a little 'untidy'. This is a feature of such data. Handling real data enhances interpretation skills of those involved.

Experience with a spreadsheet also allows more than data issues to be explored. Linking cells allows number relationships to be explored in a way not possible in other mediums. This issue combined with the data issues already identified make it a very powerful medium for teaching.

> A spreadsheet environment allows pupils to express general mathematical relationships which are far more sophisticated than those which can they can normally express in their pencil and paper work.
>
> (Healy and Sutherland 1991: 3)

Data in a variety of forms

Seeing data displayed in different forms is an advantage. The discussion of why a particular graph, as has already been indicated, is best suited to the analysis of data is a valid mathematical discussion. What this also does is to identify some areas that particular spreadsheets are not suited to. Finding that the computer will not display data exactly in the form you want is valuable for learning. This whole process has crucially helped identify the variety of possible forms by which data can be examined.

Developing pencil and paper means

Discussion and analysis of computer-generated graphs has an impact on the graphing skills of those examining it. As the structured form that the computer uses to display data is examined, there is much anecdotal evidence that this develops the pencil and paper skills of those involved with the computer. Analysis of such examples shows that in identifying why the computer uses such conventions the reasons for them are clearer to the child. This developing of experience and understanding is increasingly important to the development of data skills.

Issues revisited

The computer is only useful in developing data skills as part of the 'data handling process'. To use it outside of this generates 'beautiful but meaningless' graphs (Pratt 1994). Computers are very good at producing display pictures for classrooms. For them to be a useful tool for learning they need to be part of a process that tackles real data, that collects, analyses and displays them for a purpose and is one involving interpretation. Without this its effect is stunted.

What's in Logo?

Logo[1] is a means to develop a number of mathematical concepts and this can be downloaded free from the website referenced. Used to its full potential it can develop a range of key skills. It is also a chance for the child to develop 'debugging/problem-solving' skills. As such its use is founded upon key constructivist principles in which children develop their understandings from extended computer use.

The development of Logo stemmed from the use of robots instructed via a computer introduced by Seymour Papert (1980). Current classroom robots like 'Roamer' and 'Pip' are direct descendants of this approach. Put simply, Seymour Papert's pedagogy asked children to resolve broad problems by breaking them down in to a series of lesser ones. In resolving these smaller issues the more complex problem is brought to solution.

This pedagogy is made clearer in the following example where Logo is introduced to a new group. This style of introduction is suited to most groups new to Logo. As such it is a good basis for any group of whatever age, with knowledge of angle and shape, to start.

A start with Logo

Introduce the class to the opening Logo screen. You have a place to write instructions and a turtle that you will control. At this point draw a circle/stick some Blu Tack on the top right corner of the monitor (Figure 5.3) to act as a target. Ask the group to move the turtle to the target using the fewest possible instructions.

The group's prior experience will determine the level of discussion. Clearly they will want to turn and move the turtle. This raises and develops issues and problems for them to resolve.

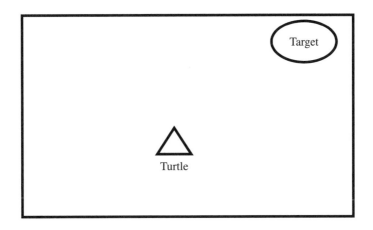

Figure 5.3 Using Logo

Estimation and angle

Normally groups want to move the turtle right. The first question the children ask is by how much? After some discussion the teacher will need to show the children how to instruct the turtle, preferably by putting in instructions which the children have agreed. This is a key point. Controlling the turtle needs to be demonstrated using the group's instruction.

Thus the teacher instructs, 'It needs to turn right so I can type in "right turn" but it is easier to type 'rt' then space 60.' This will cause the turtle to make a right turn of 60 degrees. The turtle moves and discussion as to the desirability of the move should now develop.

The skills that have started to develop through this one demonstration are:

- accurate estimation using degree;
- establishing concretely that angle is concerned with amount of turn and not the shape that two connected straight lines make.

Estimation and distance

After turning the turtle it now becomes important to move it. What is crucial here is that Logo novices will not know the units that the turtle uses. It is likely that this will cause a discussion. Crucially it is an interesting mathematical one involving the nature of measure. Depending on the group, this can be lengthy, concerning why we have a standard measure, or a brief one. Clearly the group needs to find out. Whatever the outcome the group will have to put in a test number and see what happens. Normally this is a number less than ten. If this is the case, the Logo turtle will move fractionally. In order to move into the target area, discussion and estimation will be required. This again is a nice mathematical discussion to take place in solving a Logo problem.

The instructions for moving the turtle need to be modelled as well, 'I could move the turtle forward by typing "forward" but it is easier to type "fd" space 8.'

Concluding this part

However many instructions this process eventually takes, it is likely that the group will move the turtle into the target area. Having done so, if the screen is cleared (cs), they now have the information to do the same thing in fewer moves. The level of teacher input is dependent on the group's interaction with the problem. Most versions of Logo allow you to review your instructions. Using these and mental calculation it is possible to refine your instructions more accurately so that it can be done in two inputs.

Learning outcomes

In the short interaction described above a group has been engaged with a number of key mathematical and problem solving issues. Aside from the issues of estimation and understanding of angle identified and calculations, they have also been engaged in problem solving. This has been developed on the basis of rapid feedback and, further, this feedback has been used to revise and re-calculate on the basis of experience.

Task setting for personal Logo experimentation

It is at this point that the group needs to work with Logo by itself. It is also at this point that the seemingly perennial problem of resources needed to teach mathematics through computer use is at its most difficult. In schools with a suite of computers an effective way of setting a task that novices can embark upon is to set up by using a story (Activity 5.1). This can be modified for a classroom with a single computer but it is not as effective.

Groups working without the computer are an issue (a) because they are removed, if only temporarily, from the experience of controlling the turtle and the learning this engenders and (b) because in my experience the disappointment of not using the computer can influence behaviour and attitude to work. Whatever your situation, how the computer is managed is now pivotal (Chapter 8 provides ideas about classroom management).

Crucially, even in those rare situations where a group has a computer each, using Logo requires peer discussion. Individuals need to discuss problems in order to solve them. Discussion is crucial for success and essential for the problem solving upon which this group will now engage.

Creating a 'realistic' problem with Logo can sometimes be a little awkward. It is possible to set the task of drawing a variety of shapes. There is some useful maths involved with creating a square and other simple shapes. This is not an avenue that I would explore now. What needs to be offered is an element of experimentation with a purpose.

Activity 5.1 Semi-structured group task: developing mathematical thinking using Logo and a story

If possible, try the following activity developed by Metz (1985) and evaluate the learning outcomes arising from this work.

Ask the group to tell you a popular story. A good one for this purpose is 'Goldilocks and the Three Bears' (Metz 1985). Different versions abound and there is much interest in agreeing a version. Was the porridge too hot, too salty or too sweet? Why did she reject all the chairs except baby bear's, etc.? This is a good but not particularly mathematical discussion to have.

Once this discussion has been completed and a version debated, a task can be set. Ask the group to select a scene from the story and draw a picture of it using Logo. This is open-ended in that the class select what to draw, but mathematically sound because to draw the scene they will be using key mathematical principles: orientating the turtle with angle, using calculation to complete any window frames or chairs they draw and developing their estimation skills when they consider how large to make objects. Erasing is also often highly mathematical, requiring an exact retracing of steps.

If you have only one computer, it is at this point that others in the group could design their scene on paper. Also at this point you need to stress the limitations of Logo as a draw package. This task is concerned with developing children's use of maths to portray a picture rather than ICT to develop art.

Extension activities in Logo

Creating shapes and writing procedures

Once familiarity with Logo has been established there are key areas to develop. Writing procedures is one of these. Creating a procedure that draws an object when that command is typed is a stimulating challenge. This is best tackled after a number of shapes have been explored.

Creating a square gives an insight into this process. The properties of all rectangles become evident through the process. All angles are 90 degrees and they have two sets of parallel lines. As much as these are straightforward properties to most of the groups working with Logo, the creating of them using Logo emphasises the significance of their properties. Other shapes whose properties may be well known to groups can have a further learning effect.

Equilateral triangles

Equilateral triangle creation draws out a number of geometry principles. Many groups will have an understanding of their properties. Angles are all 60 degrees and all sides are of equal length. This information is only useful in their construction if applied properly (see Figure 5.4).

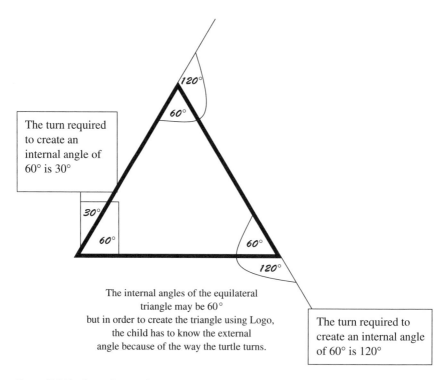

The turn required to create an internal angle of 60° is 30°

The internal angles of the equilateral triangle may be 60° but in order to create the triangle using Logo, the child has to know the external angle because of the way the turtle turns.

The turn required to create an internal angle of 60° is 120°

Figure 5.4 Equilateral triangles

Circles
Circles are best created using the repeat command in Logo. This develops understanding of the properties of circles since in order to do it the turtle

has to move and turn 1 degree 360 times. The size of the circle is dependent upon the distance moved and the direction the circle forms is also dependent upon a left or a right turn. To use the repeat command effectively the user needs to be able to make a prediction as to what will happen when the command is enacted.

In developing understanding of the properties of circles using Logo, children come to an understanding of the fact that there are 360 degrees in a circle. The speculation that a circle rather than having one side may have an infinite number is an issue also worth exploring.

It is possible to create some visually impressive patterns using the 'repeat' command but the mathematical value of such patterns without the creator attempting to make the pattern through picturing the effect of their commands is limited.

Procedure writing

Procedure writing requires the ability to create a shape in Logo. The commands are then entered. Depending on the version of Logo, the commands are entered using [To <enter the name of the procedure>] or [edit <enter the name of the procedure>]. Often when creating procedures they do not function as you expect. This requires more problem solving as you examine the commands you have included to spot an error or 'bug'. I have always found the help menu useful in this process.

Learning outcomes using Logo

The key learning outcomes when logo is used effectively centre upon developing pupil understanding of the properties of shapes through the hands-on manipulation of the turtle. Thus learners develop their mathematical understanding through building upon existing understanding with experimentation. This is an example of constructivist theories of learning in action.

To be used effectively users need time to work with Logo and time to reflect on problems that they are tackling. There are ways to stretch computer time further in classrooms, as many teachers do. The further issue to using Logo (and most programs examined in this book) is that the beneficial effects can be lost due to a lack of resources not just of access to computers but also of time to think about the work being done. But that's another issue!

Additional technologies for mathematics

We do not touch on the issue of the use of calculators in this chapter except to draw your attention to Graphical Calculators which are large enough to sit on top of an overhead projector for whole class mathematical use. These are invaluable tools for mental arithmetic as well as a whole range of mathematical thinking.

Summary

To use constructivism as a model for the use of the computer it is necessary to allow those under instruction the freedom to explore the issues with some independence. This independence must be concerned with encouraging the mathematical discussion that allows the revising and confirmation of understandings. Although only a few of the programs available for use in maths and ICT have been examined here, what is clear is that the work that learners are expected to do must first relate to their understandings and then to how those understandings can be developed through interaction between learners, the computer and the teacher.

This is only possible where learners have time with a computer and time to reflect upon their work on the computer without too long a period between experiences. The 'more rapid learning' identified by Ofsted (1995) is only possible in situations like this.

The conclusion to this chapter is clear. Learners require time with the computer to develop their skills and thought process with it, they need to be able to discuss the 'computer action' with peers and a teacher and 'computer action' needs to be regular.

Note

1 *MSWLogo* is an educational programming language. Logo can be downloaded free from here: *http://www.softronix.com/logo.html*

References and further reading

Harlen, W. (1985) *Primary Science Taking the Plunge*, Oxford: Heinemann Educational.

Haylock, D. (1991) *Teaching Mathematics to Low Attainers 8–12*, London: Paul Chapman Publishing.

Healy, L. and Sutherland, R. (1991) *Exploring Maths with Spreadsheets*, Oxford: Basil Blackwell.

Hopkins, C., Gifford, S. and Pepperell, S. (1996) *Mathematics in the Primary School, a Sense of Progression*, London: David Fulton Publishers.

Metz, M. (1985) 'Chairs for bears', *Micro Maths*, Winter, Derby: The Association of Teachers of Maths.

Ofsted (1995) *Mathematics: A Review of Inspection Findings*, Ofsted: London.

Orton, A. and Frobisher, L. (1996) *Insights into Teaching Mathematics*, London: Cassell.

Padilla, P., Mackenzie, D.L. and Shaw, E.L. (1986) 'An examination of the line graphing ability of students in grades through twelve', in *School Science and*

Mathematics, vol. 86, cited in Ainley, J. (1998) *Parallel Paths: Shared Journeys in Mathematics Teaching*, vol. 164, Derby: The Association of Teachers of Maths, pp. 16–20.

Papert, S. (1980) *Mindstorms Children, Computers and Powerful Ideas*, New York: Basic Books.
    Papert has written many books in the area of mathematical thinking and children. This is just one example.

Pratt, D. (1994) 'Active Graphing in a computer rich Environment', in da Ponte, J.P. and Matos, J.F. (eds), *Proceedings of the 18th Annual Conference of the International Group for the Psychology of Mathematics Education*, Portugal: University of Lisbon.

Thwaites, A. and Jared, L. (1997) 'Understanding and using variables', in MacFarlane, A. (ed.), *Information Technology and Authentic Learning: Realising the Potential of Computers in the Primary Classroom*, London: Routledge
    This is a particularly useful text for primary teachers. Areas covered include use of Logos, calculators, spreadsheets.

Some useful mathematics education websites

http://nrich.maths.org.uk
NRICH is an online maths club with serveral services: *Ask NRICH* is a service that aims to answer your mathematical queries, *Interact* is the monthly magazine offering mathematical challenges, articles and news, *Contribute* enables you to register for free and to send in your solutions or ideas, *Resource Bank* offers stored problems, articles, a search tree and links to other sites.

http://www.anglia.co.uk/education/mathsnet/mathsart.html
MathsNet Art
http://www.anglia.co.uk/education/mathsnet/puzzles.html
MathsNet Puzzles – MSWLogo
http://www.softronix.com/logo.html
This is an educational programming language. Logo can be downloaded free from here.

http://www.cs.berkeley.edu/~bh/
Berkeley Logo for the Apple Mac, HomePage for Brian Harvey. This site contains a variety of materials about Logo and other mathematical issues.

http://www.cam.org/~aselby/fairUse/index.html
This is a site containing a lot of material for educational use in mathematics; for example, *Teaching Algebra, Logic, Reason* (A Fair Use publication).

http://db.bbc.co.uk/education-webguide/pkg_main.p_results?in_cat=4
Within the BBC websites, you will find resources for maths at both primary and secondary levels, as well as some sites dealing with other issues in maths, like gender. The URL above refers to primary maths resources.

http://www.scottlan.edu/lriddle/women/chronol.htm
This is an interesting site dealing with women mathematicians, although many of them are from North America rather than Britain.

http://www.mathsphere.co.uk
This British site deals with the issue of mathematics at home. It claims to include 'Mathematics worksheets, test papers and other resources for teachers and parents

to download to improve children's confidence and ability in mental and written mathematics. Raising standards in mathematics, improving speed of recall of tables and mental arithmetic. Wide coverage of national curriculum, numeracy hour, education, homework.'

http://www.anglia.co.uk/education/mathsnet/

This is another British site which is developing into an excellent resource. It includes software, puzzles, articles about maths, resources and links. It also gives you help in contacting other mathematics educators. There are some interactive projects too, which you can join. There is even a MathsNet Internet Treasure Trail. To solve each task you must surf the internet for the required information, and then return to the task page.

http://www.wkap.nl/journalhome.htm/0013–1954

This site is an international educational research journal, based in the Netherlands. The book review editor is Celia Hoyles, a well-known British maths educator.

http://www.ex.ac.uk/~BBagilho/ernest/reflist6.htm

This site contains a bibliography of maths education, lots of books and articles up to about 1994.

http://www.bham.ac.uk/ctimath/

This is a site provided by Birmingham University and it concerns higher education and maths. Like many of the maths sites, it provides links to many more websites about the study of maths.

http://www.mcs.surrey.ac.uk/Personal/R.Knott/Fibonacci/

This is an interesting site devoted to the Fibonacci series of numbers and its various application in Nature and in pure maths. It also provides puzzle pages.

http://euclid.math.fsu.edu

This site at the University of Florida gives access to a virtual library of maths resources. Although it is American, there are many ideas and suggestions for work at the classroom level, as they say in the USA, from K–12, which means from nursery up to sixth form in British schools.

http://www.tech.plym.ac.uk/maths/CTMHOME/ctm.html#mm

This site at the University of Plymouth contains a number of interesting ideas, such as maths masterclasses, and the International Journal of Computer Algebra in Mathematics Education (IJCAME).

http://acorn.educ.nottingham.ac.uk//SchEd/pages/atm/

This is the site of the Association of Teachers of Mathematics, a British group of educators in schools and universities.

Further references to useful URLS can be found on *http://www.sbu.ac.uk/cme/ medsites.html*

Chapter 6

Science and Environmental Issues and ICT

John Meadows

Introduction

Science is a core subject in English primary schools, along with maths and English, although it is usually given less time than either of the other two subjects. The nature of primary science is that of a practical subject, requiring children to investigate and experiment with materials and objects in order to understand how the world works. Since there is such a lot of information which science deals with, it is easy to see how some aspects of ICT can support the teaching of primary science.

ICT can support the investigative aspects of science as well as those parts of the subject which are more concerned with knowledge. Skills and attitudes are often considered to be important parts of the science curriculum, and again, it is possible for ICT to be used to support both these areas of learning. The notion of communication is a powerful one within science, as well as in ICT. So ICT may help us support the communication which is necessary in science, as well as offering us ways of extending the limits of the communication process. ICT can also be seen as a tool for thinking, insofar as it can help children to present their results in a variety of ways. The use of a database; for example, can help to identify the patterns in data, so allowing children to use higher order thinking skills.

There are many opportunities for teachers to incorporate the use of ICT as a tool in science. This chapter is not based solely on specific case studies, but also on observations and practice over a long period of teaching and observing primary classrooms. It is also cross-referenced to other chapters where case studies focus on aspects of science, such as the multimedia project which Jane Mitra describes in Chapter 9.

Objectives

At the end of this chapter you should:

- recognise the link between science and ICT in terms of communication and constructivism;

- be able to use ICT to support information gathering in science, using CD-ROMs and the internet effectively in teaching science to whole classes, small groups and individual children;
- recognise that ICT can support teaching and learning in science, through providing information, enhancing investigations and enabling interaction;
- be able to construct effective lesson plans using ICT to support science learning;
- understand some of the characteristics of international projects in science and environmental education.

Background

Communication and ICT

One of the best ways of helping children understand scientific ideas is to encourage them to communicate their own ideas, because putting ideas into words or symbols forces learners to examine their own thinking and assumptions. Communication then enables individuals to compare ideas with others and in some cases change their minds. Communication is, of course, an important part of the scientific process, enshrined in the (English) National Curriculum in Attainment Target 1, along with process skills like predicting, investigating, making records, interpreting data.

In science, there is a danger that activities, experiments and investigations can be seen as the major ways of developing children's understanding, but unless communication is also encouraged, children's conceptual development is likely to be limited.

This is not intended to deny the importance of active investigations in science, but merely to redress the balance between activity and thought which is in danger of being lost.

Communication and constructivism

Many interactive projects are grounded in a constructivist theory of learning. Constructivist teaching and learning theories are now widely accepted as explaining how children learn in many areas of education, including maths (Novak 1986), science (Driver *et al.* 1985) and language (Vygotsky 1962).

A brief summary of the link between constructivist theory and communications is as follows:

- Learners come to any new area with some existing knowledge. So, in order to be able to teach effectively, teachers needs to recognise what learners already know, or think they know.

- In order to teach new ideas, the principle of 'moderate novelty' is important. This means that the new idea must be sufficiently novel to be of interest and unknown to the learner, but it must also be somewhat familiar too, linking in some way with the existing ideas of the learner.
- Getting learners to identify and express their existing ideas is a good starting point for developing new understandings, since it is only when you examine your own ideas about some scientific principle that you begin to realise your limits. This begins the process of communication, which is strengthened when an audience is prepared to listen to these ideas and suggest some alternative ideas or disagreements of their own.
- Learners cannot be given conceptual understanding, they need to construct concepts. They do this by confronting their existing ideas with new and conflicting evidence, or with someone else's ideas.
- Communication is a powerful tool for encouraging learners to examine new ideas and compare them to their own existing ideas, that is, to construct concepts.
- Telecommunication, and especially email, is a relatively cheap and easy way to carry out this communication process on an international scale.
- The international dimension[1] adds extra motivation for children, as well as their teachers, to research and to communicate; it helps to widen the range of ideas to consider and compare, as well as the scientific data which can be collected and analysed.

What do we mean by communication?

Communication, which results in learning, needs a responsive audience which will participate in discussion and argument so ensuring that the learners are challenged to explain and defend their ideas and explanations. Mere reporting back of results of practical activities is not real communication. If pupils are to engage seriously in learning, they need to be involved in discussion, argument, questioning and the consideration of alternatives to their own ideas.

One of the more novel ways of communicating, of increasing importance, is electronic communications. Computers are more frequently used in primary classrooms for word processing than most other functions. It is only a short step from this to using the computer as a true communication tool by linking it directly with other computers. One of the great advantages of the internet system is that messages can be sent to and received from many far-away countries for the price of a local phone call (Milligan 1991;[2] Keep 1990[3]), allowing teachers to communicate cheaply with others who share interests and ideas. This can support the learning process if teachers can co-operate to set up and run curriculum projects (see also Chapter 10).

Information gathering and ICT

CD-ROMs

There are many science CD-ROMs produced for use by children in primary schools. You can often find reviews of CD-ROMs for science in the educational press, especially *Primary Science Review*, published regularly by the Association for Science Education, as well as on the web at the BECTA site.[4] Encyclopaedias, such as *Britannica*, are also a valuable source of scientific information. But there may be issues about their use which need to be explored in order to make the most of their potential, such as the ways in which children actually use them – questions need to be asked: Do they understand the material which is being presented? Are they just 'pressing the buttons' in some random way because the buttons make things happen, or are they actually navigating through the material in some logical or intuitive manner to find the answers to specific questions?

Using CD-ROMs

You need to consider the learning objectives when children use CD-ROMs; for example, are they used as a reference, like some information books, so that children can look up answers to the questions which arise, such as how many legs does a woodlouse have, or how do fish breathe? Are you working to develop thinking skills, in which case, you can choose CD-ROMs which have built-in quizzes or activities which lead children from place to place, as in a virtual museum. In this sort of CD-ROM, the intention is that the package stands alone as a resource, rather than being used as a reference. Children are guided through the CD, rather like an adventure game, with the learning objectives pre-planned. Although teachers have little flexibility in their plans to use resources like this, this can be an advantage, as they can employ such resources more immediately in their classrooms.

Group, whole class or individual?

The ways in which CDs can be used depends, to some extent, on the size of the group of children interacting with the computer running the system, as well as the size of the screen which displays the material. Some teachers prefer to plan whole class lessons with the resource of a CD to support the science teaching. Although it is possible for a class of thirty-plus children to see a normal size screen, it is unlikely that they could all interact easily with it, or see enough detail to make the most of the information available. However, a teacher might wish to introduce some features of the CD in this way, perhaps as the children sit on the carpet or in the book corner, or in the school library. It may be possible to link up the computer to a larger screen, such as in a school video system, or through a projector, so that the resource could be more easily seen. The teacher could use it as an information source, as she might use a 'Big Book' during the Literacy Hour. In this scenario, it is possible that the material in the CD-ROM could be presented in a more systematic way than if children are exploring on their own, or in smaller groups without the teacher. Making one's own CD-ROMs is now a possibility, as multimedia authoring programs are available at a reasonable price (see Chapter 9).

Activity 6.1 Using CD-ROMs in the classroom

Test ways of making CD-ROMs more useful in the classroom by preparing a simple factually based worksheet which children could use to focus their exploration of the information in a science CD-ROM to which you have access. In order to be able to do this, you need to spend some time exploring the material on the CD, evaluating its importance in terms of children's learning, perhaps by cross-referencing it to the National Curriculum programmes of study, or to other areas of the curriculum, such as English or Maths.

You might want to look at the Microsoft site,[5] which has some examples of such worksheets, or Research Machine's Eduweb site,[6] or the National Grid for Learning and the associated Virtual Teachers' Centre.[7]

The internet

There is plenty of scientific data available through the internet, some of which could be adapted for use by children in the primary school. There has been an enormous amount of interest in the internet in education, but not much has focused on its use as an information source in the primary school. Later in the chapter, there are examples of how scientific projects can be managed through the use of the internet as a communication device. Teachers need to explore the various sites of scientific interest to see whether the material is at an appropriate level for the children in their care. Few teachers would envisage a situation in which children are left to search and surf the internet on their own, since there are so many possible dangers in doing this, as well as the cost of such a strategy.

Sites which might be valuable

As more teachers and educators in the primary sector use the internet, it is likely that more appropriate materials will become available for children's use. Schools are developing their own internet websites, containing not only material about the school, but also examples of writing and graphics produced by the children themselves in a variety of subjects. Check the Lambeth project, formerly known as Brixton Connections,[8] for examples of work from children and teachers which have been produced over a period of several years. There is an extensive list of websites on the website which accompanies this book.[9] This makes available all the websites listed at the end of each chapter.

Information about Insects[10] could be used with children aged above 8 years, almost without editing, although the children would probably find some of the associated text difficult to understand. However, this problem often arises with similar information in books, where the graphical information is often more relevant and easier for children to understand than the text. Some might suggest that children should be using information of this sort in small groups or pairs rather than on their own, since this is likely to engage them in discussion and searches for meaning (Underwood 1994).

Investigations using ICT

Data collection and sensors

Many small data collecting devices are now available for primary schools which help children collect, record and display their measurements. Temperature measurement can be difficult with normal glass thermometers, as the scale can be hard for them to read. Glass and mercury thermometers are not popular in primary schools because of the potential for breakage, with broken glass and spilt mercury as health hazards.

Time measurement can also be made easier using electronic timers with digital displays, although younger children might find it hard to understand reading which give tenths or hundredths of seconds. It is also possible to record some data, such as temperature or light measurements, automatically as a graph using E-mate or pocket book computers in the field.

Databases: a case study on parachutes

The use of a database program to record data from an investigation into the performance of parachutes was made in a Year 3/4 class. Pairs of children first made their own parachutes, using plastic bags or fabric, with string or sewing cotton and small weights. The decisions they had to make included the shape and size of the canopy, the number and length of the strings and the weight of the load. They decided to test the parachutes by dropping them from a standard height of 2 metres and to measure the time of descent with stopwatches. They also estimated the stability of each parachute, giving them a mark between one and five depending on how they fell, and then measured the distance each fell from the vertical. So they had collected a lot of data, which they then entered onto a database.

There were problems about the interpretation of the data in this instance, because there are many factors which affect the performance of a parachute and it was not easy to identify any pair of variables which could be proved to be linked. Scattergraphs were used to check cause and effects, but the children did not find these easy to understand. However, the use of the database to produce ordered lists and simple graphs did enable the children to grasp some of the patterns in the data. If the parachutes investigation was to be repeated, it would probably be better to control a number of the variables during the manufacture stage, such as using the same canopy material and string lengths, etc.

Multimedia tools could also make this work more valuable for younger children. In Chapter 9 Jane Mitra describes a project involving science, about bones, where the children had co-operated with a variety of others, including adults like doctors.

Activity 6.2 Using databases

Read the case study example above on parachutes then consider the following questions about databases for recording and presenting the results of scientific investigations.

- Was this a good context for the use of databases?
- How could you improve on the investigation?
- How many data are needed in an investigation of this sort, in order to make the graphs useful?
- How could you put together data from the whole class?
- Would a scenario with 3/4 computers be more convenient, since data entry takes a long time?
- Do you think children improve keyboard skills when engaged on repetitive tasks like data entry?

Now look at the sample lesson plan below, which uses portable computers (E-mates in this case, which can be linked to sensors for light, temperature, etc.). Could something similar be carried out in your own context? How might you have to adapt the plan in order to fit in with your own requirements and with the equipment to which you have access? After reading the plan, try to answer some of the questions about assessment in Activity 6.3.

Sample lesson plan

Content of the lesson – observation of minibeasts in the classroom, having collected some earlier in the day from a garden site. Use a light meter linked to an E-mate computer to measure the amount of light in different places as you set up a choice chamber for woodlice or worms.

Introduction

The session can begin with a discussion with the whole class about where woodlice live and their habits, that is, what they eat, what eats them, how they reproduce and grow, what they look like, how they move, etc. Then you might suggest some investigations to examine the ideas children have expressed about woodlice habitats, setting up a place which contains dark and light areas, or perhaps damp and dry areas, or even warm and cold areas. The E-mate computer can be supplied with a variety of sensors, which can measure and record temperature and light, so children can be taught how to set up and collect these data through digital readouts as well as graphs. They should then place a number of woodlice in the 'choice chamber' and allow them to move and choose the places they prefer to stay. After a time, children should record the numbers of the woodlice found in each part and compare the result with their predictions, based on the previous discussion.

Learning outcomes:

- Scientific concepts about minibeast behaviours and their ability to sense light, or temperature or damp.
- Technological methods of sensing light and the skills needed to use them.
- Co-operation in groups in order to plan the investigations, carry them out and record the results.

Assessment opportunities

Children might be assessed by formal and informal ways during this activity. As a teacher, you need to decide whether the purpose of the assessment is summative or formative or diagnostic. You also need to decide on the precise details of the assessment, in terms of what the

continued

pupils are expected to be learning, which might be ICT skills, or skills related to data handling in science, or conceptual notions, or memo-risation of factual information. Even attitudes towards science or ICT might need to be assessed.

Children could be observed while they are co-operating in the investigation, during the planning stages as well as while actually working with the minibeasts and collecting the data. You might prepare a checklist of the technological skills which children are expected to acquire or develop further. You might also expect some children to produce written reports of their work, which could be used for assessment purposes. The results produced and saved on the E-mate computers could also produce evidence of children's learning.

Activity 6.3 Assessing the learning

How would you assess what children had learned about science itself by doing the activity in the 'Sample lesson plan' above? Would you expect them to know something about the science of light, or about the way in which we sense light as opposed to the way in which the light meter works? Probably not, since light itself is a difficult concept for children in primary schools. However, the fact that light travels into the sensor and also travels into our eyes or into the 'eyes' of minibeasts is likely to be one of the aims of science teaching for children in Years 5 and 6.

You could also look up the schemes of work on ICT which were produced by the Qualifications and Curriculum Agency (QCA) in late 1998. These are available online from the Government Standards site.[11]

Interactive projects using ICT

Introduction

Projects from countries like Australia, New Zealand and the USA are often more useful for British teachers and children than European ones, because we use the same language. However, British teachers need to be aware of the very different dates of terms and academic years in the Southern Hemisphere. This difference may make the organisation of projects more problematic over a year period as suggested below. The academic year in Australian and New Zealand schools begins in February, rather than in September as in Britain. Time differences also complicate projects with US schools, which tend to have their summer break much earlier than is common in Britain.

Shadows

An example of the use of international electronic communication occurred during the intervention phase of the SPACE project (Osborne *et al.* 1994) in one London primary school. Children were discussing the positions of their shadows at 11.00 a.m. and 11.45 a.m. on a particular day and shared their results and ideas with children in an Australian primary school, through the use of email.

Kobir and Yasdan (aged 10 years) wrote:

> We went into the playground to look at our shadows and where the sun was. The sun was almost directly north and our shadows were almost directly south. We thought it would be opposite for you, the sun to the north and your shadows to the south. Were we right?

The Australian children replied:

> Our class enjoyed measuring our shadows at 11.00 and 11.45. Because we have daylight saving time on the east coast of Australia, we were actually measuring at 12.00 and 12.45. Of course this was an hour more than real time. It was strange that your shadows were north and south. Ours were quite different. The sun was directly in the east and our shadows were directly west. It was quite evident that our height and shadow length were related. Our shadows would have been nothing in about 15 minutes.

In this extract, real communication was taking place, with some interesting anomalies arising, which were then used as the basis for further research from books and discussions within the London class. Instead of just visualising Australia as a Southern Hemisphere place, they realised that it is a very large continent with a variety of time zones and that the Northern part is almost equatorial, rather than being as far south as the UK is north of the equator.

Weather

This project originated in a primary school in New Zealand. The extract below comes from the teacher's message to an internet mailing list, which is often used as a way of inviting participation in projects. It is not a very sophisticated project, leaving quite a lot open to chance and with plenty of flexibility, compared to some others which specify tight deadlines and timescales, as well as describing in detail exactly what each participating school should do. It is never clear which sort of project is most likely to succeed, but teachers should at least be aware that there is a variety of ways in which such international projects can be organised.

> Our project is to collect and analyse weather data for the whole academic year. We have a local weather station in the school grounds recording data onto a computer and we would like to have some schools in other countries to send us weather data. Countries send us data about their particular location, preferably on a daily basis. Data such as temperature, wind speed and direction, hours of sunshine, rainfall etc. would be most helpful. Each of the three Year 5 classes will spend a term collating this 'International Data' and pass it on to another class for the production of a newsheet for parents.
>
> We are not really bothered about which countries but we did think that possibly Japan and Spain would be ideal as they have very diverse climates.

So there are specific learning outcomes from the project for the children in New Zealand, but teachers in Britain would have to set their own objectives and would probably be constrained in the amount of time they could give to such work. Certainly schools with weather stations of their own might want to link up with this project and compare data over a period of time, and the science aspects could be balanced by reference to other subjects, especially geography and ICT. The science elements would need to be focused a little more sharply, perhaps by asking the children to make predictions based on the early data, or on their own prior knowledge, as in the previously described project about shadows above.

Environmental science

Environmental projects are increasingly common in the international arena, although the concepts dealt with are not always at an appropriate level for primary school children. The following extract is from a Japanese project, called GeoTouch, which did attempt to separate the participating schools into levels according to the age of the participants:

> During the first session of GeoTouch, all participants filled out a questionnaire in order to compare the geography of their regions, environmental problems, and what measures were being taken to address those problems. The results of each school's questionnaire, along with the chat room logs and other resources, have been made available in our web server and mailing list archives.
>
> We divided schools into discussion groups according to age and the results of their questionnaires. By providing a mailing list for each

discussion group, students were able to compare, contrast and analyze the similarities and differences between the environmental problems they each face locally.

But there can be problems associated with such work, as children do not always gain knowledge and understanding from them which can be put into practice in their normal school work. A Swedish teacher in another environmental project (a European-wide email discussion about the environment, problems and solutions) mentioned that students do not easily link the science they learn in school with the issues they hear about outside. He also highlighted the rigidity which may result from curriculum requirements, preventing teachers from taking advantage of unexpected happenings to reinforce environmental understanding. One hopes that the curriculum in British primary schools will never become so rigid and inflexible that teachers and pupils are prevented from taking part in cross-curricular projects like these.

SPACE: a project organised by NASA

This project was advertised through mailing lists in December 1995, but the website for NASA is still in operation and projects continue to be supported from the site.

> NASA is pleased to announce another exciting opportunity for K–12 classrooms to interact with our scientists, engineers and support staff. This time, the men and women of the Galileo project will provide a behind-the-scenes look at what it's like to be part of the flight team on a pioneering interplanetary expedition through the ONLINE FROM JUPITER project.
>
> Galileo scientists and mission engineers are opening their notebooks to classrooms, museums and the public via the internet to share their observations and experiences working on the NASA spacecraft mission to Jupiter.
>
> The flight team will write brief field journal entries describing the scientific puzzles, engineering challenges and excitement of discovery as the Galileo orbiter and atmospheric entry probe begin their scientific investigation of Jupiter. The atmospheric probe is set to descend into Jupiter's atmosphere on Dec. 7, the same day the Galileo orbiter begins circling the giant planet for a two-year mission.

Also on the NASA website Dr Jo Pitesky, a member of the Galileo Mission Planning Office, commented:

> For the first time, we're providing a window on the inner workings and interactions of a scientific deep space mission. In sharing the journal

entries, we hope to give readers, particularly students, an idea of the tremendous efforts that go into controlling and collecting data from a robot spacecraft a half-billion miles away.

After reading background material and the journals, kindergarten through 12th grade students and their teachers can ask project members questions – via email – starting in late November and running through January 1996. They will receive personal responses, corresponding with experts on subjects ranging from atmospheric science to spacecraft systems. An archive of all questions and answers will be available online.

Activity 6.4 Learning outcomes in science or ICT?

If you were taking part in a project like the one above, what learning outcomes would you set for children in a British primary class? Would the children be learning scientific skills or concepts, as well as specific ICT skills? How could you find time to undertake such projects in a busy schedule which includes literacy and numeracy work every day? Try looking at the website of the Montage project, which is a collaboration between schools in Australia and elsewhere, especially the section called 'Teachers Guide'.[12] Other useful sites to explore include the European SchoolNet and the Global School House.[13]

Summary

Traditionally, there have been connections between science at all levels and the use of ICT, but in the primary school this has often been restricted to using generic tools such as word processors and databases to record the results of scientific investigations. The equipment needed for more specific science experiments was not usually available for primary schools, in terms of either cost or difficulty of operation. In some cases, equipment originally intended for secondary science was adapted (sometimes rather crudely) for use in primary schools, but often the software was not compatible with the hardware. The situation has now changed, with more appropriate equipment for linking sensors with laptop or palm-top computers, and robust sensors, which can be used easily by younger children. In recent years, schools have been taking advantage of various offers from government and business to upgrade their computer and ICT equipment, so that the most likely scenario now in primary schools is one in which there are a greater number of powerful, internet-linked and multimedia machines. It should now be possible in most primary schools to carry out most of the ideas suggested in this chapter, from creating multimedia science presentations, to searching the internet for science knowledge or partners with whom to co-operate on projects.

In this chapter, you have examined the link between communication in science and the theory of constructivism. You also looked at ways of using ICT as a source of information, which could be used by whole classes, groups or individual children. ICT as a tool to support investigations in science was discussed and finally we looked at a few examples of international scientific and environmental projects which used the internet to support communication.

Notes

1   International links can be facilitated by a number of organisations, such as the European Schoolnet *http://www.eun.org* and also the British Council and the Central Bureau for Educational Visits and Exchanges *http://www.britcoun.org/cbeve/index.htm*

2   Milligan (1991) describes an email project between schools in the UK and the Netherlands. Although there were many problems with the exchanges, there were some small successes which could be built on in a project with a longer timescale.

3   Keep (1990) describes an early email project involving ten local authorities in a variety of different styles of email exchange, some of them on an international scale.

4   *http://www.becta.org.uk*
The BECTA site has a number of useful reviews of CD-ROMs and software. The CD-ROM reviews are searchable and divided into age ranges, although there is often a lot of overlap between these.

5   *http://www.microsoft.com/education/k12/*
The Microsoft organisation is making partnerships with educators and other businesses to provide support for teachers and pupils through this website and other links.

6   *http://www.eduweb.co.uk*
This is the website provided by Research Machines Ltd, a company which makes many of the computers used in British schools, particularly in primary schools. The website holds many school web pages, as well as ideas for projects, discussion groups and links to other educational resources.

7   *http://vtc.ngfl.gov.uk/vtc/index.html*
This site is intended to support the inservice training needs of teachers across the UK by providing information on classroom resources, professional development, school management, as well as a virtual meeting room and library.

8   *http://www.rmplc.co.uk/eduweb/sites/bricoftp/index.html*
Brixton Connections is an internet project for primary schools in the Brixton area of London.

9   The website which accompanies this book can be found on: *http://www.dmu.ac.uk/Faculties/HSS/SEDU/primaryict.html*

10   *http://www.insect-world.com*
A comprehensive site providing information about insects which teachers are finding useful.

11   The DfEE Standards website has copies of schemes of work designed to help primary school teachers manage the curriculum. The scheme of work for IT can be found on these pages *http://www.standards.dfee.gov.uk/schemes/it*

12 *http://www.bc.org.au/montage/guides/guide.asp*
This site is a link between the British Council in Britain and Australia which supports international projects and links between schools in the two countries.

13 *http://www.eun.org/*
The European Schoolnet is a series of networks for teachers and pupils across Europe. The site contains a schools collaboration area, a virtual teacher college, news and information about Europe and a technical centre and internet guidebook. The Global School House projects pages can be found on *http://www.gsn.org/pr/index*

References and further reading

Driver, R., Guesne, E. and Tiberghien, A. (1985) *Children's Ideas in Science*, Milton Keynes: Open University Press.

Keep, R. (ed.) (1990) *Communique: Summary of the Final Report of the Communications Collaborative Project*, Coventry: NCET.

Milligan, F. (1991) *Email and Europe: An Anglo-Dutch Connection*, Coventry: NCET/ Shell UK Ltd.

Moore, P. (ed.) (1995) *Teaching and Learning with the Internet*, London: British Telecommunications Plc.

Novak, D.J. (1986) 'The importance of emerging constructivist methodology for mathematics education', *Journal of Mathematical Behavior*, **5**, 181–4.

Osborne, J., Black, P. and Meadows, J. (1994) *SPACE Research Report – The Earth in Space*, Liverpool: Liverpool University Press.

Peacock, A. (1990) 'Building a multi-cultural dimension into primary science', *Primary Science Review*, **12**, Spring, p.11.

QCA (1998) *Schemes of work for ICT*, London: DfEE.

Underwood, J. (1994) *Computer Based Learning: Potential into Practice*, London: David Fulton Publishers.

Vygotsky, L.S. (1962) *Thought and Language*, Cambridge MA: MIT Press.

Useful websites

Association of Science Education website: *http://www.ase.org.uk*
Sci-Journal website: *http://www.soton.ac.uk/%7eplf/Sci-Journal/index.html*

Chapter 7

History and ICT

John Sampson

Introduction

The purpose of this chapter is not to promote particular software packages above others, though I do report on those I have used frequently. Any attempt to provide a guide to software would be quickly out of date and readers are better advised to refer to the BECTA pages[1] where an up-to-date guide is given to CD-ROM-based material. Instead I intend to demonstrate some ways in which ICT and history can be linked so learning in primary school history is enhanced. I have set out a number of principles that need to be observed if children's learning is to be effective in history through the use of ICT.

Objectives

At the end of this chapter you should be able to:

- identify the links between history and ICT;
- determine when it is appropriate to use ICT to enhance historical learning;
- recognise the ways in which ICT can support teaching and learning in history through enhancing children's historical investigations.

Linking ICT and history

The English National Curriculum informs us that

> Pupils should be given opportunities, where appropriate, to develop and apply their information technology (IT) capability in their study of history.
>
> (DFE 1995: 1)

Clearly when children are studying history they should have opportunity, where it is appropriate, to develop and apply their ICT skills. I would assume that none of us would disagree with this statement, it seems fairly clear and unequivocal. However, I would like to examine this statement a little more closely, in particular I would like to consider that part of the statement that suggests that the development of ICT capability occurs 'where appropriate'. What does 'where appropriate' mean?

NCET guidance is useful here,

It is necessary to identify situations where

- subject and IT capability development take place
- subject development takes place and IT capability is consolidated
- IT capability is developed and subjects are consolidated.

(NCET 1995: 3)

Whichever of these points we consider, it is clear that ICT and history meet where children have something to gain from the bringing together of the two subjects – the children's learning should be enhanced in both history and ICT. We should note that it is not appropriate to use ICT packages that purport to be history but only develop ICT capability and add nothing to the child's subject learning.

At this stage I do not want to explore the nature of meaningful learning in ICT but, since it seems to me that there is some danger that ICT capability will be developed without careful consideration of history as a subject, I want to further explore the notion of ICT contributing to effective learning in history.

Effective learning in history

What then is effective learning in history? Historians are mostly concerned with the process of history: they undertake investigations using the historical evidence, they hypothesise and they attempt to justify their interpretation by reference to the evidence and, perhaps, to the writings of other historians. They are concerned to answer questions such as:

- Why did this happen (cause)?
- What is different about this period in the past compared to others (change)?
- How do we know (evidence)?

To enable them to do this they need a good understanding of time and to enable other historians to benefit from their work they need to be able to communicate their views.

We can see this process reflected in the English National Curriculum, which encapsulates the notion that history is a combination of knowledge, skills and understandings. Here the study of history is broken down into Key Elements:

- Chronology
- Knowledge, Cause and Change
- Interpretations
- Use of Evidence
- Organisation and Communication.

(DfE 1995: 5)

However, historians are not only concerned with process, since the study of history does have a knowledge base. It is this balance between historical fact and historical process that is crucial for the historian, the teacher and the learner. This is a debate that has been summarised well by Peter Lee: 'A substantial part of what is learned has to be knowing-how, not just knowing-that' (1994: 47).

The historical knowledge studied will be context bound. For instance, the knowledge coverage of the English National Curriculum at Key Stage 2 (7–11 years) is described in Study Units and these appear largely unchanged in the QCA Curriculum Review for 2001 (DfEE 1999):

- Romans, Anglo-Saxons and Vikings in Britain
- Life in Tudor times/The Tudor World
- Victorian Britain
- Britain since 1930
- Ancient Greece
- Local History
- a past non-European society.

(DfE 1995: 4)

In other words, the content of history is described in terms of knowledge, skills and understanding and it is important that this mixture of historical knowledge and historical process is maintained.

Activity 7.1 Developing your understanding of history

Make two headings – historical knowledge and historical process. Under each note down what you understand by these two terms and how that is reflected in your own curriculum:

Historical Knowledge   Historical Process

This view of the nature of history helps us to determine the way children's developing ICT capability can contribute to their historical learning. I would like to suggest that to make a worthwhile contribution, ICT packages need to be able to:

- develop knowledge that is historically accurate;
- encourage investigation;
- encourage the use of historical sources;
- enable the development of historical concepts of cause and change;
- develop an understanding of historical time;
- organise and communicate historical findings.

Develop knowledge that is historically accurate   There are few 'right' answers in history, which is one of the difficulties of studying history in the classroom when children expect firm answers, and it can seem fairly vague to say that a child's answer seems reasonable given the evidence they have used. It can be even more frustrating for the child to then be asked to consider further evidence. Nevertheless we can present children with fairly accurate representations of the past that can at least be authenticated by a strong body of evidence. Therefore we need software that gives children an authentic view of the past and that has demonstrable links to historical evidence.

Encourage investigations   As outlined above, the nature of history rests on the assumption that the historian undertakes an investigation. In the classroom this may not be of great significance to anyone except the child and the teacher but nevertheless it is difficult to claim that children are engaged in history unless they are engaged in an investigation. Good ICT packages will therefore either help to pose historical questions or suggest answers to them; ideally they will engage the child in both.

Use historical sources   It is increasingly common to see documents and printed sources, artefacts, pictures and photographs used in classrooms while visits are often made to historic sites and buildings. Children's books increasingly attempt to make clear the links between the text and pictures the children are working with and the relevant historical evidence. ICT packages must develop this theme.

Enable the development of historical concepts   Historians want to investigate why things have happened, they are also concerned to know what has changed and why it has changed. ICT packages should, therefore, either pose questions about cause or change that the children can investigate or they should provide sources of evidence to enable children to answer such questions.

Develop an understanding of historical time   Children need to develop both a sense of chronology, a framework into which they can place their study of the past, and the necessary vocabulary to express the notion of time past. Much of this will be as a result of acquiring knowledge about the past that gives them a sense of a specific period and enables them to place this period or event into their already developing framework.

Organise and communicate their historical findings   Historians have to communicate their understandings to others, generally this is through the written word. Children will need to both organise the findings of their investigations and communicate them. Within school contexts this may be through writing (e.g., report, writing frames, diaries, comparison charts – see also writing frames in Chapter 2) but may also be through a variety of other forms of communication including oral work which may include drama and role play, pictorial representation, and modelling. However, children do need to develop the ability to sustain their writing and ICT can provide a particularly good means of encouraging children to write in a variety of genres.

Having established a number of criteria by which I can judge the appropriateness of bringing ICT and history together I would now like to apply them in practice to a range of common ICT packages.

Communicating in history using ICT

Word processing packages have tended to be used to enable children to present their history work rather than to meet any of the six criteria I suggested earlier. While this may, and only may, be developing the children's ICT capability, it does not contribute to their historical learning.

In some cases the ICT package can provide the starting point for a historical investigation, typically this can take the form of reporting events such as the Armada or the Great Exhibition by using the word processor to produce newspaper style reports. More recently simple desk-top publishing packages have enabled children to formulate their own reporting format. Where children are not simply repeating facts learned elsewhere but have been encouraged to base their report on an investigation of a variety of historical sources, there is abundant opportunity for effective historical learning to take place. Clearly much depends on the teacher's own understanding of effectiveness in historical learning.

Activity 7.2 Writing reports

Too often children are asked to write empathetically without having the necessary knowledge base. Plan for children to write a 'I was there report' on an event in the past. Decide what historical knowledge children would need to get them started and identify key sources that they could investigate to obtain that knowledge. These key sources should be wider than a book base.

ICT capability can also be developed through simple writing frame activities (see Chapter 2 in this book; Wray and Lewis 1997, 1999; Lewis and Wray 1997) where again the key factor is the way in which the teacher structures the work to include investigation and the use of sources. Imported graphics or sprites can make these writing frames more attractive to the children though do not in themselves lend anything to their historical validity. The use of writing frames is a well known method to promote structured writing with children, particularly in Key Stage 2. Making ICT writing frames that encourage children to develop a variety of writing genres will not only develop ICT capability and historical understanding but will also help provide opportunities for the sort of sustained writing that seems to be missing from the National Literacy Strategy (DfEE 1999).

Activity 7.3 Constructing writing frames using ICT

Look at the variety of writing frames in Lewis and Wray (1997) to determine an appropriate format. Using a word processing package, construct a writing frame that enables children to report back in structured sentences on an investigation they have carried out. Consider how this can be extended so that children are made to refer to their evidence base.

Investigating the past using ICT

Databases

The place of databases in primary history is well established (see for instance Ross 1983; Sampson 1986, 1987). Typically a database will be constructed using local Victorian census material for use in either a locally based study of the Victorians or an in-depth local study focusing on a particular period in time.

Such databases will include information that is historically accurate. They will include information about real Victorian people on:

- the surname and first name of individuals;
- where they live;
- their relationship to the head of the household;
- their age and sex;
- their occupation;
- their birthplace.

Some databases may not include all that material but will contain enough information to make it worthwhile using a database rather than merely hunting through the actual printouts.

Databases can only be successfully used if they are a focus of an investigation. This may be as simple as 'Who lived at Holly Lodge in The Grove in 1871?' (see Table 7.1), or it may require the searching of the whole data base, 'What jobs did people in Victorian Bedford have?'

Questions that reflect national events can also be asked; for example, 'how many children were at school in Victorian Bedford and what age were they?' (Figure 7.1). Information gained from investigations such as the last might call into question views that Victorian children were all down the mines or up chimneys!

Table 7.1 Data extracted from 1871 census material using Junior Pinpoint[2] – Who lived at Holly Lodge?

Name	Address	Relationship	Age	Job	Birthplace
LESTER THOMAS	HOLLY LODGE THE GROVE	HEAD	36	LACE MANU-FACTURER	BEDFORD
LESTER MATILDA	HOLLY LODGE THE GROVE	WIFE	26		BEDFORD
LESTER LAURA	HOLLY LODGE THE GROVE	DAUGHTER	4	SCHOLAR	BEDFORD
LESTER AMY	HOLLY LODGE THE GROVE	DAUGHTER	2		BEDFORD
LESTER ALICE	HOLLY LODGE THE GROVE	DAUGHTER	1		BEDFORD
PARKER ELLEN	HOLLY LODGE THE GROVE	WIFE'S SISTER	20		GODMAN-CHESTER, HUNTS.
WITTERMORE EMMA	HOLLY LODGE THE GROVE	SERVANT	34	GENERAL SERVANT	BEDFORD
WILLIAMSON ANNE	HOLLY LODGE THE GROVE	SERVANT	15	NURSEMAID	BARFORD, BEDS.

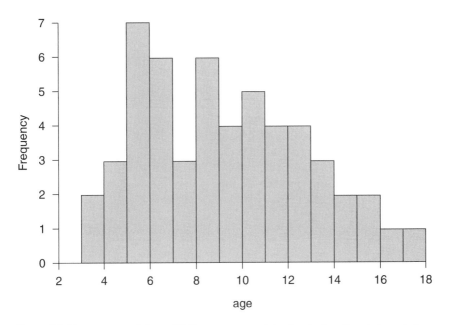

Figure 7.1 Data extracted from 1871 census material using Junior Pinpoint – what age were the children in The Grove who went to school?

The database is firmly rooted in a historical source – the census return. Other sources such as street directories and maps (perhaps there is scope here for including the work on a concept keyboard) can be added to a local study. Children can be encouraged to compare local life to the national scene and then a wider set of sources can be called upon.

One of the major advantages of a database is that it throws up further questions, particularly concerned with cause: 'Why are so many people working as ... ?', 'Why did so many children go to school?', etc.

Finally, databases give some clear indications of change over time which are enhanced once the sources are extended to include maps, stories, artefacts or museum visits. The 'Case study of using a Victorian census' below provides an examples of an application in the primary curriculum.

Case study of using a Victorian census

A class of 9 year-olds challenged a primary school historical text on home and family life in the Victorian period by asking 'How do we

continued

know it's true?' At this point it was suggested to them that they could produce their own materials based on local Victorian families. They were introduced to a range of evidence including a visit to a street of Victorian housing, the street directories for that street, maps of the area, some old photographs of the area and a database of the 1871 census return for the street. Children then investigated the evidence to build up a picture of life for particular families in the area. Some children extended this work to looking at wider issues such as one-parent families in Victorian times and the range of local occupations. Children quickly realised that even the interrogation of the database did not provide all the answers and became quite adept at using hypothetical language such as 'I think that . . .', 'The evidence suggests that . . .', etc.

Timelines

There are a number of computer timelines programs available and as a generic set they share many of the same principles. These programs have a basic framework for a period to which the children or the teacher can add information. All are designed so that when an item on the timeline is opened, further information is revealed (or a blank information sheet is provided). They also give the opportunity to link events to one another.

Clearly programs such as this will enable children to develop a better understanding of time since they will be able 'to place the events, people and changes in the periods studied within a chronological framework' (DfE 1995: 5). The program provides the class with the equivalent of the time-line around the room (which often takes the form of a washing line complete with pictures) but has the advantage that it can include considerable text and also duration as well as sequence. If children are encouraged to develop their own information sheets on the timeline, their knowledge will be enhanced, and where teachers with a good understanding of the historical process have encouraged children to research historical sources for this information, another of my criteria will have been met. It is then only a small step for the teacher to pose questions about change and cause.

A good example of work carried out in a classroom using a timeline program is provided by Smart (1996) where he shows how it is possible to address a range of historical processes in a study of the Tudors.

Simulations and games

Anyone with a home PC shared with their children will know that there are many games that have vivid graphics and are based on the past or possible futures. Most importantly these games allow the player to make decisions and suffer the consequences of such decisions! Thus supporting the development of problem-solving skills.

Software that immerses children in a 'real' (or at least accurate or authentic) historical situation should give them plenty of scope for effective historical learning. Such simulations should develop knowledge of the period and encourage the children to make investigations either within the software or elsewhere. The importance of historical sources will be evident either in the program itself or in its supporting materials and children should be given the opportunity to think about change over time and why people acted as they did. Packages such as *Time Detectives – The Victorians* (Hosler 1994) immerse the children in a historical period, in this case the Victorians, and allow them the opportunity to play a game – can they rescue the children from the present who have been stranded in the past. The power of learning through play must not be underestimated, nor must it be thought of as a methodology sound only for the Early Years.

Using the World Wide Web

At the present there are few pages that could be used by children in pursuit of their historical investigations, but the number is increasing. Most are still very knowledge based and allow little scope for meeting the criteria given above. However, this is a growing area and websites such as the National Grid for Learning[3] enable the teacher to get some good source materials and some useful ideas on how these can be used.

Activity 7.4 Using the web as a learning resource

Examples of useful sites that set interesting tasks and refer children back to a variety of written and pictorial evidence are: The Public Record Office Resources for Primary Schools: Using the National Archives for History at Key Stage 2 at *http://www.pro.gov.uk/education/primary.htm* and the Sainsbury's Virtual Museum website on *http://www.j-sainsbury.co.uk/museum.htm*

Access these pages and devise a series of lessons that have learning objectives focused on historical processes, skills and understandings in addition to historical knowledge.

Additional museum sites can be found through the Scottish Cultural Access Network and the UK based 24 Hour Museum.[4]

Summary

When ICT is to be included in the teaching of history there should be gains for the children's historical learning and not just in their ICT capability. Six criteria have been suggested:

- develop knowledge that is historically accurate;
- encourage investigation;
- encourage the use of historical sources;
- enable the development of historical concepts of cause and change;
- develop an understanding of historical time;
- help children organise and communicate their historical findings.

These need to be carefully considered to ensure that ICT packages do contribute to historical learning.

Notes

1   BECTA can be found on *http://www.becta.org.uk/index.html*
2   Junior Pinpoint. Available from Longman Publishers, Harlow, Essex. The Grove is a Junior Pinpoint file of the 1871 census material held at De Montfort University.
3   The National Grid for Learning can be found on *http://www.ngfl.gov.uk/ngfl/*
4   Museums: You will find a UK map giving you the opportunity to click on areas and then museums of your choice *http://www.24hourmuseum.org.uk* and Scottish Cultural Resources *http://www.scran.ac.uk/*

References and further reading

DfE (1995) *History in the National Curriculum*, London: HMSO.
DfEE (1999) *The Review of the National Curriculum in England. The Consultation Materials*, London: QCA.
Hosler, S. (1994) *Time Detectives – The Victorians*, Malmesbury: Sherston Software Ltd.
Junior Pinpoint. Harlow: Longman.
   The Grove is a Junior Pinpoint file of the 1871 census material held at De Montfort University.
Lee, P. (1994) 'Historical knowledge and the National Curriculum', in Boudillon, H. (ed.), *Teaching History*, London: Open University.
Lewis, M. and Wray, D. (1997) *Writing Frames: Scaffolding Children's Non-fiction*, Reading: University of Reading.
National Council for Educational Technology (1995) *Approaches to IT Capability*, Coventry: NCET.
Ross, A. (1983) 'Microcomputers and local history work in a primary school', *Teaching History*, **35**, 82–5.
Sampson, J. (1986) 'Children as historians: a study of local Victorian families, Greater Manchester primary contact', *History and the Primary School*, Special Issue Number 6, pp. 49–51.

Sampson, J. (1987) 'The computer as an aid to using evidence in the primary school', in Blyth J. (ed.), *History 5 to 9*, London: Hodder and Stoughton, pp. 85–6.

Smart, L. (1996) *Using IT in Primary School History*, London: Cassell.

Wray, D. and Lewis, M. (1997) *Extending Literacy: Children Reading and Writing Non-fiction*, London: Routledge.

Wray, D. and Lewis, M. (1999) 'Bringing literacy and history closer together', *Primary History*, **20**, October, 11–13.

Chapter 8

First Steps in Organising ICT in the Primary Classroom

John Potter

Introduction

This chapter is intended for all teachers using ICT in a primary school setting, particularly those just beginning to use computers. It is concerned with finding practical organisational solutions for teachers or student teachers attempting to deliver the National Curriculum for ICT as a discrete subject or in every subject area. Any teacher who wishes to address ICT in their classroom for the first time should also find the advice helpful. The emphasis throughout is on classroom-based organisational strategies which could be used to raise the profile of ICT in the school. So we deal with organisational strategies, including ideas for whole class teaching of ICT skills. You will also see discussions about computer rooms and rotas, as well as ideas for supporting writing with ICT. The opportunities provided by portable computers and the internet are introduced.

There is a section dealing with common hardware and software in primary schools, as well as with roles of teachers, pupils, classroom assistants and others. In the appendix to this chapter, you will find a list of some of the ICT tools likely to be found in schools.

Objectives

By the end of this chapter you should:

- be able to manage ICT in the primary school classroom; recognise what can be done in terms of introducing the computer to children and managing the learning in situations with differing levels of provision;
- recognise the background to the use of computers in the classroom in the UK and identify some of the variables at work which impact on the use of the computer in the primary school classroom, from government policy through to school management structures;
- be aware of what you might see in a primary school classroom anywhere in the UK in terms of hardware and software, as well as consider the

sorts of things you might hear people say about computer use in those schools, and what that reveals about the provision for ICT in that institution.

Some organisational strategies for using ICT in the primary classroom

This section looks at some general principles and follows up with what it may be possible to achieve in terms of children writing with computers. This has been chosen as an example because it is perhaps the most common use of computers in primary schools.

To begin with, here are some general principles. First, on a regular basis and always with new computer programs in the classroom, arrange a whole class session. In a low resource setting, that is, a single computer to a class of thirty children, first bring the computer to the carpet area where everybody can see it. This immediately brings the computer out of its corner and into the world of the classroom. There may, of course, be physical reasons why you cannot do this. If there are, do what you can to overcome them or borrow areas big enough to do it somewhere else in the school. Just getting started with a piece of software should involve the whole class. This does not need to be of the same order of time as for the initiatives in literacy and numeracy. Although at the beginning with a new package, when screens look very unfamiliar to the class, it would be worth spending longer on them.

What format should such a whole class session take? It should be strictly limited to fifteen minutes two to three times a week, ideally at the start of a session, morning or afternoon. In my own classroom, with a computer adjacent to the carpet it became a fairly regular feature which involved the children.

What mode of delivery should be adopted? If the aim is to instruct, but at the same time to allow the computer to come into the world of the classroom more fully, then a question and answer style lends itself to this situation – definitely not a lecture format. Avoid the outcome of producing another forum for promoting the idea that there are experts with all the knowledge.

Allow the children to provide tips for other users. Discuss with them the difficulties that they have to overcome in familiarising themselves with the onscreen layout of the particular piece of software. Print out screens to help the children become familiar with new layouts they will be encountering.

Ask the children to discover, and then report back on, different ways of doing the same thing.

In introducing a writing program, for example how to make text appear in a different font size or colour, you should:

- stress regular, practical instructions by giving a mantra-like tone to them;
- question children who do not always jump up and down with the answer (good primary practice, in other words . . . do not favour the loud over the quiet);
- invite children to contribute to the discussion strictly girl–boy–girl–boy etc.;
- do not allow one sex or group of children to dominate;
- stress the team building aspects of sharing strategies so that we can all use the computer efficiently and safely;
- involve children in a discussion about safety – monitor position, length of time, seating and so on;
- let everyone become an expert . . . do not always ask the same child (who is managing their own internet business from their bedroom at home);
- value what they say even when it is patently wrong ('That's a good suggestion but . . .').

Above all, have a bank of regular class sayings which are published on a class noticeboard near to the computer and which emphasise good practice; for example, 'Save Before You Print'. (This is perhaps the first and most important thing to have written up in your classroom in – at least – 72 point type.)

What are the benefits of whole class input?

There are a number of benefits to be gained by starting with the whole class approach:

1   Sharing knowledge
Regular whole class input increases the shared level of knowledge in the classroom about the use of the computer. It increases the overall standard of ICT work and the number of areas for which you can use ICT with some feeling of security.

2   Reinforcing learning
It will also repay you in terms of stress reduction to have a regular period of whole class instruction in the basics of a particular piece of software. You will reduce the number of times that you have to say the same thing over and over again to groups of two to three children. You will not be followed round the room by children desperate to save or print work which it has taken all morning to complete. They will know by reference to the noticeboard or by questions raised in whole class sessions, how to carry out the most basic tasks.

3   Developing independence

Becoming independent and increasingly competent in basic ICT skills will engender in the children a sense of responsibility for their work. From an early age, as children progress through the school, they are expected to take on more responsibility for knowing where their equipment is, where their possessions are, where they are going next and so on. Why should ICT be any different? Children can be shown the importance of looking after electronic forms of their work, just as they can the importance of looking after their draft books. They will need to be shown how to save and retrieve their work and the importance of backing up work. Children be will less inclined to ask how to print, how to save, how to underline, how to centre text, how to make a picture appear, etc. if these tasks have been publicly outlined in whole class sessions.

All these activities allow you and the children to start to think of the computer as more a part of the world of the classroom. More than that, they foster a belief amongst all users in the classroom that they can become competent and confident manipulators of ICT.

The cascade model for introducing new software

The alternative model of instruction, a version of the cascade model, whereby one or two children learn it and teach others over a period of time discreetly while other children get on with the real work, allows the more negative messages about ICT to be disseminated. Amongst these more negative messages are:

- There are ICT experts who know everything and must always be consulted before you do anything.
- ICT is something that happens in a corner of the room away from the mainstream and is never discussed and nothing to do with the rest of the school day.

However, there is sometimes a case for giving the children themselves responsibilities for passing on their skills and knowledge to each other, as long as every child has an equal chance of becoming an expert and teaching others.

Creating a learning ethos for ICT

We suggest that you show the children that you too are a learner. ICT will be less threatening to you as a teacher if you enter into the situation as a learner alongside them. It is wrong to give children the impression that you or anyone else knows all they need to know about computers; the truth is that we are all learning about ICT. Once one thing is learned you can be sure another parameter will enter the equation. It is OK to make mistakes. If the basic care of the equipment is known and respected, there is not much harm that can be done.

Finally, if it is not obvious within, say word processing, how to carry out the basic functions, why is it not obvious? Is it always your fault or theirs? Occasionally the software you use will deliberately obscure the issue. Encourage children to think about software as a tool and to question its ease of use or appropriateness to the task. Sometimes they will need to change the tool to undertake a different task or to refine an existing one. Thinking about software as a tool fosters an idea that they are in control, or will be in control with practice.

Access to computers: the arguments for computer rooms

Areas in primary schools which have been networked as a computer lab – or where all computers in the school have been placed – obviously allow for more of this direct instruction to take place.

Computer rooms have a place in a school where previously poor practice – or non-existent practice – has been identified; for example, by Ofsted. In some schools, there is uneven provision for computer use, perhaps because equipment is not repaired quickly, or because a few teachers may lack confidence in ICT teaching. A computer room may make the organisation of ICT more equitable and encourage all teachers to use ICT regularly, when they are timetabled for the use of the computer room. One of the risks being run in this organisational strategy is of going too far into lecture mode and expanding the initial input to the point where the children get very little of their allotted time actually working at the computer. The other risk is of further divorcing ICT from the business of the classroom.

Ideally, a mixed economy of whole class teaching in a lab in a very directed way would be balanced by some continued input back in the classroom which allowed the children to develop a project over time.

Rotas in the normal classroom

Rotas ensure that there is equality of access and of opportunity in the classroom. However, fixing them once and for all at the start of an academic year can limit the development of teacher and pupils skills. ICT skills acquisition is dynamic, always changing. After whole class input, at the beginning of working with a new piece of software or hardware, children need time to practise. Longer rota periods can be gradually shortened as children become more skilled.

Rotas should always be public. They should be large, on the wall, and clearly visible so that children can see that there is equality of provision. Older children can be involved in the drawing up and monitoring of time on the system.

With software which has specific content, such as a game or simulation or where the software is of the Drill and Practice sort – such as Integrated Learning Systems – there are fixed, tighter, more specific timetables of use involved. The software itself monitors these.

Translating National Curriculum demands into classroom practice

Activity 8.1 What are the demands on you?

Review the demands made on you as a teacher by your own version of a local or national curriculum. What are the skills needed by the pupils you teach now? How are you planning to deliver those skills and techniques to the children? Do you have access to a computer suite, or do you propose to set up a rota so that pupils manage to practise these skills in an appropriate context; for example, in developing their writing of poetry, stories or scientific reports? Do you plan maths lessons in which some children use ICT to help them calculate and handle data? You could use the QCA[1] *scheme of work* (1998) or a school version of it to provide you with the framework for planning your own scheme.

When younger children are writing with computers, they should be given time to generate and communicate their ideas, using text, tables, pictures and sounds. This notion of communicating their ideas implies that they should have a number of recognised audiences for their writing. Using email to communicate with experts or with other children carrying out similar activities is one way in which ICT can support this process.

As they get older, pupils should also begin to respond to the needs of their audience, perhaps by using email to continue a longer conversation with one or more partners. You will need to monitor any email messages sent out by your pupils, since it is possible that unintentioned meanings may be transmitted by inexperienced writers.

Children's jokes may be misunderstood, especially if they are communicating with others whose first language is not English.

The QCA *Scheme of Work* (1998) provides a map of activities which allows for progression in all areas of ICT throughout Key Stages 1 and 2 (pupils aged up to 11 years). It can be used on its own or as a supplement to a school scheme or as a template for a school scheme. It has been organised into units labelled by year group. Each unit is broken down further with contexts for its operation under headings such as:

- Where the unit fits in
- Technical Vocabulary
- Resources
- Expectations
- Learning Objectives
- Possible Teaching Activities
- Learning Outcomes
- Points to note.

The key element for translating this into action in the classroom is how to map the learning objectives into your own particular setting, in terms of both the wider schemes of work in your school and the resources at your disposal. We have discussed ways of understanding the patterns of influence on IT in the school and have noted some solutions in organisational terms for introducing new packages and systems into the classroom. The next step is to situate the work within the given context.

In a school where the only computer is still shared between thirty children, the expectations of the curriculum you are following need not necessarily be lower than in more richly resourced environments. Using whole class teaching sessions initially to develop basic skills of starting, saving, printing, closing down, these skills can be refined over time to include sessions which focus on developing writing skills. If children are secure about where they are saving work and know that they can find it again, the computer will become a tool which they can rely on and feel confident about using much more rapidly. This basic training can prevent children losing motivation because of long queues and the boredom of copy-typing.

Whole class ICT sessions in lab environments

You may find yourself working in a school which has made the decision to go for a lab environment, or computer suite, if they can no longer manage to deliver the curriculum with smaller numbers of older computers in the classrooms. As a result, computers have been collected in and used in a group area. The rota question no longer applies at class level. It now becomes an issue for the various managers in the school to manage the equitable provision across classes.

Whole class demonstrations can, and should, still take place. But they need to be a sensible length, enabling the children to make the best use of what may be their only time in the week when they are on the machines. After all, lesson management ought to be easier with no other activities going on other than computing. The teacher can provide more direct input for the children. Where these grouped computers are networked, saving and logging of progress is even easier. Networking solutions are becoming the norm for schools just beginning to address the issue with recently released funds for ICT development.

There are advantages to working in this way:

- The computers can be more easily maintained by ICT co-ordinators and by service contractors.
- There is a slot booked in to the week which must be devoted to ICT, raising the prospect of all children gaining their entitlement to ICT.
- Reluctant, non-confident teachers can observe more easily the use of ICT and use such a lab for their own professional development.

There are disadvantages to working in this way:

- It further perpetuates the concept of IT being outside of the main agenda of the class.
- Follow-up is very difficult and continuity, such as is required by the curriculum and by the QCA scheme of work, is very much harder to maintain.

There is only one solution which allows for all the different elements to be satisfied. That is, to have both a lab and a classroom connection to a network. Work which has been launched in whole class sessions in a lab setting can be followed up in the world of the classroom on one or two classroom stations. The business of saving and routines for writing with computers can be outlined in the lab. The other elements of the teaching of writing can then be followed up in relation to the rest of the classroom work.

Working in more richly resourced environments: using the internet

In schools which have much higher levels of ICT provision, the organisational issues are of a different but still significant nature.

Schools looking for uses of the internet for children's writing, for example, will find that they are limited only by the kind of connection that they have. Teachers and children who can compose text in a word processor will find no particular problems with using email packages. The organisational issues presented by writing email with children aged about 8 or 9 years include:

- How to compose off-line (if you do not have a cheap, reliable, fixed connection).

- How to sustain motivation and interest when the correspondents do not reply for long periods of time.
- What particular forms of writing are appropriate to email.
- How to introduce children to the concepts of netiquette.

Working in more richly resourced environments: using portable computers

In schools fortunate enough to have portable computers which are connectable to their desktops, there are opportunities for more creative use of IT, in particular, seeing the portable as an electronic draft book and the desktop as a publishing centre. Children have access to IT from the very beginning of the composition. There is none of the sometimes awkward working from drafts in books which is often seen in school. And, naturally, there is less temptation to use the computer as a typewriter to type up from best copy!

We are fortunate to be working in an education system which, on the face of it, is richly resourced for ICT in the primary classroom. Furthermore, we have in place legislation which makes it a compulsory subject from the very earliest years in the primary school up to the ages of 16. In addition to this, the National Curriculum places ICT in every subject order. Thus there is a legal imperative to teach it and the equipment to do so.

And yet the Stevenson[2] report found that the evidence, from inspections by Ofsted and others, suggested that the take up and quality of use of computers in our classrooms is actually low. Even in areas where there is rich provision of equipment, and/or internet connections, it was possible to find little evidence that the computer was fully or usefully integrated into the curriculum.

One of the main reasons for the low take-up of ICT, as identified by Stevenson and its companion report with accompanying statistics (McKinsey 1997), was the actual age of the computer equipment in classrooms throughout the UK. They found the situation to be such that it made the use in the classroom difficult or impossible. The National Grid for Learning; for example, the central initiative of educational ICT strategy for the incoming administration, was poised for a launch, but, without significant investment would be available to only a limited number of connectable schools. Age of equipment would disqualify many from all but the slowest sort of connection.

The other main factor was the perceived lack of confidence and skill of the teaching profession. Sometimes this is characterised as 'reluctance'. It is certainly true that some teachers find it enormously threatening to be delivering a subject which employs skills which they do not themselves have.

Once elected, the Labour government set about investing large sums of money in training. In its White Paper, *Connecting the Learning Society* (DfEE

1998), the government envisaged such training to be supplied by providers working to recognised 'kite marked' standards. Each teacher in the country would receive a level of basic IT skill training, some of it to be worked on by independent study, some provided in approved centres. All teachers were to be trained and fully competent to use classroom IT, access online services through the National Grid for Learning and use IT for their own administrative tasks by the year 2002.

For the National Grid for Learning strategy to work, teachers would need to be shown how the computer can take its place in the world of the classroom, in whatever setting, whether there are large numbers of networked computers in the primary school or a mixed bag of older and slightly unreliable work stations lurking and occasionally working in the corner.

Support within school

A further background factor in the previously low uptake of ICT nationally is that there may be no support structure for teachers in their school situation. At school level, there may be no ICT co-ordinator. Good ICT co-ordinators who attend training, pass it on to colleagues, give generously of their time and knowledge are in short supply, perhaps because the demand for people with these skills has increased dramatically. However, the training initiatives instituted by Government funding is likely to redress this situation. Governing bodies of schools and management teams will see the need to offer incentives and further training in order to make sure that their school has a place on the National Grid for Learning.

Success with ICT in the primary school?

Even in a school with fast internet access in all classrooms and many other ICT resources there are still issues of curriculum integration to consider – at a different level. The starting point is to bring the world of ICT closer to the world of the classroom, away from the corner of the room or the lab visited once a week, and situate it within the main business, the main discourse of the classroom.

Before discussing some of the ways in which this may be achieved, the following section attempts an overview of what you might see in a primary school in the UK in the way of ICT equipment.

What will you see in the way of ICT in a primary school classroom?

The following sections offer comments on observations that you can make about three areas which impact strongly on ICT in primary schools: the hardware, the software and the people therein.

What hardware is available to you?

Activity 8.2 Identifying computers and other hardware

If you are a student teacher, this would make a good observational task early on in your time in the primary school. If you are a classroom teacher, there may be particular sensitivities you need to consider before undertaking this inventory. Have a look at all the classes, and all the places in the school where computers may be in operation. What do you see?

Make a list – suggested headings are in Table 8.1.
Compare it to the one in the appendix to this chapter.
Use a table like the one in Table 8.1 to help you collect and organise this information.

Table 8.1 Identifying the hardware available in your school

Equipment type	Who uses it?	What is it used for?

What software is available to you?

Activity 8.3 Evaluating the software resources

Find the software associated with your age phase in the first instance. Note down particular curriculum content or applicability. Then widen your search to see if there is a similar range available for other classes in the school. Are you able to use the current software to its full extent? Do children need to spend a lot of time learning new skills in order to use this software, or will some of their current skills just need updating?

Which curriculum areas will you choose as a focus for the ICT skills and the software you have available?

You might want to organise the data you collect into a table like Table 8.2.

Table 8.2 Evaluating software resources

Software item	Intended age range Curriculum application

You may see software which came bundled together with the computer. It was pre-loaded and intended to form a basic toolkit of software which could be used as a starting point for the school. The toolkit is a common concept across platforms and is usually organised to the labels or similar set out in Table 8.3.

Table 8.3 Toolkit labels

Programme type	Examples
Word or Text Processing	Talking WriteAway or Textease – PC
	Talkwrite or Pendown – Acorn
Desktop Publishing	Microsoft Publisher or Creative Writer – PC
	Ovation Pro – Acorn
Internet	RM Edu Web or through an LEA
Image processing or graphics	Dazzle or First Artist – PC or Acorn
Data handling	First Workshop or Information Workshop – PC
	Junior Pinpoint – Acorn or PC
Multimedia authoring	Hyperstudio – PC, Acorn or Apple
Early Years	MyWorld – PC or Acorn
Monitoring or DataLogging Software	Junior Insight – all platforms
Controlling and Modelling Software	Logo or WinLogo – all platforms

There may be additional CD-ROMs in use, bought for specific teaching purposes such as *Talking Animated Alphabet*[3] from Sherston (for early literacy) or *The Way Things Work* from Dorling Kindersley[4] (for science, design and technology).

As a general rule of thumb, seek advice before installing unchecked older software on newer machines. Early Windows programs will happily install all sorts of arcane files and folders all over your brand new hard disk, crippling its operation. Seek advice from the ICT co-ordinator or LEA advisor, or manufacturer of your new machine (you may even find the soft-ware house is still in existence). Always seek advice before installing new software onto a network.

Maximising support development

Activity 8.4 Support systems

There are many people in the primary school who have an influence on the level of support for the organisation and use of ICT. Find out who they are in your particular school situation. Interview them and discover more about their views on the whole school development for ICT. Consider how this information can help you achieve your goals for ICT in your classroom.

Before going on to list some of the things you might have discovered about people who impact upon ICT in your institution, it is worth noting that, in general, far too little attention is paid to the human resources in schools. A great deal of agonising goes on about hardware and software and much, often increasingly successful, appealing for money from the school budget for equipment. Sometimes, training is included in such planning and budgeting. Far more rarely is there consideration for who will oversee the management of the resources and their continued development once they are actually in the school. Who will provide the leadership in both the technical and the curriculum sense? And, more significantly for a smaller school perhaps, how will they be remunerated and what will their status be within the school management structure? You may include in your list such people as ICT co-ordinators, senior managers, heads and deputies, other teachers, parents, governors, classroom assistants and, of course, the children themselves.

Furthermore, with so much pressure on 'the basics', curriculum develop-ment is often focused on literacy and numeracy initiatives. Strangely, hopefully not for much longer, these initiatives and the managers' under-standing of them, fail to address the opportunities for ICT to provide valuable activities and support for delivery of the 'basics'. The two could, indeed should, go hand in hand. Chapters 2, 3 and 4 provide advice on these issues.

Certainly, there are opportunities for record keeping and assessment and ICT (I am NOT talking about incomprehensible reports for parents auto-matically generated from National Curriculum statements but about creative electronic profiling and records of achievement such as may be found in; for example, the Newham Primary Toolbox).

Table 8.4 Statements on computer use in classrooms

One extreme ...	... to the other
'You've finished your work now, go and play on the computer.'	'Why don't you stop writing that story in your book and co-operate with Jimmy on a shared story on the computer?'
'We hardly ever use the computer because of the literacy hour, the numeracy hour and everything else, there just isn't time ...'	'The computer can be really useful in Literacy and Numeracy work. Spell checkers and thesaurus functions are great!'
'Ask Forida (or Faisal), (s)he always knows how to do it ...'	'Have a look at our book of "Frequently Asked Questions" whenever you have a problem.'
'We used to use it all the time but now it's broken. We haven't switched it on for months ...'	'Well, the printer ran out of ink yesterday, but we managed to get some more from the local stationers.'
'It's wet playtime ... OK, you can go and play on the games on the computer ...'	'During wet play, the usual rota system will be working.'

There are of course some negative aspects of computer use in a few classrooms, but consider the sets of statements in Table 8.4 and decide where you would prefer to be in the debates.

The children

Children are the best source of information about what is going on with ICT in the classroom, if you are new to it, or just visiting. They know about the equipment. If it is old, they know which keys stick. They tend to know how to get round the deficiencies of the equipment. Some of them, as in the case of a 6 year-old I encountered recently, are surrogate ICT co-ordinators, wearily sorting out problems for people in the classroom (including the teacher).

Many children now have access to computers at home. What they say about the computers in school can be quite interesting in this regard. I have overheard young children discussing the relative merits of Word97 over other writing packages, others talking knowledgeably about computer viruses and what can be done about them.

The games-playing children, those who have consoles at home of one kind or another, often have a robust attitude towards computers of all sorts. They are aware of 'cheating' to get to different levels. Sometimes they will indulge in various key presses which may cause havoc with onscreen displays, sometimes they may discover for the class, newer, more efficient ways of doing things. Whatever the situation, it is always worth listening to what children say about computers and considering and valuing their contributions to the whole class body of knowledge about ICT.

Other issues to be considered

Health and safety

One other issue you may observe is connected to health and safety. Children may be sitting at a table which is not designed to hold a computer and which could provide a lethal dose of electricity were any small hand to come into contact with certain wires at the back. They may also have inadequate space in which to use the mouse. They may be sitting too low down and craning their necks to look at a display monitor.

Good quality computer trolleys with earthed sockets are available at less than one tenth the cost of a new computer. Again, trolleys are often low on the list of budget items when people sit down to plan for computers in schools. They will, however, prevent injury and protect the equipment in the longer term.

If a school is being newly networked, reputable companies will always advise on seating and benching considerations. The same will apply to safer power points. These facilities will not safely operate on multiple 4-gang sockets hanging from leads and connected endlessly together. Higher voltages in such rooms need to be delivered from surge protected sockets in new trunking.

Maintenance

Before we leave the general observations on computers in schools, it is worthwhile considering the maintenance situation in the school. One of the obstacles faced by teachers in schools is the lack of working equipment. If you add poorly maintained equipment into an equation which already includes old equipment, reluctance and even fear on the part of some staff members, you have a recipe for poor ICT provision.

Maintenance is a serious issue and a school should have a procedure for dealing with non-functioning equipment. Some LEAs offer central support contracts which ensure that the equipment is kept at a decent level of operation for large periods of time. In other LEAs, schools organise their own maintenance contracts. Whether or not this is the case, there should be a procedure for logging defective equipment and regularly servicing it. If there is not, you need to take action to start logging it yourself and asking awkward questions of senior managers. One question might be 'How can I provide the ICT entitlement for children in my class when I don't have any working equipment?'

Newer providers, such as those taking money from schools benefiting from central government standards funding, should provide high-quality service contracts. Indeed, maintenance is an issue which has led to increasing numbers of schools entering leasing arrangements.

Virus protection

Be aware that the authors of the infamous pieces of malicious code which can harm computers do not have exceptions for educational computers. Before running any old software or looking at any disks you have, your colleagues have, your children have, make sure that something on the computer can examine it for viruses. Many suppliers of newer equipment have virus protection as standard in their particular toolkits. It is worth asking if that is the case or not with the computers in your care. The latest virus protection software may be downloaded for a trial period from certain sites.[5]

Summary

This chapter has attempted to provide a broad overview of some factors which impact on organisational strategies for ICT in the primary classroom. It has attempted to be non-specific and generic in order to be applicable to a number of different settings. It has, furthermore, attempted to break down the notion that expertise around a particular piece of software or hardware is a prerequisite of sound classroom practice. Rather, good use of ICT in the classroom is about fostering an ethos in which the expertise is jointly shared and used to empower all members of the class. All the ideas for projects in all curriculum areas with ICT will not operate successfully without consideration for how this ethos may be established. Once it is up and running, the classroom or school with ICT as a central part of its life and operation will experience no limits to what can be achieved.

Appendix 1: What you are likely to find in your school

Ignoring other ICT devices for the moment and focusing on the computer and its related equipment (apologies if I have missed anything out, this is a *broad* overview):

Computers (Stand-alone)

- PCs with management software and toolkits of various kinds, e.g. RM Window Box PCs with Windows (3.1, 95, 98 etc.)
- RM 480Z computers
- RM PC 186 computers
- RM Turnkey systems
- RM WindowBox PCs with Windows (3.1, 3.11, 95 and beyond)

- BBC Micros
- Acorns (all ages, A3000, A3020 . . . A7000)
- Apple Macs (of all ages and types)

- Old PCs donated by businesses with inappropriate software and dangerous hardware.
- Good condition, renovated PCs donated with guarantees and good software (same source as above).
- PCs donated with inappropriate software and no training (a business might have tried to help out local schools towards the end of a financial year).
- PC given by a parent or governor (in any of the states mentioned above).

Networks

- PC Networks recently set up by LEAs responding to the National Grid for Learning. (Many companies previously only associated with businesses are bidding to provide such resources.)
- PC Networks running Novell or similar with Independent Learning Systems (ILS) packages running on them.
- PC Networks with Windows NT Workstation running; for example, RM Connect Management tools or networks supplied by Apple Xemplar.
- Acorn EcoNet round a school, or in a 'Computer Room'.
- RM Net 3.0 with PC 186 stations.

Printers

- Laser printers of all shapes and sizes. Quiet, efficient and better value than many people realise. Some connected to networks as a single printer in a lab setting.
- Large, robust dot matrix printers with continuous feed paper very noisy in a classroom but economical (when it isn't jammed).
- As above but smaller with a cut-sheet feeder.
- Higher quality inkjets, quieter, cheap to buy but very expensive to maintain. Some popular models will even persuade you that the ink has run out when it has not.

Portable computers

- Pocketbooks, I or II or III
- E-Mates
- Ancient laptops from Acorn or Apple or RM

- Multimedia laptops (some perhaps in the hands of teachers in the BECTA Multimedia portables project)
- All of the above used by children OR teachers OR the headteacher. (Sometimes with a portable printer that is very difficult to get going)

Internet access

- Via a modem (external or internal) of varying speed and quality
- Or via an ISDN line
- Or via cable
- Or via a Local Authority or Higher Education internet connection
- Access will be standalone in the enthusiast's classroom or the library
- Or it will be across the whole school (or just in the 'Computer Room')

Some internet access will be unfiltered. Most schools will have opted in to an education provider like RM Internet for Learning which provide a measure of protection from undesirable sites and which provide links to national curriculum content without the need to search the World Wide Web in the first instance.

Programmable toys

- A Roamer, Pixie, Pip or other programmable toy
- A Valiant turtle (infra-red linked to an Acorn usually)
- A Jessops turtle (linked by cable)

Imaging equipment

- Digital cameras
- Flatbed scanners with parallel printer port connections
- Hand scanners requiring 'podules' (Acorn)
- Flatbed scanners with cards

There will be more in the cupboard. It will be in varying states of disrepair.

Older equipment

Beware of writing off the capabilities of all but the very oldest equipment. The Acorn A3000 computer; for example, has been able to handle mixed text and graphics by drag and drop for many years. PCs with reasonable amounts of memory and later versions of Windows are only now in a position to compete. Apple Mac enthusiasts will happily demonstrate the capabilities of their older machines, famously regarded as user friendly and graphically sophisticated.

Notes

1   The QCA produces schemes of work in ICT, as well as in science and other subjects, which has been sent to all schools. The schemes can also be downloaded from the Standards website *http://www.standards.gov.uk*
2   The Stevenson report (1997) was commissioned by the Labour Party, in opposition, to examine the extent of ICT use in schools.
    Two key conclusions were made:
    1. that ICT in our schools is primitive and not improving,
    2. that there should be a national priority to increase the use of ICT in the schools.
3   *Talking Animated Alphabet* is a CD-ROM from Sherston Software which helps young children with literacy.
4   Dorling Kindersley produces many high quality products for schools.
5   Try this site for downloadable software giving virus protection: *http://www.datafellows.com*

References and further reading

Particularly useful for teachers in training:
Trend, R., Davis, N. and Loveless A. (1999) *QTS: Information and Communications Technology*, London: Letts Educational.

Useful reading for getting started with computers and thinking about the organisational aspects of their use would include:
Bennett, R. (1997) *Teaching IT at Key Stage One*, London: Nash Pollock.
Chandler, D. (1985) *Young Learners and the Microcomputer*, Buckingham: Open University.
Crompton, R. (ed.) (1989) *Computers in the Primary Curriculum*, London: Falmer Press.
DfEE (1998) *Connecting the Learning Society*, London: DfEE.
McBride, P. (1998) *The Schools' Guide to the Internet*, Oxford: Heinemann.
McKinsey and Company (1997) *The Future of Information Technology in UK Schools*, McKinsey and Company, 1 Jermyn Street, London.
Nash, G., Wilson, A. and McDougall, R. (1997) *The Internet Guidebook*, London: Peridot Press.
QCA/DfEE (1998) *Information Technology – A Scheme of Work*, London: DfEE.
Somekh, B. and Davis, N. (eds) (1997) *Using IT Effectively in Teaching and Learning*, London, London: Routledge.
Straker, A. (1997) *Children Using Computers*, London: Nash Pollock.

There are books to which it would be a good idea to turn for some theoretical basis to bringing the computer into the world of the classroom. One of these would be:
Crook, C. (1998) *Computers and the Collaborative Experience of Learning*, London: Routledge.

Useful websites for organisational ideas for work with children

Virtual Teachers' Centre – Literacy Time: *http://www.vtc.ngfl.gov.uk/resource/literacy/index.html/*

BBC Learning Station: *http://www.bbc.co.uk/education/schools/#top*

BBC Primary English Guide: *http://db.bbc.co.uk/education-webguide*

Berit's Best Sites for Children: *http://db.cochran.com/litoc:theoPage.db/*

Funschool: *http://www.funschool.com*

Epals: *http://www.epals.com*

Chapter 9

Creating and Using Multimedia Applications

Jane Mitra

Introduction

You will come across multimedia software applications on the world wide web, in libraries and information centres, in kiosks on the High Street, in the classroom, games arcade and at the cinema. What does the term multimedia actually mean?

Multimedia software is any software which uses more than one medium, that is, text, sound, pictures, video, animation. There is a strong argument for the view that using multimedia software to communicate creates a whole new kind of literacy (see for example, Chapters 2, 3 and 4). The key to understanding this new literacy is to become an active participant in using the software – to create your own rather than be a passive consumer of commercially produced products. In the same way that writers learn about writing by doing it, you will learn most about multimedia by making your own multimedia texts.

One powerful feature of multimedia texts is their interactivity – the reader can choose how to explore a text, how to read it, hear it, watch it. The author can no longer predict how their text will be experienced, and that gives power to readers to create a virtually new text of their own. At the same time the reader has lost the predictable structure of traditional book-based texts – it is no longer obvious how much the text contains, how it is cross-referenced, how to move around within it, how it can be measured or evaluated. The skills needed to read and appreciate multimedia texts are different skills to the traditional literacy skills needed to read and appreciate a book.

Creating an interactive multimedia text can be easy to do if you choose the right software. There are many authoring programs designed for pupils to use, and some will allow quite sophisticated texts to be built.[1] Once you have become a multimedia author, just by putting together a couple of screens to convey a particular message, you will realise the new power you have. The same thing happens with pupils, and time and again I have seen pupils lifted and transformed by their own achievements.

Objectives

At the end of this chapter you should be able to:

- understand the basic structures, features and demands of multimedia software texts;
- appreciate the potential of multimedia software to empower both yourself and your pupils with a new way of communicating;
- plan a multimedia authoring project for your classroom.

Background and educational purposes

Computers have been used in education for many years, but the way they are being used today is very different and very exciting. The classroom computer has become a communication device, a publishing gateway and an aid to self-expression for all pupils irrespective of their abilities.

Multimedia software gives pupils the power to communicate using all the skills they came into school with. Think of the complete self-expression of 3 year-olds – they communicate by talking, by singing, in drawings and paintings full of colour. Once at school they are introduced to the idea of written text as the main medium of acceptable communication, with occasional opportunities for drawing, and limited time for oral expression. It is not surprising that young pupils who do not take easily to reading and writing text, begin to lose self-esteem. By the age of seven many of them will have a low self-image, and will have devised their own strategies for dealing with their lack of literacy – some will be difficult in class, others will be withdrawn and wary.

What if those same pupils have the opportunity to express themselves through multimedia in full colour, using their own voice to speak their own text, with pictures, sound effects, and more? It is not surprising that children as young as five years old take to this new authoring technology with enthusiasm and excitement. Pupils of all abilities can find something in it that they can do really well, and the software they produce is high status, long lasting and very satisfying. Later in this chapter I provide examples of work from very young children.

Basic structures and elements of multimedia texts

Before looking at projects you can undertake in school, it is necessary to know the meaning of the terms used in the production of multimedia and some of the most common are defined here.

User interface   This is simply the way the user sees and uses the software. It should be clear and unambiguous, but this is not the case with poorly designed software. There should be sufficient Help resources on screen or in an accompanying User Manual – these may include an initial tutorial on how to make best use of the software.

When building your own multimedia screens you should do plenty of usability testing with members of the target audience. This will show you whether your user interface is adequate. If the testers are baffled by what they see or do not know what to, do then you have some redesigning to undertake. It is best to do some testing before the whole project is complete in case the user interface needs major redesigning.

Navigation   Moving around through a multimedia text is known as navigating, and there are some common conventions such as buttons marked *Next* or *Back* for going through a sequence of screens, arrows to click on, a *Home* button or graphic icon to click on to go back to the start screen.

Some features of traditional texts are used in some multimedia applications; for example, index, contents list, glossary. They can be enhanced in a multimedia text by having instant transfer (through a clickable button) to the relevant page or section, but even as a non-interactive feature they are useful to give the user a feeling for what the text contains. Navigation can be very difficult if you cannot estimate the amount of content you will be looking through, the range of content available and the overall structure of the content into meaningful sections or themes.

When you are building your own multimedia, a storyboard or navigation map will make it easy to see where all the links on individual screens will lead. Some authoring programs offer a contents list or storyboard feature, and software for web page design sometimes includes a graphical representation of all live links so checking them is quicker. Testing all the links will take time and pupils will need encouragement to persist and be rigorous.

Using a different design or colour scheme for each section will also make navigation easier, as the user has more visual clues to remind them of where they are in the text.

Hypertext links   A text which contains jumping off points to other pieces of text can be much more flexible and powerful than a straightforward text to be read all the way through. Links are attached to particular words or phrases and when you click on these you are taken to the destination text. A simple example is that of a passage about Vikings in Britain – if you click on the phrase *Viking jewellery* you will jump to a passage about jewellery. You may not go back to the original passage, but may jump from the jewellery passage to one about food and cooking. This is how the user can construct their own text in effect. When you plan your own multimedia text you should bear this in mind, and make it easy for the user to navigate through their chosen route without getting lost.

Hot spot   Hot spots are areas on screen which react when you click on them, or sometimes when you just move over them. They may be hidden behind words or pictures, or displayed with their own icons or buttons.

Sound   By using a cheap microphone and simple sound handling software you and your pupils can enhance and transform your multimedia texts. Voice can be used to explain text, to read poems, to become part of a story, to give helpful instructions. Sound effects and music can be used in countless ways. Editing sounds on screen is an interesting exercise, and manipulating sounds to get special effects is great fun.

Text   Word processing may be included in your authoring program or text may be imported from a separate text file. The most important features which you should teach your pupils to use are: spell checker, fonts, frames, scrolling text. Too much text on a screen is unattractive and difficult to read, so blocks of text should be kept small.

Colour   Pupils will be excited by the range of colours available to them as designers, but should remember to consider the needs and preferences of their target audience. Many different combinations of colour can be tried out very quickly.

You should be aware of the incidence of colour vision deficiency in the population. This is also known as colour blindness but the term does not really describe what is actually a range of deficiencies from total colour blindness to a lack of discrimination between two or more colours. It does not appear to be linked to intellectual capability, it does not often affect females, but up to 12 per cent of the males in a population may be affected. The most common colours affected are red and green. Some useful guidelines to remember are: use blue, yellow, white and black for significant features on screen, make sure text colour is a strong, bright contrast from the background and put text labels next to colour blocks on charts etc. rather than relying on the colour as identifier.

Drawings and paintings   Pencil or crayon drawings can be scanned to convert them into computer files, and they often look fabulous on screen. Paintings can also be scanned, or if too large, photographed and then digitised (see section below on Photographs). Computer-based art work is simpler to work with as it is already in digital form. Even very young pupils can use simple art programs and the results they produce can be wonderful. They can experiment with colour, line and form, and are freed from the constraints of paint and paper supplies, and the frustration of not being able to correct mistakes on paper.

Clip art   Commercially available clip art can be very useful, but should really only be used to supplement the art work and photographs produced by you and your pupils. It is possible to buy collections of drawn or painted pictures and decorative detail, cartoons, photographs, animated sequences, and even film sequences. You should acknowledge the source of any clip art you use, and check that the copyright allows you to use it.

Charts and graphs Computers are used in many curriculum areas to help with data handling, and graphs and charts produced in other programs can be displayed and explained in a multimedia presentation. Relevant charts could be accessed from hot spots in the main text. Check that the format required by your authoring software matches the format output by your graphing program.

Photographs There are several ways to get photographs into your software: scanning a traditional photograph, choosing from a collection of images which have been transferred onto a photo CD from traditional negatives (Figure 9.1) or import digital images direct to your computer from a digital camera or from the internet (click on the image and save to disc but do check copyright allows this). It is a good idea to crop the photo images before using them, so that only the important part of the image is seen. That will keep the file sizes smaller, which means the screens will load more quickly when you run your software.

Figure 9.1 Using the photo CD

Animation   It is possible to create animations in some simple authoring programs like Magpie[2] by running a consecutive sequence of screens quickly – the effect is rather like that of using a traditional flick book. There are some specialist animation programs which allow more sophisticated effects, but they are sometimes too complex for younger pupils. Make sure that any animations you and your class produce will be able to run within your chosen authoring program.

Animation is a powerful way to explain some physical processes or phenomena, and pupils can learn concepts thoroughly by building short animations to explain them.

Video   It is possible to use short video clips in your own software, but editing and manipulating video is quite complex. As more intuitive video editing software becomes available, it will be a more realistic option in the classroom. You will need a video card in your computer if you want to digitise your own videos, and you will need software which can run video. This will probably be included with your authoring software.

Hardware   To start building your own multimedia software, you will need a computer with a hard disc for storing large files, which has sound and colour graphics capabilities, a microphone, a scanner or CD-ROM drive for photo-CDs.

Software   The basic software requirements are: an authoring program e.g. Magpie, Multimedia Textease,[3] Hyperstudio,[4] sound recording software, an art program, and some clip art to get you started (this should be included with your authoring program).

A note about classroom management

The way you organise your class to build their own multimedia texts will depend on the available resources. It is possible to produce a whole class project using one computer, but it will take quite a long time. Pupils can work individually, in pairs or in small groups. It is a good idea to organise teams who take on responsibility for certain screens, or for certain functions; for example, link makers and testers, sound recorders and importers, spelling checkers, etc. Chapters 8 and 10 provide more detail about classroom management issues.

Examples of classroom practice: case studies

The following case studies are based on work done at Northgate JMI School in Hertfordshire. Making multimedia has become part of the normal school routine, and there are many examples there of creative, enthusiastic multimedia authors at work.

Awesome Alphabet

This was a whole class project with a mixed Year 2 and Year 3 class of thirty-two boys and girls. The end product was a valuable teaching resource based on the letters of the alphabet and their phonic sounds. It was designed to be used by Reception classes, so the useability testing was done with pupils from those classes.

The starting point of the project was revision of knowledge about the alphabet, and the need for about a quarter of the class to learn initial sounds correctly. The scope for creativity seemed limited but over the course of two school terms the class designed a set of activities based on letters, words, pictures and sounds which are lively and fresh. They started in pairs and chose words beginning with the twenty-six letters, painted a picture on screen to represent their word, and then recorded the sound of the word and of the initial letter. Once those pictures and sounds were stored on the classroom computer, they thought of ways to use them which would be useful and fun for reception classes who were beginning to learn about letters and their sounds.

There was a range of developmental level and ability level in the class and about a quarter of the class had special educational needs and were withdrawn once or twice a week for small group work with the support teacher. Everyone in the class contributed to the Awesome Alphabet, and everyone was justifiably proud of it. Several pupils showed a marked change of attitude to their work afterwards, and pupils of high ability recognised the valuable contribution made by those whom they had considered lacking in ability. There was a tremendous group spirit of co-operation and tolerance.

The next phase of the project was a fascinating process to watch. The class had to design a user interface which would be understood and enjoyed by their target audience. The testing and remodelling of this interface took many weeks, and a whole shift in attitude by the authors. They had all been in school long enough to know how important it was to get things right, to avoid making mistakes public (is this not why mistakes are often scribbled over so completely in children's written work?). Now they found that in order to develop this multimedia software successfully they had to ask the younger pupils to point out their mistakes and the weaknesses in their design. The first time two younger pupils were invited in to test the software, they sat down in front of the computer and when asked 'Do you know what to do?' they both said 'No'. On screen in front of them was an icon which represented the mouse and four arrows, which indicated that a choice had to be made using the mouse. The younger pupils did not know what it meant and it took a supreme effort for the older ones not to get really cross with them. After that a system of gold stars was introduced – anyone who found a mistake on screen or who was confused by an instruction would be given a gold star for helping to make the software better.

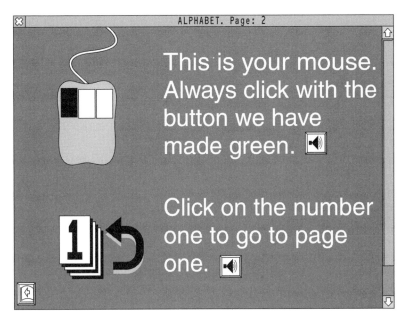

Figure 9.2 Making Awesome Alphabet

Many gold stars later the user interface included verbal instructions, a much better mouse picture, and an initial help screen to tell new users what to do to get started (Figure 9.2).

This work was an excellent illustration of the need to design and make a multimedia application for a particular audience, for it is only then that it can be evaluated in a real context.

Class management for the Awesome Alphabet project

The initial sessions to introduce the authoring, painting and sound handling software were whole class lessons. After that pupils worked in small groups mostly, with some individual work.

A volunteer parent helper was available for several hours once a week and she worked with individual pupils in the library, teaching them how to use the authoring software. After an initial session with her, most of the class were independent and confident Magpie users.

Resource management for the Awesome Alphabet project

The computer-related resources used for the project were: an Acorn 5000 computer in the classroom, an Acorn 5000 computer in the library, an Oak

Recorder microphone and Sound Lab 3 software, a simple painting program called Easel 2, an easy to use multimedia authoring program called Magpie, individual floppy discs for transferring picture files between computers.

This project won a National Educational Multimedia Award and several clips from the software, including an audio clip, can be found on the NEMA '96 website.[5]

Bones

This was a whole class project done with thirty Year 3 boys and girls. The pupils designed and made a high quality, interactive reference text about bones. The starting point was the study of the skeleton, muscles and movement in science. Their project eventually included work in English, maths, science, IT, design and technology, PE, art (see Figure 9.3).

The pupils interviewed medical experts (Figure 9.4), did some individual research on bones, handled and drew real bones, made models of joints, did a school-wide survey about broken bones, wrote an illustrated story about the school secretary's broken wrist, wrote poems about bones and made an interactive quiz about bones. Aspects of all this work became part of the multimedia text called BONES. It has a total of 101 screens, starting from a main menu screen and incorporating sub menus within the six main

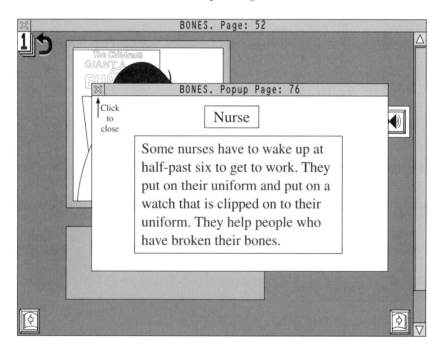

Figure 9.3 Example from the Bones project (written by pupils)

Figure 9.4 The physiotherapist in the classroom

sections: Learning About Bones, Bone Experts, Broken Bones, Bone Quiz, Reference and Bone Gallery.

The testing process was long and hard at times, but the class never gave up, and there was a good level of collaboration. There was a strong sense of ownership of the final multimedia presentation and that caused a group awareness of quality issues which seemed unusual for pupils of that age.

Pupils 'policed' each other with regard to spellings, even borders round text, neat layout and accuracy. Possibly this change was because they would not normally be critical of each other's work as it had taken a long time to do but here it was easy and quick to make corrections so they pointed out all the faults they spotted.

Class management for the Bones project

Whole class sessions introduced the class to the authoring software, the sound recording process, computer-based art work, the use of a photo CD, the use of a scanner, the data collection software, questionnaire design, the use of an Instamatic camera, recording interviews on cassette tape, conducting a survey using their questionnaire, data input from question-naires, analysis of gathered data, using traditional reference sources (books, posters, TV programmes), observational drawing, designing and making models of joints from found materials, investigating breathing rates by observing and timing movement of the ribcage. There were also many whole class sessions of voting on possible design options such as content, navigation methods and screen design. The above teaching/discussion sessions took place in the classroom over a six-month period.

Teams were allocated tasks to be responsible for, and actual work at the computer was done by individuals, pairs and teams. A flexible approach was necessary as there was only one computer with the authoring software on it and all thirty members of the class were eager to use it.

Resource management for the Bones project

The computer-related resources used for the project were: an Acorn 5000 computer with a CD-ROM drive, an Oak Recorder microphone and Sound Lab 3 software, a black and white Logitech hand scanner, Junior Pinpoint data handling software and, most important of all, Magpie, a simple multimedia authoring program.

The timescale of the project was six months to allow each pupil time to learn to use these resources. Routines developed in the classroom to make it easier for multimedia work to go on in the corner while the rest of the class worked at their desks. When sounds were being recorded; for example, one person would put up their hand high in the air and call out 'Recording!'. The rest of the class would be silent for a few seconds, and then carry on as normal with their work. The system worked because they knew it would also help them when it was their turn, and because everyone was committed to making something really good.

The hand scanner was attached to an old PC in the library, which was next door to the classroom. Pupils soon learned the routine of going in to scan a picture perhaps several times until satisfied with the quality, saving it onto a PC floppy disc, taking it to an Acorn computer in the library, converting the picture file to an Acorn file, saving it onto an Acorn formatted floppy disc and returning to the classroom with their picture ready to be loaded onto the classroom Acorn computer. They had their own individual floppy discs for this work, and were responsible for them. This scanning, converting and saving process was quite complex for 7 year-olds but it caused them no problems because they knew why they were doing it, and were motivated to do it well.

An excellent six-minute sequence showing the pupils at work on the Bones project is part of *Communications and IT* Programme 8 of the Channel 4 series for Primary Teachers called *Making Sense of Science.*

This project won a NEMA award and clips from it are featured on the NCET NEMA '95 CD-ROM.

Activity 9.1 Making your own multimedia: choose a topic

Having considered these case study examples, discuss what you and your pupils might like to do. Make a list of six school related topics, events or themes which could be communicated to a particular audience most effectively using multimedia. Some useful categories to think about are:

- learning resource
- entertainment
- reference resource
- fiction
- interactive branching stories
- carousel of art work
- diary of an event
- history topic
- interactive newspaper.

Multimedia supporting English as an Additional Language (EAL)

Pupils who do not use English as their first language can use multimedia communication to express themselves in their other language or languages. They may be able to act as a resource for the rest of the class and gain status during the production of a multilingual dictionary; for example.

One example of successfully using multimedia in this way was with two pupils, brother and sister, who came to live in the UK speaking French and Arabic, and very little English. There was already a tradition of children creating multimedia resources in the school, so it was suggested to the newcomers that they could work on a small presentation to let everyone know something about their languages and where they came from. They were delighted to take part in what was seen as a treat. They quickly understood what to do, despite their lack of fluency in English.

The first screen they made has a map showing North Africa and Europe. There are arrows going from the words English, French and Arabic to the respective countries where those languages are spoken. The subsequent screens showed some artwork done in class by the two pupils, with a commentary in the three languages. Their mother was pleased to hear about the project and agreed to come in and make a contribution to the software herself.

Class management for supporting EAL

These two pupils were taken out of their classes to do this work. They worked with the school ICT Classroom Assistant, who regularly works with groups of children from various classes under the direction of their class teachers.

Activity 9.2 A self-audit of your multimedia skills

Consider which of the following you can do and then identify where you may get help and training to improve your skills:

- Do I know how to save, retrieve and make back-up copies of all my computer files?
- Can I draw and paint on screen?
- Can I record sounds to be used in my software?
- Am I familiar with a multimedia authoring program?
- Do I know how to use hypertext links, hotspots and navigation icons?

Resource management for supporting EAL

The computer used for this work was in a resource area outside some classrooms. The sound recording could be done while the rest of the pupils were in class, so the resource area was quiet.

Activity 9.3 Auditing hardware and software and allocating funds

What sort of computers do you have access to?

- Are they suitable for multimedia work, that is, colour and sound capable?
- Is there a microphone?
- Is there a scanner?
- Is there a CD-ROM drive?
- Which multimedia authoring programs are available?
- Which program is most suitable for the age range within my class?
- Can more than one computer be used to build the software and the files merged together later?

The allocation of funds to the purchase of hardware and software is usually done by senior managers. Consider the process for making those decisions in the context in which you are working and whether there are ways in which you can be involved in influencing these decisions. Some schools operate an annual bidding system for funds and staff responsible for a certain area are expected to put forward a bid, others may allocate set amounts to subject areas. Funding is usually linked to the priorities for development identified through the school development planning process.

Where can you go for help?

- The ICT Co-ordinator in school may be able to give you some training, or at least arrange for you to try out the range of software available in the school.
- Read the ICT policy and the School Development Plan to see what structures are already in place to support teachers' professional development.
- Find out if there is a Teachers' Centre nearby where you could book some time to use their computers and software and even some training sessions.
- Ask your teaching colleagues for help and advice.
- Find out if any of the pupils in your class have multimedia skills which they could share with you and/or other class members.
- Look for support online,[6] where you will find groups of colleagues ready and willing to exchange expertise and experiences.
- Look in detail at multimedia work done by other teachers and pupils.

Making multimedia with your pupils

Taking the ideas you identified for Activity 9.1, use the activities below to plan a multimedia project with your pupils. My advice is to start small so that both you and the pupils can gain a sense of achievement and confidence fairly quickly.

Activity 9.4 Skills pupils need to get the most from multimedia software

Make a list of these skills using these headings and consider how you are going to organise this learning:

- pictures
- sounds
- text
- colour
- navigation
- hypertext
- hotspots
- animation
- storyboard/contents map.

Having a clear plan of the overall structure allows a number of children to work on the project at once. Building a storyboard provides a tool for this planning.

Establishing criteria for what makes an effective multimedia project will help the children evaluate their work. Undertaking a modified activity covering aspects of Activity 9.6 as a class may be useful in establishing this shared vision of a good project.

Activity 9.5 Build a storyboard on paper for one simple multimedia project

This could be done with the pupils in your class or by you for them if they need help to get started. By drawing out a map of screens with all their links marked, you can test each possible route a user could take and make sure that there are no dead ends. The quality of your quick sketches will not matter, as it is the overall plan which is being described. This is a very useful activity to ask your pupils to do and can reveal any confusion they may have about the project and how it all fits together.

Activity 9.6 Evaluating multimedia software

Points to consider when evaluating your own multimedia or commercial products include the following. Using these headings as a starting point, evaluate one or two pieces of multimedia software:

- amount of content
- depth of content
- ease of navigation
- language level
- relevance of illustrations/animations
- use of sound
- motivation and enjoyment
- appropriateness for target age group.

Consider the evaluations undertaken by teachers and reported on the Virtual Teacher Centre[7] and TEEM project websites.[8]

Involving parents

Once you and your pupils have learned to be multimedia authors, many of their parents will probably be very keen to find out what it is all about. They will hear snippets at home which may not make sense to them, and they may ask to see what the pupils are doing. This is a wonderful opportunity to involve them and perhaps turn their curiosity into enthusiasm.

The parents of the children in the first two case studies above came into an evening meeting in school to hear more about their children's achievements. Over thirty of them agreed to become voluntary ICT helpers in the school. Many of them had never touched a computer before and were very nervous about starting. The deal agreed with all the ICT helpers was to give them some training from the ICT Co-ordinator in exchange for some of their time given weekly to a particular teacher to help with computer-based work. A reporting sheet was drawn up to help with the teacher's assessment, and teachers had the opportunity to state their preferences and timetable their helpers' sessions on the computers in the library and the other resources areas in the school.

The head teacher was very supportive and arranged for some non-contact time for the ICT Co-ordinator so that training could be done during school time.

The helper scheme has been very successful and still continues. Several interesting developments have been linked to the multimedia authoring activities in particular. Some parents have taken multimedia on as a family project and have developed not only personal authoring skills, but also skills in the critical evaluation of commercial multimedia. They can see beyond the merely novel features of titles and can appreciate good design.

Summary

Multimedia communication is rich in possibilities for teachers and pupils. It requires new skills and brings new benefits. It is the literacy of the future, and the skills learned through multimedia authoring today will be transferable to new kinds of global communication along the Information Superhighway when it is finally a reality in schools and homes.

As soon as you start making multimedia you will see its potential for differentiated learning in the classroom, for independent and collaborative projects, for high quality useful resources created by pupils and teachers, for living, talking, laughing stories, for liberated self-expression for all your pupils. It is not difficult to resource or manage in the classroom, and it is not expensive either.

Through multimedia authoring your pupils will learn to communicate in an exciting, interactive way. Your role is one of facilitator and guide, and once you have taught them the skills to get started they will probably teach you many valuable lessons in return – about creativity, determination, motivation and persistence.

Notes

1   Examples of multimedia authoring software which teachers find useful include:
    • Multimedia Textease for PC and Acorn, demo available from Softease: *http://www.textease.com*
    • Hyperstudio for PC, Apple and Acorn, demo available from TAG: *http://www.tagdev.co.uk/hs/hs.html*
    • Magpie for Acorn, available from Logotron: *http://www.logo.com/catalogue/titles/magpie/index.html*
2   Magpie for Acorn, available from Logotron: *http://www.logo.com/catalogue/titles/magpie/index.html*
3   Multimedia Textease for PC and Acorn, demo available from Softease: *http://www.textease.com*
4   Hyperstudio for PC, Apple and Acorn, demo available from TAG: *http://www.tagdev.co.uk/hs/hs.html*
5   The NEMA '96 website is on *http://www.becta.org.uk/projects/nema/awesome/awesome1.html*
6   Chapter 11 provides advice about joining online communities.
7   The Virtual Teacher Centre multimedia evaluations are available on *http://www.becta.org.uk/information/cd-roms/*
8   The TEEM project (Teachers evaluating multimedia project) is on *http://www.teem.org.uk/what.htm*

References and further reading

Educational Computing & Technology, November 1997, Cambridge: Hobsons/ABC Business Press.

This edition of the magazine has an article entitled 'Multimedia in Action' by Paul Heinrich and also reviews of seven authoring programs suitable for use in primary school: Pages, TalkWrite, BookMaker, Magpie, Ultima, Key Author and Illuminatus. The article draws on materials submitted by schools for the National Educational Multimedia Awards (NEMA) run by NCET.

Lachs, V. (1998) 'Surviving the Jungle', *Times Educational Supplement ONLINE EDUCATION magazine*, 9 January.

This article is subtitled 'A 10-step guide to using multimedia for classroom projects'. The author is an advisory teacher for ICT and the examples cited in the article are taken from work she has done with classes in the Borough of Hackney in East London within the age range Year 5 to Year 8. She gives some good advice on the practical implications of introducing multimedia authoring to your class.

Shreeve, A. (1997) *English Case Studies and Materials*, Coventry: NCET.

This booklet was produced by the national IT in English project funded by the DfEE and managed by NCET (now BECTA). It is one of a series of publications from the project and it contains examples of writing and using multimedia texts successfully at Key Stages 2 and 3. It also contains references to further material on the project website (*http://vtc.ngfl.gov.uk/resource/cits/english/*).

Whitehorn, A. (ed.) (1996) *Multimedia The Complete Guide*, Bristol: Dorling Kindersley.

This is a very clear, well designed book aimed at adults. It is a highly visual guide to the way the different elements of multimedia are combined, online multimedia, the internet, interactive TV, games and more.

Chapter 10

Managing Curriculum Projects Using ICT

Darren Leafe

Introduction

Over the last few years the internet has become a popular and effective means of communication for many people. Industry has been using communication technologies of one form or another for some time and home use is developing at an unprecedented rate. Many schools are already connected and even more are looking into the opportunities that this form of technology can offer. This chapter examines some of these opportunities and why schools might embrace new and existing means of communication.

The term Information and Communication Technology identifies the two main elements of the internet: communication and information. Each has its advantages and disadvantages, however, it could well be argued that at the primary level, pupils will benefit from ICT strategies which have a bias towards the communication aspect of the curriculum. This chapter looks at some aspects of planning, implementing and evaluating communication projects.

Objectives

By the end of this chapter you should:

- understand some of the aims and learning outcomes of curriculum projects;
- recognise some of the advantages of using email for project communication;
- identify the possible roles of teachers and pupils in conducting projects;
- know how to assess the learning and evaluate the overall benefits of the project.

Background

It is not possible to explain the term 'curriculum project' without identifying exactly what we mean by 'curriculum'. How should 'curriculum' be interpreted within the context of an ICT project? Is the curriculum element of a project prescribing the content to be taught, which in part refers to the National Curriculum, or is it to be used as a more general term which embraces the wider view of the whole curriculum?

Barrow and Woods (1998) argue that we should concern ourselves with the content that the term refers to and not its definition (1998: 46). If we take this view, we should focus on the *learning outcomes* which have been identified by the class teacher. The relevant planning will naturally be related to the National Curriculum Programmes of Study, but the project should not be controlled by them. A teacher should identify where the use of a communications-based curriculum project is appropriate in relation to the objectives being delivered within the classroom.

It could well be argued that if a project embraces a wider view of the curriculum, it will lose its focus and that outcomes for the pupils will be very generalised. Whilst on the other hand, a project which is so tightly focused that it takes no account of the possibility of any additional learning taking place will result in a narrow project with a limited range of outcomes.

Activity 10.1 Learning objectives

In the outline of the project in the case study below, there are a number of possible learning objectives. Try to identify these and link them to the curriculum documents which you currently use. Is it necessary to go beyond the current stipulated curriculum in order to set objectives in an international project?

Case study: please join our global schools project

This is adapted from a message posted to a website by a teacher looking for partners (see for example, projects in the European School Net[1] sites)

Project: Global Schools

Date: September to October
Purpose: To compare primary schools across the world.
Subjects: Reading, Writing, Geography, Maths
Age range: Year 1 to 5 (age 5 to 10 years old)

Summary:
Class 4 of Beacham Primary School in the UK will collect data from schools in different countries regarding their unique educational

continued

systems. This data will then be collated and published and sent to other participating schools.

Number of participants:
A total of ten primary schools from various parts of the world.

Activities:
First of all a questionnaire will be sent out to participants.
The questions are about your schools and communities; for example:

> How many children and teachers are in your school?
> How many pupils in your class?
> When do you start school and when does it finish for the day?
> What subjects are taught and which are your favourites?
> What festivals do you celebrate at school?

We hope you will also ask some further questions and tell others about any special things in which your school is involved.

The answers to these questions will be organised into a table and sent to all participants so that everyone can draw their own conclusions about similarities and differences.

The project is expected to last six to eight weeks and an evaluation will be sent out to all at the end of the work.

We therefore have to reach some form of balance where a project does not only state the subject to be taught, but also focuses on the learning objective that a pupil will cover, whilst at the same time acknowledging that there is the strong possibility that a number of additional outcomes will be identified.

What exactly does the content of the curriculum consist of? The orders for Information Technology (DfE, 1995), referring to children from 8 to 11 years-old, stated that:

> Pupils should be taught to . . . use IT equipment and software to communicate ideas and information in a variety of forms . . . showing sensitivity to the needs of their audience.

> (DfE, 1995: 69)[2]

Therefore we could argue that teachers should provide pupils with the opportunities to use ICT as a tool for developing other areas of the curriculum. The Teacher Training Agency's consultation document *The*

Use of Information and Communication Technology in Subject Teaching (TTA, 1998) states that teacher trainees should be taught how to use the most suitable ICT to meet teaching objectives (1998: 8).[3]

It should be noted that a communications-based project may not always be the most suitable ICT method for delivering a planned objective. However, if such a project is identified as being the most appropriate tool, then the tool should be used as the medium through which specific content is delivered to enable effective teaching and learning to take place.

In addition to this the TTA rightly point out that:

> ICT is more than just another teaching tool. Its potential for improving the quality and standards of pupils' education is significant.
>
> (1998: 2)

Clearly, the opportunities that new technologies offer should be investigated by teachers.

Will the use of a particular aspect of ICT enhance the pupils' learning beyond the existing confines of the classroom? When studying aspects of another country, teachers and pupils are able to extend the boundaries of the classroom and bring the topic to life and give it an element of real-time. The ability of a class to access up-to-date information and use this in their work provides valuable opportunities for teachers to improve the quality and the standard of education for the pupils.

As we have already suggested, the communication aspect of ICT, and in particular the interaction of pupils from different countries, provides additional opportunities which, when managed effectively, can have a direct effect on the quality and standard of education provided.

When discussing learning within the school environment, Morrison and Ridley suggest that it is dependent on the interrelationships between the teacher, the child, the context and the task (1998: 58). In addition to this we should note that this is also dependent on the relationships between the partners of the project. This in turn relates to the teacher activity, pupil activity, learning outcomes and emphasises the point that objectives need to be shared, focused and realistic.

The level at which interaction between pupils, staff and partners takes place will have a direct effect on the quality of learning taking place. Without careful planning and effective communication, an ICT curriculum project will not enhance the overall quality and standard of education provided within the school.

Equipment needed for projects

It is widely accepted that the internet enables staff and pupils to access an enormous amount of information. However, this raises a number of issues including quality assurance, access to undesirable materials and information overload. The proportion of information specifically aimed at pupils in the primary sector is low, as the majority of internet pages are written for an adult audience. There are, however, a growing number of internet sites which provide excellent resources for use by both staff and pupils. One hopes that the National Grid for Learning[4] and the Virtual Teacher Centre[5] will provide good routes towards finding and using these sites, especially for a UK audience of pupils, whose needs may be different from those of an American audience. These sites commonly provide up-to-date information or tackle specific subjects where there are few book-based materials available. However, resources need to be carefully selected and pupils effectively directed to ensure that effective teaching and learning takes place.

Activity 10.2 Resources and ICT

What sort of equipment, besides a computer and printer, will you need in order to teach effectively with ICT? Is the full range of equipment available to you in school, or is it necessary to borrow some from elsewhere? Chapter 8 provides a list of equipment you are likely to find.

What sorts of books will you use to supplement the use of ICT in your classroom? Will these be information books; for example in science, if you were studying the Earth and the Planets?

How will you use the various ICT tools to help you carry out a curriculum project? Would you be able to integrate the use of a digital camera, especially if you were designing a web page to go with an international project?

Your view of ICT which supports projects should not be restricted to the use of a computer and a modem with access to the internet. Fax machines have enabled schools to communicate on a global scale for a number of years, however, the use of electronic mail has provided a number of advantages. These could perhaps be grouped into three main areas.

First, the use of email is arguably more economic. Documents can be prepared off-line and a large number of emails sent together in one large bundle when a user logs on to the internet. The amount of time required to send a number of individual messages is far less than having to dial several numbers and feed separate sheets of paper through the fax. Therefore the amount of paper and call-time used is reduced to a great extent.

Second, the quality of the transmission is higher than that achieved by most fax machines. Text documents can be attached to the main message and then opened into the appropriate software package for immediate use, retaining the original format. This also applies to images which can be sent in colour, without losing any of the original quality.

Third, and perhaps most importantly, email gives the user the opportunity to develop an identity on the internet where pupils can communicate and build relationships with their peers. This identity may simply be that they are a member of an establishment, where the email address reads pupil@school-name, or it could take the form of an individual, unique email address. At present (1998) few schools are able to offer this facility. However, the government's intention is that every pupil (over the age of nine years) and teacher in the UK will be given their own email address. This will enable pupils and staff, with access to the internet, to communicate on an individual basis throughout the world.

Planning projects

It has been suggested that it is the communication aspect of the internet that can be best exploited at the primary level. One such method is through developing a curriculum project using ICT as a tool to enhance the learning taking place within the classroom. There are a number of different views as to the nature of such projects and their relationship to the curriculum, however, ICT should always be seen as the means by which learning is developed and not controlled. It is crucial that the teacher has clear objectives and is able to communicate these effectively with the partners in the project. More importantly, these objectives should be shared to ensure that the project achieves its aim and that it is directed by all involved towards the same goal.

The process of sharing aims can be made easier if all partners are prepared to make compromises in the outcomes of the work, so that different aims could be achieved by different partners. In most cases, pupils in European schools would have English language development as one of their aims, although for English-speaking pupils this will not always be the case. These pupils may be aiming to enhance their science or technology skills, or research geographical facts and concepts. The following case study shows how a teacher in the UK and a teacher in Australia, worked together on curriculum projects.

Case study: the OZ/UK treasure hunt

A joint project with Jo Emptage, Australia.

The William Alvey School, Sleaford, and South Hackham Primary School, Adelaide, established a communications link in November 1996 and worked together on a number of projects during the British Council's New Images '97 initiative.[6] After successfully completing the 'Monsters' project, they wished to continue with another ICT project which would integrate the use of communications technology with research skills.

The teachers at both schools had developed an excellent working relationship over a fairly short period of time and the physical distance between them was rarely an issue. Time zones were worked out, school holiday dates shared and professional experiences discussed. A private, virtual staffroom was created between the two key members of staff. A short email would often turn into a detailed message of epic proportions, discussing a wide range of professional and social topics!

From the UK perspective, the objective for this particular curriculum project was to develop the pupils' geographical skills where the pupils were to be given the opportunities to:

- Observe and ask questions about geographical features . . .
- Collect and record evidence to answer the questions;
- Analyse the evidence, draw conclusions and communicate findings.

(DfEE, 1995: 88)

The pupils had worked on a number of curriculum projects and had been developing a range of geographical skills in class. A project which would combine these skills and develop them further would benefit the pupils to a great extent.

The Australian group had recently been involved in another internet project through the 'Global Schoolhouse'.[7] The Trans Asia Expedition followed the adventures of five explorers who retraced Marco Polo's route from Venice, Italy through Europe, Russia, the Balkans, China and down to Hong Kong. All the children had been given the opportunity for hands-on use of the internet and had become competent in using that technology.

The 'Where in Oz/UK' project was designed to reinforce a range of skills, to encourage and provide a meaningful purpose for research and to extend the pupils' knowledge of another country.

It could have been argued that the objective, and related statements, could have been covered by other means, however, there was a strong case presented for developing such a project. It was proposed that an activity which involved the pupils examining the geography of their own country would achieve the objective, develop a high level of motivation and provide opportunities for additional learning outcomes to be supported and encouraged. Most importantly, the use of communications technology was seen to be able to improve the quality and standard of the pupils' education by providing a context within which the objective could be met.

The project, therefore, had a focused objective which was directly related to the teachers' planning, allowed for a certain degree of flexibility as regards learning outcomes and used ICT as a tool through which learning would take place.

Working arrangements were established and the following issues were addressed:

- What were the pupils going to learn?
- What were the pupils going to do?
- What were the staff going to do?
- How was the project going to be assessed?

The pupils were to be taught the necessary geographical and ICT related skills which they would need before communications between the schools began. The project provided the context through which the objective was to be met, however, it was crucial that the skills that the pupils would need were identified and taught. The pupils' participation in the link provided opportunities for these skills to be reinforced and developed.

The pupils at each school were expected to use their geographical skills to produce a number of clues which related to a major town in their country. This would then be emailed to the partner school where the pupils would use the appropriate skills to find the location. They were then expected to email their answer back and wait for the reply.

To begin the task, explicit teaching, modelling and discussion occurred. Destinations were selected by the pupils; groupings of pupils were negotiated; critical discussion and decision making occurred in regard to the categories for the clues; for example, a natural feature, a tourist attraction, a historical event, a geographical feature such as a mountain, river, etc. Explicit teaching and modelling of appropriate language was necessary. Then the groups of pupils worked together to write their emails where the final and deciding clue was to be the latitude and longitude of the destination.

The pupils in Australia made use of their school's Resource Centre to research their clues and finally they wrote their clues using the computer in their classroom and saving the information on disk. The pupils then logged onto the internet using the connection in the Resource Centre and sent their email message to their partner school.

In the UK, the pupils discussed the clues in class and then took the information home to research. Some pupils made effective use of the local library, whilst others asked their family for assistance or used other information sources including the internet and CD-ROMs. Time was allocated within school for further research to be completed and emails sent.

On receipt of a set of clues from their partner school, the next task for our intrepid researchers was to research the information provided in the clues and to deduce the correct destination. Sometimes this research was quite difficult and the commonly available sources such as non-fiction books or encyclopaedias could not provide the answers. Often several differing conclusions were reached and so, using the enormous resources of the internet was the only avenue of detecting the correct solution. The final conclusion was emailed back to our partner school for verification. Due to the immediacy of email, questions and answers were rapidly exchanged so that there were no long aggravating delays.

The staff were expected to manage and co-ordinate the project as partners. This required a large amount of communication by email where project details were discussed. This included the project's objective which, whilst referencing the National Curriculum for England and Wales, also needed to be of benefit to the pupils working in Australia. They were to have developed the appropriate ICT skills and provide time in class to allow the pupils to complete their tasks. In all, staff were expected to provide relevant support at all stages of the project and communicate effectively with the partner.

The major area of assessment was focused on the original learning objective and related success criteria.

- Had the pupils been able to develop the relevant geographical skills and apply them to their work?
- Were the pupils able to observe, question, collect and analyse information and communicate their findings?

The pupils had demonstrated that they were on the whole able to achieve both statements. Actual levels of attainment in both areas varied, however, the pupils had been well motivated and applied their skills well to the set task.

Extension activities may have included: mapping the destinations; keeping a log book of the distances travelled from one destination to another; completing the mathematical computations of changing miles to kilometres; presenting the work on a web page, using photographs taken with a digital camera and written descriptions of students' reactions to being involved in the project.

There could have been many more activities included but a realistic approach meant limiting the activities to those which were practical, achievable, within budget and time constraints and, most importantly, would achieve the goals set at the beginning of the project. This emphasises the importance of planning and co-operation between the participants and setting limits and reasonable expectations as well as clear learning outcomes for students.

Activities

The following activities are aimed at promoting a number of issues associated with curriculum projects using communications technology. Identify one aspect of class planning which may provide opportunities for pupils and staff to become involved in an ICT-based curriculum project and complete Table 10.1.

These questions, and others, need careful consideration and possible outcomes planned.

Table 10.1 Planning an email/internet curriculum project

1 Identification and planning

Learning outcomes
- What are the pupils going to learn?
- How are pupils with learning difficulties going to be catered for?

Pupil activity
- What are the pupils going to do?

Staff activity
- What are the staff going to do?

Assessment arrangements
- How are you going to know what the pupils have learnt?
- What assessment criteria will be used?

2 Implementation

Key skills input required
- Are there any skills which need to be developed before the project begins? (Example, logging onto the internet, sending an email)
  - Staff?
  - Pupils?

Project management
- Who will manage the project?
- What will they have to do?

Timescale and budget
- How long will the project last and how often will the partners be expected to communicate?
- What costs are involved?
- On-line costs
- Additional costs (example, posting paintings by air mail)

3 Follow-up activities

Extension activities
- How could the project be extended?
- What effect will this have on the original objective?

Further development
- How can learning outcomes be built upon within the classroom?
- What further project may be possible in the future?

Establishing your criteria for successful completion of the project will also be useful for both the project you are undertaking and the planning of subsequent projects.

Pupil involvement

Perhaps the first step is to find suitable partners for the project. In the case study 'Please join our global school project', you can see how one school tried to find partners for a comparative study of primary schools. Similar requests are made daily, often by USA schools, through a variety of organisations, using their websites or mailing lists.[8] The project may involve the pupils using email to discuss with their partners a typical Christmas Day or they may be required to answer a number of searching questions about their own local community. Off-line tasks may be set where the children have to complete an activity which is then used and developed further by the teacher within the classroom; for example, painting a monster from a description emailed to the pupil from another country. Chapter 13 on networks offers advice with regard to partner finding.

Staff and other adult involvement

The project will probably involve both pupils and staff at both ends of the link and clear objectives for them should be set. Will any technical support be required? If a link with another school has been difficult to establish, a link with an industrial partner may provide the answer. Year 5 pupils were studying St Lucia as part of their work and the school found it very difficult to locate a suitable school-based partner to work with on the island. A hotel offered its support and over a period of time, the project was discussed and clear objectives set. The pupils developed a set of questions about St Lucia and emailed them to the manager of the hotel. He acted as a communication link and passed the pupils' work onto his daughter and her friends who provided the vital answers.

Activity 10.3 Finding the time for travel buddies

Look at the Panda project outlined below, on a common theme of travel buddies, which has already set up objectives and arrangements. How could a British teacher fit their involvement into an already overcrowded timetable? Would it be possible to participate in a project like this one on a partial basis, or would that prevent the achievement of the aims for others? Do schools in Britain have such resources as librarians, who might help organise the project? There may

continued

---

be adults other than teachers, such as classroom assistants, parent volunteers, who would be interested in supporting such projects. The organiser of the project would be doing more work than other participants, since they would be maintaining the website, while others send in information about the Panda bear's journeys and adventures.

Joining a travel buddies project

Below is an example of how to find a travel buddies project posting on a partner finding website (e.g., The European School Net).

PANDA PROJECT: Our Travelling School Mascot

We would like to have our School Mascot, a PANDA BEAR, travel around the world. While he is travelling, we would like to keep track of his route and learn a little about his host classrooms. We would like to start his travels in November '98 and track his travels through April '99. We will also be designing a web page, so all of his host 'families' can also keep track of him.

When he arrives, he will come with his scrapbook of his life here in Ohio, and a journal for you to write about his visit to your classroom. We will also include a videotape, and a Teacher's Guide, including a checklist of what to do during his visit. He will visit your classroom for ONE week, and then you'll send him on to his next family. You will be sending out many email messages to all participants while he is visiting, and you'll receive messages throughout the entire year, to hear about his/her travels.

YOUR COST will be: the cost of mailing the entire package – by PRIORITYMAIL – to the next school after you are finished. (This could be as much as $10+) Or AIRMAIL to an International address.

Managing a curriculum project

Managing a curriculum project is an important task. Teachers should ensure that the objectives are shared and should work together before, during and after the work has been completed by the pupils. This allows discussions concerning the planning, implementation and evaluation of a project to take place. Careful planning is therefore required to ensure that ICT is used effectively within the classroom. It is often the teachers and other adults who use email more frequently during the planning and assessment stages of international projects, rather than the pupils. Curriculum projects need clear objectives which are shared and are relevant to the pupils' learning.

What are these objectives and how should they relate to the school's long, medium and short term planning?

Objectives

Objectives for a communication technology-based curriculum project need to be carefully planned and agreed between the partners involved. As with any other activity planned for the classroom, objectives need to be focused, realistic and form part of a school's overall planning. When developing a project, the partner needs to be carefully chosen and a positive working relationship developed. Projects are most successful when the objectives have been developed by both partners and when staff have had the opportunities to communicate with each other to ensure that expectations are shared and understood.

There are perhaps four major elements which need to be considered: pupil learning outcomes, pupil activity, staff activity and assessment arrangements.

Pupil learning outcomes

The key question of course is what are the pupils going to learn? Any task, even if it is using some exciting new technology, is only worthwhile if a pupil's learning is going to be developed. Projects should relate to the long, medium and short term planning for the pupils and should not be developed for the sake of using the technology. Central to this theory is that ICT should be viewed as a tool through which a wide variety of knowledge, concepts, skills and attitudes can be developed.

Whilst the main focus of the task presents itself as a specific objective, there may be other learning outcomes which are not expected. Some of these can be anticipated and strategies put in place to ensure that additional outcomes are supported, however, this raises the question of how tightly the project should be focused. We discuss this issue in more depth later.

Pupil activity

The teacher needs to consider exactly what the pupils are going to do. The staff have to arrange for the appropriate equipment to be made available and to assess whether any additional skills will be required.

An analysis of the pupils' current skill level will give an indication of the types and complexity of projects in which they will be able to participate. The development of newer technologies and their application in the

Activity 10.4 Exploring your city: what are the learning objectives?

How would you define learning outcomes in a project which linked two schools in Britain and the USA? In this project, the pupils in two classes explore their own city and send reports and artefacts concerning their homeplace to their partners. Penpal links are made between some of the pupils, who send each other details about themselves and their interests, as well as stories they have written, pictures they have drawn, etc. Some of these exchanges go through the normal post, others through email and websites. Some of the teachers and pupils in the project manage to visit their partner's school and city. The project leads to further involvement of other teachers and classes in both schools. The work now expands to environmental studies of rivers and water quality, of litter and its collection and eventual resting place and of books being read by pupils in the two cities.

classroom demands continual updating of the skills of teachers and pupils. Many primary schools now possess digital cameras and colour scanners, which can be used to provide images for web pages or other multimedia presentations. But these devices do need some introductory training and familiarisation.

The level at which the pupils will be involved in communicating with the partner needs to be established. Will all the pupils be expected to communicate on-line or will the majority participate through the follow-up work in class where email is used to keep both parties informed of each other's progress? If one aspect of the project's objective is ICT-based, then arrangements will need to be made to ensure that all pupils have an equal opportunity to interact with the technology. Some consideration needs to be given to establishing groups of pupils in most communication projects, so that the time taken to prepare and send messages can be reduced. Not all children will expect to communicate directly with individuals, and groups' activities make fewer demands on computer time.

Another important consideration is who exactly are the pupils going to be communicating with? It may possibly be pupils of a similar age, an expert from industry or perhaps a manager of a retail shop in America, for example. Whoever it may be, the pupils need to be aware of the audience with whom they have contact and the partner needs to be made aware of the learning objective established for the project. It is important, though, for teachers to be wary of divulging personal information about pupils in public internet places, like websites. If pictures are published on the web, especially photographs of children, then teachers must not identify them personally to avoid unwanted contacts with unsuitable people. Personal contacts should be conducted through email, which is less likely to be intercepted or accessed than web page information.

Staff activity

What exactly is the teacher going to have to do and what skills, if any, need to be developed further by the member of staff? The teacher should be able to communicate with the partner through email and be able to support the pupils' use of the technology. As staff become increasingly familiar with the use of ICT the range and depth of curriculum projects will inevitably increase.

The project must also be managed and co-ordinated effectively. If the class teacher is going to manage the project then they will need to communicate with the partner school to ensure that the objectives of the project are shared and that it relates to the overall planning for the class. In some cases it may be that one member of staff co-ordinates several projects and provides both technical and skills-based support to the teachers involved. The development of the project towards establishing an agreed objective is, in the majority of cases, the responsibility of the individual class teacher with additional support if required. They will have the task of implementing the project within the classroom and therefore need to be its driving force.

Assessment arrangements

The issue of assessment needs to be considered from the very beginning of the project. What is the purpose of the assessment and what procedures are already in place? The assessment of a communications-based curriculum project should have two strands that evaluate the learning outcomes achieved by the pupils and the technological process involved. An assessment based on ICT could be used to identify some aspects of pupils' progress and to record these, possibly as a multi-choice questionnaire which could also be marked by a software program.

A formal evaluation at the end of the project should relate back to the original objective and indicate whether or not it has been met. This will give some indication as to the success of the project, however, additional learning outcomes should also be noted and analysed. Conclusions should be recorded and used to inform the planning of further class-based tasks and future ICT projects.

If a school has a set procedure in place for the evaluation of pupil's work, then this should be followed, as the work that the pupils have completed should not be viewed as separate from any other work that they produce in class. Aspects of the pupil's learning and the effectiveness of the technology involved will be informally evaluated throughout the project. These observations should be noted as they provide an important first-hand analysis of the project and a significant contribution to the overall assessment of its success. It might be worth commenting on children's attitudes to communication projects, since this is likely to affect other learning that takes place. In some international projects, there may be negative attitudes from one set of pupils about people or cultures in other countries. One of the learning objectives of an international project could be to confront such attitudes and to make progress in changing them, through the direct contacts which are possible. If children are encouraged to communicate their thoughts and ideas, as well as information about their lives, they may alter their stereotyped impressions about their partners. Some surveys reported in the media have suggested that many British children still have negative attitudes towards Germans, even so long after the Second World War.

When assessing the communications link, we need to consider how effective the partnership was and what changes would be made to the development of future working relationships. Did the staff and pupils already have, or were they able to develop, the appropriate skills required to achieve the objective of the project? How realistic were the objectives in the first case? Until schools have taken part in a few of these types of projects, they will not realise the many potential problems which occur, and consequently may have initial aims which are unlikely to be achieved until further experience has been gained. If a project consists of too many sophisticated technological processes, then a number of barriers are immediately raised for some staff and pupils, which have to be negotiated before the true objective of the project can be tackled.

Teachers should expect to make mistakes on their first attempts at interactive projects using email and the internet, but should also expect to learn from mistakes and gain new skills and insights. Subsequent projects with the same or new partners should then be more successful and might try out more complex technologies, such as video conferencing or web-based ideas.

A question often raised is whether any overall assessment of the project should be made jointly between the partners involved or left to the individual teacher. The reality is that in the majority of cases both will happen. A successful partnership will facilitate a degree of communication between the teachers for some time after the project has come to a conclusion, where the partners will be able to share their final assessment of the project and relate this to their future planning.

Summary

In this chapter, you have seen some of the ways in which international projects could be managed. The issues of pupil and staff involvement have been raised, along with pupil learning outcomes and assessment arrangements. It has been suggested that international partnerships can be organised and managed, if participants or partners are willing to make some compromises, as well as being clear about their aims and abilities. Some examples from projects have been presented so that you could think about how they might be useful in teaching in a British classroom. The curriculum itself was discussed at the beginning of the chapter and a question raised about content and delivery. Finally, we looked at assessing such projects, in terms of pupils' learning objectives, as well as evaluating the overall success and learning new skills which could be used in the future.

Notes

1   European School Net is on *http://www.eun.org*
2   DfEE (1995) Statutory Orders for IT in the National Curriculum. This is the National Curriculum document which deals with the subject of ICT, rather than the way ICT supports other curriculum areas.
3   DfEE (1998) Teaching: High Status, High Standards, Requirements for courses of Initial Teacher Training. These documents set out the standards which trainee teachers must achieve in ICT before they can become qualified.
4   National Grid for Learning: *http://www.ngfl.gov.uk*
5   The Virtual Teacher Centre: *http://www.vtc.ngfl.gov.uk*
6   The site for this project is on *http://www.bc.org.au/montage*
7   The Global Schoolhouse can be found on *http://www.gsn.org*
8   Mailing lists are useful ways of finding partners for your own projects, or for finding suitable projects organised by others in which you would like to take part. One group in the UK which runs mailing lists is Mailbase and you may be able to find partners there *http://www.mailbase.ac.uk*
    Another group in the USA dealing with a variety of projects for schools and colleges is IECC *http://www.iecc.com*

References and further reading

Barrow, R. and Woods, R. (1998) *An Introduction to the Philosophy of Education*, 3rd edn, London: Routledge.
DfEE (1995) *National Curriculum Orders for Information Technology*, London: DfE.
Morrison, K. and Ridley, K. (1998) *Curriculum Planning in the Primary School*, London: Paul Chapman.
TTA (1998) *Consultation Document: The Use of Information and Comunication Technology in Subject Teaching*, Londom: TTA.

Chapter 11

Talking to the World through Video, Sound and Text

Gordon James

Introduction

There is a significant difference, particularly for children, between communicating synchronously, in 'real time' as one does when making a telephone conversation, and asynchronously, as happens when you exchange letters with a friend. In the first case you need to think quickly and be able to respond instantly to changes of direction, in the later case you have time to consider your response and research any subject which you are unsure of. The vast majority of computer-aided communications which occur in schools have been of the asynchronous type, mainly through text-based email exchange. With the availability of much faster computers and lines of communication at an affordable price, schools are starting to explore the possibilities of synchronous collaboration.

This chapter will deal with a few examples of synchronous collaboration over computer networks based on our experience at Wickham Market CP School, a village school in East Suffolk serving a socially very mixed community with around 300 children on roll, from Nursery to Year 6. Since 1995 the school has enjoyed a fruitful partnership with BT Laboratories at Martlesham Heath, Suffolk. In order to investigate how a primary school would use 'cutting edge' ICT equipment, BTL established a test-bed of schools within the UK of which Wickham Market was one. BTL provided the school with a network of computers and video conferencing facilities. The work described in this chapter stems from this collaboration.

Objectives

By the end of this chapter you will have been introduced to ways in which one primary school sought to develop literacy through:

- online synchronous collaborative working between pupils in the UK and internationally, using audio and video conferencing;
- a pilot project networking a selection of families from the school community;

- involving parents, pupils and teachers in audio conferencing and email communications with 'experts'.

Working collaboratively online

For our first venture in collaborative working we shared a joint science and history topic on the theme of 'transport' with Cwmaber Junior School in South Wales. The general philosophy behind this project, and much of our subsequent work, came from Margaret Riel's experiences[1] in setting up 'Learning Circles' in American schools. She emphasises the importance of agreeing a clear time scale and a 'product' to be jointly authored by the collaborating classes. Although much of the planning for this project was carried out through asynchronous email exchanges and the research and investigative work carried out separately within the two schools, regular synchronous sessions lay at the heart of the project.

These sessions used a software package called 'Timbuktu',[2] which allows the full functionality of a computer to be shared across a network, either within the school, or at a distance across telephone lines. Children sitting in front of a computer in Suffolk and South Wales would jointly author and edit pages of our multimedia transport book situated on a hard disk in Wickham School. Each group had full control over mouse and keyboard functions. So long as graphics were kept to a reasonable size, the speed of working, particularly after we acquired digital ISDN lines, was quite acceptable. Audio links were maintained through standard 'hands-free' telephones. The number of classes which can collaborate in this way is only limited by the memory of your computer. At first we thought that arguments might arise over who should have control of the mouse or keyboard. In practice the opposite was often true, with both groups being unduly polite and reticent, with a computer version of 'no, after you – no, please, after you' conversation occurring.

An unexpected educational benefit from this form of synchronous collaboration was the way in which each school could share their area of computer expertise with the other, and this form of peer-tutoring became a very powerful tool. The extracts from the children's own evaluations (each child word processed a evaluation immediately after each session) provides a flavour of these sessions.

Introduction of video

The introduction of a video-conferencing computer into our collaborative work with Cwmaber made less of an impact than might be expected. The children enjoyed being able to see each other at last but this, in itself, did little to sustain useful communication, which was provided by the task which had to be achieved, such as joint writing or editing a poem or

> ## Pupils' evaluations of a typical peer-tutoring session
>
> 'I found it really fun talking to people who live in Wales. We taught Kate, Helen and Danielle how to fill in a block graph. – I thought it was really interesting talking to the three girls in Wales because I learned quite a lot of things and got to know them quite well.'
>
> 'The second group showed us how to make frames and add a title and writing to the picture. They used a different picture and they let us have a go. They also explained a lot better than the first group. It worked very well but sometimes the telephone line went fizzy – I really enjoyed talking to the children in Wales, it was great fun and really interesting and I would really like to do it again.'

comparing the shopping habits of their respective communities. At best the video image gave useful visual clues. In subsequent collaborative sessions we tended to open the video link in order to introduce ourselves and maintain a visual contact and used computer-sharing software to carry out the substantive task. However, using video conferencing with pupils abroad was particularly helpful in aiding communication. Once we had established close working relationships with schools in Europe, where English was their second language, the video-conferencing link, together with its audio channel, came into its own. During these sessions the main learning objective of the session was often the verbal communication itself and the ability to see who you are talking to seemed to help this communication process.

Through a weather project which we ran during 1997–98 we began to work closely with Tommola Primary School in Finland. This relationship developed to a stage when two teachers from the Finnish school spent a week in Suffolk and I was able to make a return visit a year later. Whilst at Wickham, the Finnish teachers kept in touch with their own school through the video link and during one session with the headteacher and a colleagues in Tommola School, the headteacher swung their camera around to point out of the window and show us their playground deep in clean white snow and in the distance the frozen lake, our pupils were both impressed and jealous!

Later in the year Tommola school suggested that we undertake a project focused on learning about each other's cultures. To do this, we arranged four daily video-conferencing sessions using the European Net Days initiative[3] as a focus. In preparation, groups of Year 6 pupils in Tommola worked with their English teacher in planning a set of questions for our pupils at Wickham. These questions concerned our daily life, starting with home and family and working outwards to questions about our country and its culture.

The extract below contains my own evaluation of these four short sessions and Figure 11.1 shows the video conference in action.

Using video conferencing to find out about other cultures

The first session seemed a little stiff with little development of two-way dialogue, however, the Finnish pupils' English came over very well and the consensus on both sides was that it had been fun. The second day was far more lively, with children at our end engaging in dialogue and turning the questions back to Tommola. Wednesday's session was better again, with a noticeable increase in animation of their side and a lot of laughter. The final session on Thursday proved more difficult for us, since it demanded a knowledge of our own country which we didn't necessarily have and which a little more research might have provided!

These sessions proved a great success and at the end of each we sent a written response to their questions. The English teacher at Tommola asked us for these written replies in order to support his 'follow up' lessons with some written communications. The full text of these replies can be found

Figure 11.1 Video conferencing between Tommola school in Finland and Wickham Market in the UK

on Tommola's web page.[4] The two schools have maintained regular video contact and supplemented with synchronous text-based conferences using a 'First Class'[5] v groupware, undertaking projects such as 'What are we looking forward to' in which 10 and 11 year-old pupils from both schools came together near the end of the school year to 'talk about' what they were looking forward to in the future.

HomeLearn – linking home and school through audio conferencing

When considering our children's progress in the use of computer technology, it would be foolish to ignore the influence of the technology that they have available in the home. Some significant Australian research[6] has shown how the percentage of households owning a computer rose dramatically in the households of school-aged children, where home computers were purchased 'with the idea that they will enhance the educational and employment prospects for both the children and adults in the family'.

In this section we deal with a project called 'HomeLearn' which BT and Apple Computers collaboratively sponsored in our school over two terms in 1998. Apple provided eight computer systems, including printers and digital cameras, which were placed into the homes of a selection of our Year 5 or 6 pupils. BTL installed the dedicated telephone lines for the duration of the project, provided access to the internet and maintained the project server. The three teachers responsible for the Year 5 and 6 classes were also provided with computers and telephone lines and it was these three teachers who, with the support of BTL's Education and Training Research Team, ran the project on a daily basis.

The purpose of the project was to investigate how ICT equipment in the home can help to bring the home and school closer together, building a stronger learning community. We were seeking to achieve this objective on several fronts, through:

- Developing special projects for the group, which involved the pupils and families in using the equipment at home, conferencing together and communicating the results of their work with the school. These projects always related directly to work which was going on at school.
- Keeping an interactive homework diary on the server which could be checked by the pupils, parents and teachers.
- Providing a variety of communication channels on the server for different members of the group; for example, a 'Kids-Chat' area, a 'Parents' Area', a 'School Discussion' area, etc.
- Placing on the server all the long-term and medium-term curriculum plans for the current school term and providing links from the server to the school's own web pages.

Layers of literacy built into the project

From the point of view of the school the main educational purpose of the project was to see how this type of approach could help to develop a broad range of communication, research and general literacy skills. Table 11.1 lists the forms of communication which were planned into the HomeLearn project:

Table 11.1 Forms of communication developed through the HomeLearn project

Communicating groups	Type of communication	Means of communication
Communication between pupil trialists.	Written communication in an informal mode.	Email within 'Kid Club' conference area.
	Oral communications in an informal mode.	Telephone communications between pairs or larger groups of pupils using the audio-conferencing facilities.
Communication between pupil trialists, school (and outside agencies).	Written communications in a formal mode.	Emails between pupils and school (both ways) concerning homework, special projects or other project business.
		Written responses (with or without graphics, either as word processed files or web pages) to homework or project assignments. This type of response is usually based on some form of set 'research task'.
	Oral communications in a formal mode.	Telephone communications between pupil and teacher, usually used to clarify some aspect of project business.
		Audio conference between group of pupils and teachers and often an invited visitor from outside the school community.
Communication between parents within the trial.	Written communication in an informal mode.	Email within 'Parents Conference Area'.
	Oral communications in an informal mode.	Telephone communications between pairs or larger groups of parents using the audio-conferencing facilities.
Communications between school and parents.	Written communications in informal mode.	Email messages, usually messages alerting parents to forthcoming events and messages concerning clarification of project business.

Table 11.1 (continued)

Communicating groups	Type of communication	Means of communication
	Oral communication in informal mode.	Telephone communication between parent and teacher concerning some point of project business.
	Oral communication in informal mode.	Audio conference between group of parents and teachers in a formal conference to discuss project developments.

Establishing the HomeLearn community

Parents of all the Year 5 and 6 pupils were invited to join the project and a sample of eight was chosen. Despite the provision of a computer and unlimited internet access for a limited period, only fifteen homes showed an interest. Possibly the majority were put off by the commitments required by the project. From this short list we tried to achieve both a social and a gender balance, whilst ensuring that the homes selected would be supportive of the project and its aims.

The hardware and software platform

The computers arrived in the homes preloaded with Claris Works (for general work), Claris Homepage (for web page authoring), photo-editing software for handling the images from the digital camera and Netscape Communicator (for internet access). In addition to this software each home also received a colour printer, modem and digital camera.

BTL's Education and Training Research Team had developed an experimental conferencing tool, Real-Time Interactive Social Environment (RISE),[7] which had been trialled in Higher Education and was now tailored to the requirements of the HomeLearn project. When users log into RISE they are presented with a homepage which provides project news and access to a number of conferencing folders from which and to which they can send and receive emails and attached files. Access to individual folders depends upon the user's status; for example, teacher, pupil, parent, etc. The system allows audio conferencing where up to thirty users can come together in a 'conferencing room' and talk to each other over an ordinary phone line. Several separate conferences can be going on at the same time and the position of different people within these 'conference rooms' can be tracked graphically. The audio conferencing facility allows any member of the conference to record the conversation and store their recording either in their own folder or within a 'public' folder, thus making it available to the whole community.

During the first term the hardware and lines were installed, the school placed their curriculum plans onto the server and we held a meeting at school to brief the families as to the purpose of the project and provide initial technical training. Then we got down to business.

The first conference: *The Herring Girls*

This conference focused on the development of oral literacy through audio conferencing. During the trial we held two main 'conferences' and for each of these conferences we invited an outside 'expert' to respond to questions set by the pupils, and in each case the subject of the conference tied in closely with work going on in the classroom. Each conference took place in the evening in order to involve the parents.

During literacy lessons the Year 5 and 6 classes had been studying a book called *The Herring Girls* by Theresa Tomlinson, set at the end of the nine-teenth century amongst the fishing community of Whitby, and for our first conference Theresa was invited to answer questions about herself, the writing process and her book. The conference was 'moderated' by one of the class teachers. Prior to the conference the pupils had prepared some questions which were submitted by email to the conference moderator who sent a selection to Theresa.

The conference took place with a member of the BTL research team ensuring that the process ran smoothly, this was still early days and not everybody was very familiar with the technology. The moderator intro-duced the members of the conference to Theresa and invited each pupil to ask their question. In all the whole process lasted just under one hour.

Everyone who either 'attended' or listened to the recording of this confer-ence has been impressed by the level of discipline shown in both asking the questions and listening to the answers. However, there was compara-tively little evidence of children trying to take the discussion forward by developing points from the answer. Typically they asked their question, listened to the answer, said 'thank you' and then waited for the next ques-tion to be asked. One 11 year-old girl was the only pupil during this conference who regularly supported Theresa in her answer by 'encouraging interjections' and asking ancillary questions at an appropriate place, as shown in the short part of the transcript included below. In Chapter 3, the importance of developing pupils' talking skills is discussed in detail.

Part transcript showing pupils starting to respond to answers

GIRL PUPIL: Hello, um, this is my first question. How long does it take you to write one of your books?

TERESA: Well, I think that is a very good question and I think you might be a little bit shocked by what I am going to tell you.

GIRL PUPIL: Right.

TERESA: Because the first book I wrote took me six year –

GIRL PUPIL: Oh, my gosh, wow!

TERESA: I know that probably seems a bit dreadful, doesn't it?

GIRL PUPIL: Yes.

TERESA: (developing a long answer) – some of the bits of the story have been written seven or eight times.

GIRL PUPIL: Oh right. How long did it take you to write *The Herring Girls?*

TERESA: Right, well what happened was that as time went by I speeded up a lot –

GIRL PUPIL: Yes.

TERESA: – and so by the time I wrote *The Herring Girls* it took me about one year –

GIRL PUPIL: Oh that's good.

TERESA: – so that was a bit better –

GIRL PUPIL: Yes.

There was one further example (shown below) of a more developed oral style when a 10 year-old boy, having already asked his question, picked up at a later stage in the conference on some information Theresa had provided about her younger son whilst answering a question from a girl pupil.

Part transcript showing a more developed oral style

TERESA: – it is at the beginning of the book.

BOY PUPIL 1:   Yes –

TERESA: Good.

CHAIR: Lovely, I think –

BOY PUPIL 2:   Just a little bit out of interest. Could I just say good luck to your child on his GCSEs.

TERESA: Oh! Thank you very much, I think he needs it.

CHAIR: Very kind, I think you need a lot of help with your GCSEs.

BOY PUPIL 2:   You need all the luck you can get on them I suppose.

Following the conference, a homework activity was posted onto the server which asked the children to listen to the conference recording and extract the main points in the form of a bullet-point list which they then shared with the other pupils during a follow-up conference.

The second conference: the Met Office

The subject of the second conference developed from our ongoing 'international weather project'. We invited Andy Yeatman from the Met Office in Bracknell to join us to answer questions about the weather and weather forecasting. We retained the general form of the first conference, with children submitting questions which were moderated by a class teacher, who then chaired the conference. An extra element was added to this conference when two of our weather project schools, one in Oregon (USA) and one in Finland, each submitted questions for the conference by email.

Since Theresa's conference the group seemed to have developed a little more flexibility in the use of audio conferencing and to have gained in confidence, using ancillary questions and helpful interjections to keep the discussion flowing. The short transcript below shows how the process was becoming more interactive. Neither of the questions asked by Boy pupil 1 (aged 11) or Boy pupil 2 (aged 11) were submitted or scripted beforehand.

Part transcript showing two-way dialogue developing

CHAIR: OK –

BOY PUPIL 1:   I've got a question here.

CHAIR: Who's that –?

BOY PUPIL 1:   Yes. What is precipitation?

ANDY: Precipitation? Anything which falls from the sky really, it can encompass rain, snow, drizzle, hail –

BOY PUPIL 1:   Frogs?

ANDY: It could actually include frogs and there were some of those not so long ago falling out of the sky.

BOY PUPIL 1:   Cats and dogs.

ANDY: (laughs) Yes, cats and dogs as well.

CHAIR: So that was Boy pupil 1 –

BOY PUPIL 1:   (interrupting) What actually causes hail.

ANDY: Causes hail? Well – (Andy described the process of hail formation.)

BOY PUPIL 1:   Yes, OK, that was quite interesting actually.

ANDY: (laughs) Good.

CHAIR: There you are –

BOY PUPIL 2:   Hello, this is – Who actually started the Met?

ANDY: Who actually started the Met? It began in 1864 –

The conference continued in this mode for some time, with Andy Yeatman, and the two boys taking a leading role and the chair taking a back seat. It is interesting that following Pupil 1's light hearted interjections about frogs and cats and dogs, he returned to another serious question about hail, picking up on something Andy had said some time before in response to someone else's question. As before, homework activities were posted on the day after this conference which provided a transcript of part of the conference recording. The activity required the pupils to extract information concerning the El Niño effect from the transcript, carry out some research using an atlas and the internet, organise their findings on their computer and post the results of this research into the project area.

It is worthy of note that in neither conference, both of which lasted well over three-quarters of an hour, did any pupil leave the conference or show impatience with the process. We intended to set up some conferences where one of the pupils will take the role of the 'chair' and moderate the conference. This process would have demanded some very high-level communication and organisational skills but unfortunately the HomeLearn trial ended before we could arrange such an experiment. However, a lot was achieved during the two terms of the trial.

Development of written literacy through homework and project tasks

During the HomeLearn trial specific improvements in the pupils' written literacy skills have been more difficult to pinpoint than the developments in their speaking and listening skills. One girl triallist presented her class teacher with a seventeen-page word processed story of considerable quality following one homework assignment, but she always was an enthusiastic and skilful story-writer! The use of computers for this kind of written assignment might well repay closer analysis, however, word processed homework certainly is not restricted to the HomeLearn triallists. Over the past few years the use of the word processor in straightforward written homework tasks has been increasing, though now, of course, children can email it to their class teacher directly. The issue of schools adopting a policy with respect to pupil/parent/teacher email contact is further discussed in Chapter 14.

The following specific literacy skills have been used within this project (though again, the pupils are quite adept at many of these through involvement in collaborative projects within school time):

- Using the word processor to assemble and organising materials from diverse sources.
- Production of non-linear narratives, using presentation, web-authoring and multimedia authoring packages.
- The use of maps, charts and graphics to communicate meaning, with or without words.
- Giving consideration to your audience when using email as a communication tool.

The two examples of homework tasks below, developed from HomeLearn, illustrate how the development of these skills were built into the project. Both examples were messages posted by the class teacher in the pupils' project areas.

**Homework task set following the conference with
Theresa Tomlinson**

Following the very successful conference with Theresa Tomlinson here is an English Project for you to work on. Either working on your own, or conferencing with a partner:

< Listen to the recording of the conference which is stored in the 'recordings area'.
< Identify the main points from Theresa's answers and record them on a word processor under useful headings.

Send a copy of your notes to this 'projects' area.
Soon we will organise a conference where you will all be able to discuss your work and decide on a group response.

**Homework task set following the conference with
Andy Yeatman**

I have transcribed (written down) parts of the weather conference and placed the text onto our Weather Project Web Pages, with a link from the front page.
   Read the transcript and note down, on a word processor, all the facts or information about weather that you have learned from this text. Use bullet points and keep the items short and clear.

< Write a short review of the conference; good points and bad points.
< Use an atlas and see if you can follow the discussion about how El Nino works. Use the computer to produce a diagram explaining it in your own words.
< Find at least one Web page about El Nino (you will need to do a search) and send it in.

Send in the results of this work to this 'projects area' by Thursday 7th May please.

These tasks were demanding and we actively encouraged the triallists to work together using the conferencing facilities and to draw their family and friends into the process.

Some lessons learned from the HomeLearn project

- Audio/video conferences are like any other meeting and to be successful they need to be well planned, with an agreed agenda and moderator. Conferences which were left open ended and lacked a clear voice in the 'chair' tended to be less successful.
- Conferences with a clear purpose and an outside 'expert' proved to be more successful than 'internal' project conferences, though the later did serve a valuable and necessary purpose.
- The ability to 'ask an expert' questions which would be difficult or impossible to answer by other means proved a powerful incentive for using this kind of technology.
- Getting quality follow-up work from all the triallists proved more difficult. The conferences seemed to be viewed by some triallists as one-off events rather than as part of a larger educational programme.
- Involving the whole family was not always as easy as we had anticipated. We had to work hard to develop strategies which brought the whole family together to support their children within the various project activities.

After HomeLearn: developing a virtual community

Once the HomeLearn trial came to an end we were sufficiently convinced of its value to want to develop our own school website[8] as a vehicle for maintaining these close links between school and home. To this end we placed all our school policy documents, school brochure and newsletters onto the site, as well as our long-term curriculum plans together with a selection of medium- and short-term lesson plans. We have also developed curriculum areas where examples of pupils' current work were placed and they are actively encouraged to develop their own 'special interest' web pages. On each of these pages we invite parents, or any other visitor, to feedback comments and offers of help. The use of the web for these purposes is further discussed in Chapter 14.

This process is still in its early days and in common with any new educational initiative it demands even more time and effort from an already over-stretched teaching staff. However, it is beginning to prove itself through positive comments from children and parents who access the site from home and by promoting a very positive image of the school to the outside world. This was made clear when a prospective new parent rang up the school to request places for his children and was asked if he would like to be sent the school brochure and visit the school. He replied that this would not be necessary as he had accessed the school website and was sufficiently impressed by what we do already!

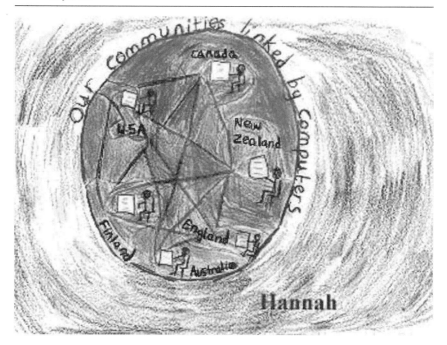

Figure 11.2 Navigation map for the communities project – developed by a Year 5 pupil

Alongside these developments we have been actively building a more dispersed 'local communities' web site through another internet-based project. Initially six schools from New Zealand, Australia, Finland, UK, USA and Canada gathered together to build a dispersed website around the idea of 'a local community'. Each school was invited to sponsor and develop one or more topics concerning 'local communities', using the other schools to draw out similarities and differences. This website, which is itself dispersed amongst the participating schools with ourselves maintaining the home page (see Figures 11.2 and 11.3), is starting to merge our interest in international links, with our commitment to developing closer links with our pupils' homes and our immediate community. All these aspects will draw upon our full range of communication skills: visual, audio and text.

Summary

In this chapter, you have been introduced to:

- How pupils can work collaboratively over computer networks.
- How pupils can use these collaborative sessions to learn from each other – 'Peer tutoring'.

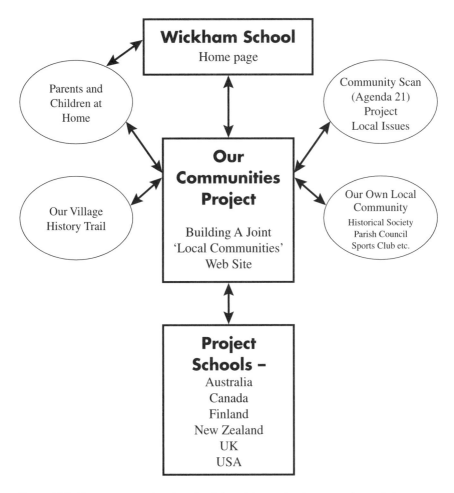

Figure 11.3 Concept map showing the links with our local community and the project schools abroad

- How video conferencing might be used to enhance language work.
- How one school brought teachers, pupils, parents and experts together using audio conferencing facilities.
- How project-based homework tasks can be managed across a computer network.
- How a group of geographically dispersed schools can work together to develop and build a website around a theme.

Activity 11.1 Some questions for consideration and suggestions for action research

If you have not already done so, find out:

- How many of your pupils have access to computer technologies at home and how do they use them?
- How many have access to the internet or email facilities, do they use these and if so how?

and consider

- Does access to these technologies at home isolate the child or encourage communication within the family?
- With the influx of new computers and cheaper networking options into both schools and homes schools can you see a use within your school for including your pupils' homes within your school network? Technically this does not need to be too difficult or expensive to achieve.
- Do you have any evidence from your own experience of any aspect of your pupils' literacy skills improving through the use of IT?
- If your school has a website, what is its purpose and what is its perceived audience? Do you think this might need reconsidering?

Notes

1   Margaret Riel's Virtual Office provides a page from which you can access all Margaret's papers available online: *http://www.gse.uci.edu/vkiosk/faculty/riel/*
2   Information about Netopia's 'Timbuktu' Software can be accessed on: *http://www.netopia.com/software/tb2/*
3   European Net Days 1999 homepage can be accessed on: *http://www.netdays.org*
4   Tommola School maintains an excellent bilingual website, information about our video conferencing sessions can be accessed on: *http://www.sci.fi/~tommola/heiwick/heiwick.htm*
5   Information about SoftArc's First Class Service can be accessed on: *http://www.softarc.com/homepage.shtml*
6   The online paper 'Young children talking about computers in their home' by Toni Downes and Cathy Reddacliff, University of Western Sydney, Macarthur. can be found on: *www.notebooksystems.com/linksite/DownesStg3rep.html*. They quote: Australian Bureau of Statistics (1995) *Household Use of Information Technologies*, Canberra: Australian Bureau of Statistics.
7   Information about RISE can be accessed on: *http://www.acm.org/sigchi/chi97/proceedings/short-demo/ps.htm*
8   Wickham Market School's website, can be accessed on: *http://community.labs.bt.com/public/WickhamMarketPublic/Wickham_School_Homepage.html*
    The community project can be found by following 'International projects' link from the home page.

Chapter 12

Undertaking an ICT Self-Audit

Lynn Dawes and Marilyn Leask

(Reprinted with permission from Leask and Pachler, 1999)

Introduction

As a teacher you can expect to go on learning the whole of your professional life. This means that you have to be able to analyse your strengths
and weaknesses and identify ways in which you can address these weaknesses. In this chapter we provide a self-analysis grid for you to use in
analysing your needs for professional development in the area of ICT. The
grid is based on, but in some areas goes beyond, the *National Curriculum
for the Use of Information and Communications Technology in Subject Teaching*,
that is, the curriculum for student teachers in England (TTA 1998) which
is included as Appendix 1 and can be downloaded from the DfEE website
or the TTA website.[1] This is a statutory document setting out what teachers
and student teachers are expected to be able to do but we recognise that
it provides just a starting point. The standards of effective ICT deployment
achieved in the leading schools today (some of which are have contributed
to this text), will become the standards of acceptable practice in schools
tomorrow. As the level of ICT skill and knowledge in the profession rises,
so too will the expectations of what teachers should achieve by the effective deployment of ICT in their work. This curriculum will no doubt be
revised in due course to reflect ever more demanding cognitive and pedagogic skills.

Through the use of ICT, increasingly you will be able to find information about resources related to teachers' professional development across all
subject areas. For example, professional organisations and research laboratories publish recent findings and university and LEA websites provide
information about courses, which are available including online and distance
courses as well as those conducted face to face. In Chapter 1, the role of
online professional communities in ongoing professional development is
discussed.

At the time of writing, searching techniques for finding personally relevant material on the internet are limited. Development to date has generally
required users, when they revisit sites, to read the same pages again in case

there is anything new to them – a process not dissimilar to having to read an encyclopaedia or dictionary over and over in case there are any new pages inserted. 'What's New' options on websites only partly answer this problem of finding out what is new and relevant to you as an individual. The editor of the 'What's new' part of a website has no way of knowing if all users have found the new information relevant to them, before it is removed as a 'What's new' item. This process must become more sophisticated if internet users are not to waste a lot of their time. We consider that internet personalisation software will provide this required sophistication and TeacherNetUK[2] are piloting experimental software based a personal professional online profiling system. This software should enable you to profile your needs through a web-based system which provides an ongoing and easily updated record of your interests and needs. The intention is that when you log on, the software provides updated information about resources (including but beyond websites) where your particular interests and needs may be met.

For the moment however, a national priority is to train teachers in the effective use of ICT. Therefore, in this chapter, following the self-audit which provides you with the opportunity to identify your strengths and weaknesses in the general area of ICT, we discuss options for further training. Other chapters in this book provide you with the opportunity to consider ICT applications in particular subject areas. You may also find that the chapters on ICT in the secondary subject books accompanying this series will give you further subject specific guidance.[3] The British Educational Communications Technology Agency (BECTA), which was previously known as the National Council for Educational Technology (NCET), also produces subject specific guidance.[4]

Objectives

By the end of this chapter you should have:

- developed your understanding of requirements for ICT skills and knowledge placed on teachers in England;
- defined your own areas of competence in ICT;
- clarified areas in which you require further study, tuition or practice;
- been presented with some of the options for training which are available.

Areas for audit

Much of this text is focused on subject-specific applications of ICT illustrating the pedagogic implications of using ICT in certain settings and providing examples based on what schools are doing now. Pedagogic knowledge about ICT applications to your area of work is a vital element in your professional repertoire. But there are a number of factors which can have an impact on your capability in using ICT in the classroom and we suggest you undertake an audit in each of these separately:

1   To what extent can you operate various types of equipment?
2   What knowledge do you have about the ways in which ICT can enhance and support pupil learning and your teaching?
3   In what ways is your working environment supportive or not supportive of your development in the area of ICT use?
4   What training programmes are likely to provide for your needs?

The next section addresses the familiarity and use of equipment generally and the following section provides grids for self-analysis against the Initial Teacher Training National Curriculum for ICT (ITT NC for ICT).

Your skills using the equipment

The ITT NC for ICT for student teachers identifies knowledge and skills in the use of the following equipment as essential: 'computers, the internet, CD-ROM and other software, television and radio, video and cameras and other equipment'. In the 'other' category, we would include scanners, electronic whiteboards and specify the ability to produce multimedia presentations (Chapter 9) which incorporate video, sound and still pictures. Depending on your responsibilities, you may need to be able to use specific forms of software (e.g., voice operated), other forms of computer-driven equipment and CD-ROM writers. If you have responsibilities for special educational needs, then Chapter 7 in Leask and Pachler (1999) provides additional detail on SEN. As digital TV becomes available, the distinctions between what computers, TV and video offer will become more blurred.

In this book we are focusing on the first three of the items listed, namely computers, the internet, CD-ROM and other software. Since television and radio can be viewed and heard through the computer via the internet, it is hard to draw clear boundaries. You should aim to be able to use all equipment including software which can support you in your work.

Throughout this chapter you may wish consider what training is the highest priority for you and, if appropriate, discuss with those responsible how you might access this training. In the rest of this chapter, we discuss elements of the ITT curriculum and we provide grids for self-assessment. Although this curriculum was developed for student teachers, it is also being applied to the training of teachers. Again, we suggest you assess yourself against these items and plan your professional development on the basis of your self-assessment. To start with, we provide some background about this drive to develop teacher competence in ICT.

Activity 12.1 Can you operate the equipment, the hardware and software?

Table 12.1 lists equipment which may help you to do your work more effectively, depending on your responsibilities. Various chapters in this book provide ideas about the application of the different types of equipment to the teaching and learning process and your professional development. Undertake an assessment of your strengths and weaknessess. Fill in the table below by assigning yourself to one of the three categories for each statement. The categories 'Adept', 'Working knowledge' and 'Beginner' are drawn from an apprenticeship model of learning. They imply that people within each category are dependent on one another for the survival of the ICT community of practice.

More detailed self-assessment tables follow later in the chapter.

Table 12.1 Can you operate the equipment, hardware and software?

Item	Adept	Working knowledge	Beginner
1 Computers (word processing, databases, spreadsheets, presentation software, e.g., PowerPoint)			
2 The internet (e.g., downloading pages and individual pictures for use in worksheets/multimedia presentations)			
3 CD-ROM and other software			
4 Television (to include digital television provision when available, Teletext)			
5 Radio (to include accessing radio through the web if appropriate for your pupils)			
6 Video (e.g., can you use a video recorder, can you use video in multimedia presentations (as described in Chapter 9)			
7 Cameras (to include video and digital cameras and the insertion of photos and video clips into multimedia presentations (see Chapter 9)			
8 Scanners (scanning text and pictures and using the files created in multimedia presentations/web pages (see Chapter 9)			
9 Other equipment relevant to your subject area and available in your school, e.g., video conferencing (see Chapter 11), CD-ROM writers or electronic whiteboards			

Background to the ITT NC for ICT for student teachers

When the Labour government was elected in the UK in May 1997, they brought with them a commitment to ensure that ICT was used effectively in education and in the community at large (Stevenson Report 1997, Consultation Paper on the National Grid for Learning, October 1997). This drive had a fairly immediate effect on various associated government agencies. In 1998 the Teacher Training Agency (TTA) specified a curriculum which was to be followed by trainee teachers, as they called student teachers, from September 1998.

Primary student teachers were required to have ICT training in maths, science and English (the core subjects), as well as their specialist subject. Secondary student teachers were to have training in their specialist subject. Lottery-funded training was to be introduced to enable serving teachers to train to a similar level of expertise and to develop an 'action plan' in order to continue their professional development in ICT once their initial training was complete.

This curriculum and the training of serving teachers was to be supported by a self-analysis pack provided by the TTA for every teacher. If you have access to this pack[5] you may find that it is particularly helpful to you in undertaking an in-depth self-audit of your ICT skills and knowledge.

The aim of the curriculum is stated as:

> to equip every newly qualified teacher with the knowledge, skills and understanding to make sound decisions about when, when not, and how to use ICT effectively in teaching particular subjects.
>
> (TTA 1998: 1)

Self-assessment of your ICT skills and knowledge

The tables which follow are for you to use in identifying your personal professional development action plan. The curriculum is summarised below in the self-assessment tables and is in two sections:

- Section A deals with teaching and assessment methods for the use of ICT in subject teaching;
- Section B deals with personal knowledge and understanding of ICT.

We have kept to the general structure of this curriculum in what follows. The statements in the tables are taken from the DfEE document but re-ordered and extended – we have regrouped some categories and extended others. In doing this, we have included the skills you would need to undertake the example projects in this book.

Section A: ICT teaching and assessment methods

The tables which follow are set out in a format which can provide you with an indication of your ICT status in relationship to this curriculum. The purpose of such an audit is for you to identify individual strengths and weaknesses, so that your needs can be addressed, and strengths can be consolidated. We then suggest that you identify sources of expertise perhaps within your own school or local area which can support your professional development.

Activity 12.2 Self-assessment

Read the statements in Tables 12.2–12.19 below and assign yourself to one of the three categories for each statement. Later you will be asked to prioritise your development needs. The purpose of this activity is to help you plan for your own personal development. In activity 12.4, which follows these tables, you are asked to devise your own personal action plan.

Table 12.2 Making decisions: when is ICT use beneficial, or when is it inappropriate? (TTA 1998: para. 1)

Do you understand the implications for teaching and learning of the following capacities of ICT?	*Adept*	*Working knowledge*	*Beginner*
Speed and automatic functions			
Capacity and range			
Provisional nature of information storage			
Interactive information storage			
Exploring models and simulations			
Communicating with people locally or at a distance			
Searching for and comparing information from different sources			
Presenting information appropriately			

As a profession we have a lot of knowledge, based on research evidence over the last couple of decades, about the effective use of computers in the classroom but this knowledge is not widely disseminated. Such dissemination of new professional knowledge may be enhanced by the forms of communication available through the internet. Online communities may provide one route for this dissemination, not just between teachers in the UK but also between teachers in all countries. The forms of professional communities discussed in Chapter 11 show how this professional sharing of ideas might evolve. The experimental work carried out through the Schools On Line project at Ultralab, Anglia Polytechnic University, provides other examples. What has been found so far is that for any online professional community to work, those involved must have a driving need to communicate.

Some of the websites listed at the end of each of the chapters may provide you with particular ideas in the areas above. These can be accessed through the website for this text on *http://www.dmu.ac.uk/Faculties/HSS/SEDU/ primaryict.html.*

Activity 12.3 Identifying sources of support

Having analysed your strengths in table 12.2, you should now identify the sources of support available to you. Student teachers and teachers on higher degrees at universities will automatically have access to various courses and support services. Teachers in LEA schools may have central support provided. Primary schools often cluster together to employ a technican. These staff form an obvious source of support for other staff wishing to develop their expertise. However, this public sharing of weaknesses does assume a supportive rather than competitive culture between school staff.

Repeat this activity for all the tables which follow. If you need clarification on any of the points, we suggest you read the fuller description on the TTA website.

Table 12.3 Implications of ICT functions for curriculum areas (TTA 1998: para. 2)

Do you demonstrate the following in your classroom practice?	Adept	Working knowledge	Beginner
Use ICT effectively			
Avoid unnecessary ICT use			
Prepare ICT equipment, content and methodology			
Value content over presentation			
Refine searches			
Have high expectations			
Expect pupils to evaluate and improve work			
Link ICT use and subject matter			
Link ICT use to everyday applications			

Table 12.4 Planning for ICT (TTA 1998: para. 3)

Can you do the following?	Adept	Working knowledge	Beginner
Relate ICT use to teaching and learning objectives			
Direct pupils' learning when using ICT			
Assess and record pupils' progress in ICT supported work			
Distinguish ICT and subject progress			
Ensure ICT work is at pupils' level			

Chapters 8, 9 and 10 which include issues of planning and assessment may be of help to you on these issues.

Table 12.5 Classroom organisation (TTA 1998: para. 4)

In your classroom do you:	Adept	Working knowledge	Beginner
Ensure equal access to ICT			
Ensure group collaboration			
Provide flexible access for pupils			
Consider safety issues			
Link work with work done away from the computer			

Chapters 8, 9 and 10 deal with some of these issues.

Table 12.6 Special Educational Needs (TTA 1998: para. 5)

Are you able to use ICT to:	Adept	Working knowledge	Beginner
Provide appropriate access and support			

Special Educational Needs and ICT are not dealt with in detail in this text. The SENCO forum[6] provides online support for discussions about professional issues and Chapter 7 in Leask and Pachler (1999) contains more details.

Table 12.7 Choosing suitable ICT (TTA 1998: para. 6)

Have you criteria for:	Adept	Working knowledge	Beginner
Judging the suitability of ICT for the specific group of pupils			
Evaluating its effectiveness			

Table 12.8 Developing ICT capability (TTA 1998: para. 7)

Can you do the following:	Adept	Working knowledge	Beginner
Teach ICT skills			
Use ICT terminology			
Demonstrate good ICT practice			

Discussions with staff working in the same area or with the same forms of technology could be a useful way of building effective practice in the deployment of ICT in your classroom. On a number of these issues, planning at the subject or school level is necessary if ICT is to be fully integrated into the curriculum.

Table 12.9 Monitoring and evaluating (TTA 1998: para. 8)

Through your assessment procedures do you:	Adept	Working knowledge	Beginner
Monitor progress in ICT and your curriculum areas			
Note use of computer functions			
Require referenced sources			
Evaluate individual achievement through collaborative effort			
Target objectives for assessment			

Many of the chapters in this text provide examples in this area.

Table 12.10 Nursery and reception (TTA 1998: para. 9)

Do you do the following:	Adept	Working knowledge	Beginner
Encourage ICT use			
Ensure equal access			
Use ICT to support language, numeracy and creative work			
Encourage collaboration			

Section B: personal knowledge and understanding of ICT

This section (Tables 12.11–12.19) is more skills-based and looks at the issues raised in Section B of the ITT NC for ICT in curriculum, that is, knowledge and understanding of, and competence in, Information and Communications Technology. The incentive to develop these skills comes from having a purpose for undertaking the work. Consider the work being done in other schools as described in various chapters in this book. Are there projects you wish to undertake in your area? What skills do you need to have to be able to do this effectively? Experiential learning, learning through and by doing, is particularly useful when it comes to understanding how to operate various forms of equipment.

Table 12.11 General computer use (TTA 1998: para. 12A)

Can you do the following:	Adept	Working knowledge	Beginner
Start the computer			
Open programs			
Use menus			
Select different applications			
Swap between applications			
Cut and paste text			
Copy, delete, rename files			
Cut and paste data between files			
Change font size and style			
Insert and format tables			
Save data or text			
Print			
Use grammar or spell checker			
Use help option for information			

Table 12.11 (continued)

Can you do the following:	Adept	Working knowledge	Beginner
Shut down computer correctly			
Highlight text using mouse and keys			
Minimise and maximise windows			
Connect and use concept keyboard			
Install and use CD-ROM			
Use good practice in avoiding viruses			
Draw text boxes			
Draw circles, lines, rectangles, etc.			
Use ruler, tabs, and toolbar			

Table 12.12 Information handling (TTA 1998: paras. 12B, 13A, 13B)

Can you do the following:	Adept	Working knowledge	Beginner
Access the World Wide Web			
Access information from a CD-ROM			
Be aware that information must be evaluated in terms of accuracy, validity, reliability, plausibility, bias			
Search a database for information			
Search internet for information			
Widen or narrow down searches			
Frame useful questions			
Use key words and strings			
Use logical operators AND, OR, NOT			
Use indexes and directories			
Use an internet search engine			
Save files to use least memory			
Know where information is stored			
Use ICT to present static information, e.g., picture or text			
Use ICT to present changing information, e.g., simulation			
Link information between applications			
Share applications and information with others at remote locations			
Collect and structure data			

Table 12.12 (continued)

Can you do the following:	Adept	Working knowledge	Beginner
Store data for later retrieval			
Interpret and correct data			
Use a spreadsheet			
Change the variables in a spreadsheet			
Use a database			
Model numeric relationships			
Evaluate graphical outcomes			
Programme using Logo			

Table 12.13 Using ICT to make things happen (TTA 1998: paras. 13B, 13C)

Do you understand or can you do the following?	Adept	Working knowledge	Beginner
Know the importance of grammar and syntax of ICT instructions			
Sequence actions, e.g., robotic control			
Programme feedback into a control device, e.g., computer controlled systems			
Put conditions into a spreadsheet formula			
Understand closed and open loop systems, e.g., computerised control systems			
Use ICT to communicate			
Evaluate and select appropriate technology for particular purposes			
Use electronic mail			
Use conferencing (telephone and video)			
Use a bulletin board			
Use a user or news group			

Table 12.14 Using ICT to support teaching and learning (TTA 1998: para. 14)

Can you apply the following in your professional practice:	Adept	Working knowledge	Beginner
Use the speed and automatic functions of the media			
Measure and record events which would otherwise be impossible, e.g., through simulations			
Link sensing of events with the control of actions, e.g., through robotics			
Access and handle large amounts of information			
Change time scales and remove barriers of distance			
Use the range of forms in which ICT can present information			
Use ICT to gain access to expertise outside the school			
Make use of the ability to change things easily			
Evaluate and improve text, etc.			

Table 12.15 The potential of ICT (TTA 1998: para. 15)

Can you do the following:	Adept	Working knowledge	Beginner
Adapt and differentiate materials using appropriate media to present ideas			
Recognise the potential to target special educational needs			

Table 12.16 The National Curriculum (TTA 1998: para. 16)

Do you understand or can you do the following:	Adept	Working knowledge	Beginner
Know the requirements of the NC for IT			
Know the level of IT capability to expect of pupils when using ICT			
Understand the ICT requirements of the NC for pupils working in specific curriculum areas			
Collaborate with IT specialists			

Table 12.17 ICT in subject areas (TTA 1998: para. 17)

Can you use the following which are relevant to your work:	Adept	Working knowledge	Beginner
Understand the key features and functions of ICT relevant to the subject area			
Use ICT to produce material for pupil use			
Incorporate information from CD-ROMs, the internet, into teaching materials			
Use graphics packages			
Use scanner			
Use CAD equipment			
Use sequencing software			
Use midi keyboards			
Use dynamic geometry software			
Use subject specific software			
Use Integrated Learning Systems			
Use web page authoring tools			

Table 12.18 Legal and ethical issues (TTA 1998: para. 18)

Are you:	Adept	Working knowledge	Beginner
Familiar with relevant health and safety legislation			
Able to identify potential hazards			
Able to minimise risks			
Familiar with relevant parts of the Data Protection Act (see Chapter 14)			
Able to prevent access to illegal and unsuitable internet material			
Careful to acknowledge sources of information			
Able to ensure confidentiality of data			
Explain how users of information sources are monitored			
Aware of material which may be socially or morally unacceptable			
Able to explain copyright legislation			

Table 12.19 Research (TTA 1998: para. 19)

Do you understand and can you do the following:	Adept	Working knowledge	Beginner
Know about current classroom-based research in ICT[7]			
Know about inspection evidence			
Know about the application of ICT to your specialist subject			
Know where such information can be found			
Know how to locate sources of help and support, e.g., NGfL			
Know how ICT can support your continuing professional development			

Your personal action plan

If you have repeated Activities 12.1 and 12.2 in all aspects of the tables above, you should now have a list of your development needs, together with a list of strategies for satisfying these needs drawing on individuals and other sources.

There are a number of accredited courses which support development in the area of ICT. LEAs and universities will often run courses and you can expect many of these to give credits for post-graduate certificate, diploma or MA awards. Other accredited programmes commonly used include the RSA CLAIT or the European Driving Licence[8] programmes.

> ## Activity 12.4 Drawing up a personal action plan
>
> Draw up a personal action plan indicating your priorities for development, the timescales over which you plan to achieve your goals and the sources of support for your development, which includes individuals in your own school, other colleagues and courses which are available. The headings in Table 12.20 may provide a useful framework for your planning.

Summary

Before accepting training for ICT use in the classroom, it is important to decide what areas are a priority for you. The ITT NC for ICT provides a structure for self-assessment of ICT skills and understanding. For teachers,

Table 12.20 Your personal action plan

Focus for professional development: what is your goal?	Tasks to be done to achieve the goal	Support and resources needed	Who has responsibility for providing the support and resources	Timescale	Deadline for completion	Criteria for successful achievement of your goal

knowing when and why to use particular ICT applications with pupils is as important as acquiring personal skills. Undertaking the assessment suggested in this chapter will allow you to construct a personal action plan for your professional development in ICT use. Having done this, you can then evaluate the training offered by your school, LEA or training provider, and decide which particular courses will help you to address your needs.

Notes

1   The Initial Training National Curriculum for ICT can be found on the DfEE website *http://www.dfee.gov.uk/circular/0498.htm* or the TTA website *http://www. teach-tta.gov.uk*
2   TeacherNetUK can be contacted through the website at *http://teachernetuk. org.uk*
3   The *Learning to Teach in the Secondary School* series is published by Routledge and covers most areas in the curriculum.
4   BECTA formerly NCET is at the Science Park, Milburn Park Road, Coventry, tel: 01203 416 994.
5   The Teacher Training Agency can be contacted on tel: 0171 925 3700, *http:// www.tta-teach.gov.uk*
6   The SENCO forum can be found on *http://www.becta.org.uk/projects/senco/ forums/index.html#senco-forum*
7   Sites of research associations around the world can be found through the Web Links button on the British Educational Research Association website *http://www. bera.ac.uk*
    It is now common practice for papers presented at conferences to be put on the website so that at the touch of a couple of buttons, you can find out the latest research news.
8   European Driving licence: *http://www.bcs.org.uk/ecdl/*

References and further reading

Leask, M. and Pachler, N. (1999) *Learning to Teach with ICT in the Secondary School*, London: Routledge.

Stevenson Report (1997) *The Independent ICT in Schools Commission Information and Communications Technology in UK Schools: An Independent Inquiry*, 78–80 St John Street, London EC1M 4MR.

TTA (1998) [*http://www.teach-tta.gov.uk/icy.htm*] The published version is available as DfEE (1998) *Initial Teacher Training National Curriculum for the Use of Information and Communications Technology in Subject Teaching*, London: DfEE. This is reprinted in Appendix.

Chapter 13

Networking People and Computers

John Meadows with Ken Millar

Introduction

This chapter deals with some of the issues arising from the idea of networking, in a technical sense, with computers and, in a social sense, with people. Schools no longer think of buying computers as stand-alone systems, but as networks of machines which can have a variety of links and connections to each other.

People networks can be built up through the use of the communication parts of ICT, and these might be on a number of levels and with a number of purposes. The British Government Education Departments are; for example, involved in setting up virtual networks, such as the Virtual Teacher Centre (see Notes, Chapter 1 and 2). The Commonwealth has set up a network called CENSE.[1] Inservice training too is increasingly carried out through electronic networks, with government making demands on the training providers. Then there are other independent professional teacher networks such as TeachernetUK[2] and MirandaNet.[3]

Primary school ideas for international projects are usually constrained by the language spoken[4] – in the case of the UK, it is rare for primary school children to begin learning a foreign language, so projects using networks tend to be restricted to others who also speak English. Hence links with the USA, Canada, Australia and New Zealand are popular, as well as links with international schools. Primary projects are often cross-curricular, but there are cases of single subject uses. In the case study in this chapter about Hermitage Primary School, however, you will see that there are opportunities for schools to link with others in Europe and that this situation can be supported through European Union educational funds.

Objectives

By the end of this chapter you should be:

- able to recognise the characteristics of networks using ICT;
- aware of some of the main principles in an international network – communication, methods, activities;
- able to evaluate projects and adapt the case studies presented;
- aware of how international projects and networks are organised, built up and evaluated effectively;
- able to plan your own cross-curricular projects and networks and set appropriate learning outcomes for these.

Background

At a simple level, a local computer network would mean that several computers could be connected to a single printer, with the advantage that a more expensive and better quality printer could be bought instead of several cheaper ones. This would also mean a different system of managing the printing needs of the class and a different expectation of the notion of queuing work to the printer. Local Area Networks (LANs) usually work on the principle that one powerful computer acts as the 'server' for the network, providing the programs and data for all the other lower power computers linked to it. The server and client computers may be in the same room, or linked together by wiring in the same building, or another nearby. A Wide Area Network (WAN) usually links computers to servers at a remote site, but with high bandwidth (i.e., fast) phone line connections between them. When a school links its own computers to the internet through a service provider (like America On Line), the local network of the school, or even stand-alone computers in the school, connected through a telephone line, are being linked to the WAN run by the internet service provider.

The notion of people networks is a much more complex matter. As you will see later in the chapter, there are many and varied ways of networking which teachers carry out using ICT. Some of these networks are at a local level, as schools co-operate in clusters for both administrative and pedagogic purposes. Most school administration across Britain is now conducted through computer networks set up by Local Education Authorities, separate from public networks like the internet, as the data being collated are often of a confidential nature. But teachers also co-operate in other ways in order to support the children's learning, using ICT tools such as email and the World Wide Web to communicate ideas and information, organising local, national and international projects in which children extend their understanding of curriculum objectives in a wider context.

Linda Harasim (and others) have written a book entitled *Learning Networks* (1995), giving further background on the types of computer technology underpinning networks. It is interesting to look at books on technology to see how quickly some of them become dated, even if the ideas and learning theory are still relevant, for example, *Learning Networks* has very little about the World Wide Web, yet this is the technology which has revolutionised the internet in the past few years. One wonders what breakthroughs in technology will arise to make this chapter out of date?

Organising 'people' networks for collaborative projects

1 The network needs to develop a set of aims and objectives – these can be very short and simple ones for a short timescale network, or more complex if the group intends to operate over a longer period.
2 A network co-ordinator is necessary, who maintains contact with all the members of the group on a regular basis and keeps everyone up to date with events. This person also needs to nag sometimes, so that projects keep to their deadline dates.
3 Messages need to be sent, or web pages published, according to a set timetable, so everyone knows what to expect. If breaks/delays are unavoidable, then all participants need to be informed about them. There should be some sort of backup provision in such circumstances.
4 Mini-networks tend to have a limited life time – this is an advantage because it means that members can then set up other networks of their own, if they wish, not be tied for life into one particular group.
5 Interests and classes change, so mini-networks should be flexible too.
6 Building up mini-networks – information is needed about what links already occur, especially those which could lead to mini-networks. Most schools with global experience have several international contacts which could be built into networks, if that seems appropriate. Projects can be initiated by national or local organisers on special interests, e.g., environmental topics, or exchange of cultural or historical material.
7 It is always useful for new members to give a brief description of their own circumstances, e.g., number of classes, age of students, interests, geographical location, amount of time available for the project, holiday dates.

How to set up a network project

First you need a good idea: something that would be of interest to teachers and pupils in your own and other countries! The Global Stories project (see Chapter 2) was interesting because it included multi-cultural and historical ideas, as well as the opportunity for pupils to create their own stories. Children were also interested in reading stories from other countries. Your project might cover global topics like the environment, current affairs, language learning, mathematics, science, history, religious education, etc.

Then you need to find others who wish to join your project. One easy way to do this is by joining a Listserv, like 'iecc-projects'. You can do this by sending a message to the list-owner, in this case *iecc-projects-request* @*stolaf.edu*, with no subject and the message 'subscribe iecc-projects [your email address]'.[5] The European SchoolNet[6] and British Council Montage[7] projects site offer ways of finding projects and partners.

You also need to tell participants how to send in and receive the texts. This was done in the Global Stories project through me: teachers sent me the stories and I then sent them out through a distribution list using the internet. Alternatively, you could set up a distribution system through a Listserv[8] of your own, if you have a friendly service provider who will help you, or even through the World Wide Web, if you have a home page. You can enhance your project website with pictures, photos or other graphics.

International network organisation

Many internet-based projects try to link schools and colleges one-to-one, matching up interests and age groups where possible across national boundaries. But some schools are keen to have more than one age group or class working on international links – other classes or groups within a school prefer to communicate with several other countries. The move towards multi-links needs to be supported and co-ordinated, but to do this, we need to understand some of the characteristics of mini-networks.

Activity 13.1 Mini-networks: the Global Village Newsletter

The Global Village Newsletter idea is one in which a group of up to ten participant schools takes turns to produce and distribute a newsletter to all the others. The news can be varied or it might be on one topic. Each participant receives messages every week (or fortnight) but only needs to prepare one message for transmission every ten weeks. Each member of the group can also make direct contacts with others, if they wish.

This type of network needs an active organiser who will remind the participants in advance when it is their turn to produce the newsletter. The organiser may also act as distributor of the newsletter, through email or a mailing list, or may forward newsletters from each participant to the others in the group. The organiser may also need to have a short newsletter always available from her or his own institution, in case one of the other participants fails to deliver their contribution on time.

continued

Each participant would use the newsletter within their own institution in the most appropriate ways, for example:

- printing the news direct from the system and displaying it on noticeboards;
- downloading it into a word processor and printing it in larger font for a more careful display;
- downloading, editing and integrating it into an existing printed newsletter or magazine, using desk-top publishing techniques;
- incorporating it into the school website, as a regularly updated feature.

Different types of network

Networks originating in one school

Several classes in one school may decide to co-operate in order to carry out international links. One person in that school should have the responsibility to co-ordinate all the messages going in and out, ensuring that the messages reach the right classes and teachers and encouraging the dissemination of good ideas within that school. This person would be advised to engage the help of other colleagues at times, in order to ensure continuity when she or he is busy elsewhere, or better, to seek help from trustworthy pupils/students who could be relied upon to check the mailbox daily. It is good practice in such a situation to download all new messages daily onto a disk and keep this as backup, but also to print the messages as they arrive and ensure they are delivered to the correct addressee. Those who send messages to such a school would need to be aware of the situation and would need to identify the recipient clearly in the message header. Sending out messages would also need to be done on a daily basis, with disk-based messages delivered to the co-ordinator in good time and again with clearly identified sender and receiver. On internal networks, this process may be easier than with stand-alone computer systems. Prepared messages to be sent out might be addressed to the school's own mailbox, but with copy or blind copy additions already included in the message. This would give the sender a copy of all messages actually sent, acting as a check on the operation of the system.

Networks linking a pair of schools

Activity 13.2 is based on a question from an extract of a report written by the deputy headteacher of a junior school in Bexley. Her school was part of a larger project GETN (Global Electronic Telecommunications Network), which originated as a partnership between teacher trainers in London and New York City. She and her colleagues in the London school had been using electronic mail for several years and communicated regularly with countries like the USA, Australia, Sweden and Finland (Keep 1990).[9]

Activity 13.2 Integrating networking into the curriculum

Extract from the UK teacher's report on the project:

> Christine (a young class teacher) of the primary school in New York City suggested that we should undertake a shared project. It was decided that we would look at Current Events as they were reported in the newspapers on both sides of the Atlantic. The children had already exchanged views on such dramatic issues as the Lockerbie disaster, the Salman Rushdie affair and the Hillsborough tragedy. I suggested that we should focus on conservation issues. It was agreed, the project was planned, but the problem was – when to fit it into the normal school day.

In your view, how could a teacher fit such a cross-curricular project into the school day in a modern primary school? Would there be ways of integrating it into subjects like Religious Education? Could some of the materials find a place of study within the Literacy Hour? What sorts of issues would you think suitable for children aged 10 to 12 to study and discuss? Is there a need to discuss controversial issues with children at around this age? There are often websites which deal with current controversy. Would you want to involve primary school children in these debates, or make them aware that such debates are going on?

Curriculum-based networks

Another way to develop networks is with a group of classes sharing one specific interest; for example, maths surveys or writing stories, etc.

This kind of network can be set up by local organisers, or may arise from one school's request. This network may last only a short time while that specific project takes place. It is important that the results of such networks are available to all members. This could be through email copies sent to all, or through the setup of a database to which all can get access, or through bulletin boards. In the current climate, many schools have their own websites on which some information can be presented. Web pages are now easier to prepare using selected software, such as Microsoft Word 7, which translates documents into HTML (hypertext markup language, in which web pages are written).

Special interest networks

One further network type is one which depends on similar curriculum needs; for example, teacher training colleges co-operating on aspects of student practice in schools, or vocational schools linking up to compare ways of meeting the industry-placement needs of their students. International exchanges of students could be supported by the email exchanges occurring in such groups. At the primary school level, these kinds of networks are very common, perhaps because many primary schools around the world expect to use the interests of children and teachers as motivation towards learning.

Activity 13.3 Special interest networks

Look at these examples of special interest networks and suggest ways of dealing with them in a British primary class.

For children aged between 7 and 12 years

Network focus: the importance of rules
Children would focus on identifying areas in their lives where they have to obey rules, drawing up sets of rules and the consequences if the rules are broken.

By setting up internet links with other schools, you can compare the rules imposed on children by schools; for example, why children have to wear school uniforms in some places but not in others. One internet project which I organised through email examined the children's perceptions of school rules and their own influence on such rules through organisations like school councils. It was interesting to note that German schools do not have uniforms because of the dangers associated with the Nazi period, whereas many English and Australian schools do have uniforms.

For younger children aged between 5 and 8 years

Network focus: investigating the clothes we wear – art, science and geography

continued

The work could involve the following activities:

- Art – recognising colour, pattern and texture, including similarities and differences;
- Science – materials and their properties – understanding that materials are chosen for specific uses on the basis of their properties;
- Geography – the effects of weather on the clothes people wear.

These activities could be supported through some of the web pages; for example, the Web Louvre site shows painting of people wearing an assortment of clothes. Children could be shown some of these pages and asked to describe colours, patterns, or to discuss why people are wearing different types of fabrics, or actively investigate how the colours are put into the fabrics. They might also communicate directly with children from a very different climate and ask about the clothes they wear and their favourite colours.

Centrally organised networks

Eurofood (see below) was one project in a series that ran over a two-year period. The Euro series looked at issues like European schools, environment, or food or customs. Each project has a common format, consisting of ten questions, sent out through email to schools and colleges around the world. When replies were received, they were often repackaged and shortened, then sent out to all the participants. Many of those receiving the messages were regional co-ordinators who forwarded messages to educators within their own areas.

This type of loose and open network is increasingly common these days, as educators work in partnerships to enrich the curriculum. Teacher trainers and school teachers frequently co-operate in organising and participating in such projects, since they are equally valuable for school pupils and for trainee teachers.

Eurofood project

Project description (which was emailed out to the participants and some local co-ordinators).

Young people across the world often share similar tastes in food, many of us like sweet-tasting or spicy foods, many of us perhaps eat too much fast food, which may not do us much good in the future.

continued

But there are also traditional foods in most countries, which tend to be less fashionable with young people.

This project is about your tastes in food. Please try to answer the questions in small groups and send in the response of your group, not as individuals.

Names of people in your group:
Ages:
School:
Country:

1   What foods do you usually eat at breakfast time?
2   What sort of food do you eat at lunchtime?
3   What types of food do you normally eat in the evening?
4   When you eat with the family at weekends, what kinds of foods do your parents prefer for a main meal?
5   Do your grandparents have special favourite foods, that are not very common any more?
6   What special kinds of food are linked to certain times of the year in your country, for example in Britain, many people eat Christmas puddings (at Christmas, of course!).
7   Eating too much of some foods may cause health problems – do you know of any foods that may cause heart attacks?
8   Some things we eat and drink may cause tooth decay, especially in very young children. What kinds of food and drinks should babies avoid?
9   We often associate certain types of food with different countries, like beefburgers with the USA, pizzas with Italy and curries with India, but what kinds of food do you associate with:

Spain
Germany
France
South American countries
Norway
China
England

European funding and networks

Ken Millar at Hermitage Primary School describes projects his pupils enjoy – these include Linda Bear, a Travel Buddy project, European Waterways and Renata, a sailing boat idea.

Linda Bear project

Linda Bear is an exciting project that I have been developing in Hermitage Primary School. Linda Bear is a teddy bear who is travelling between three schools. These schools are Taivis School in Helsinki, Finland, Kyrktasjo school in Hoting, Sweden and, of course, our own school. The aims of the project have been to provide a purpose for the children's writing and develop their communication skills using a range of communication technologies. Linda makes the initial contact arriving by post along with her journal of adventures which the children keep for her. She becomes a focus of great interest going on trips, being interviewed by the press and visiting the pupils' homes before she sets off on her travels again. Where, you might, ask is the ICT component? Well this is the second aim of the project that children and staff become familiar with and use email facilities to maintain contact with Linda when she arrives at our partner schools and also develop email links with the staff and children of the other institution. To date, this project has been remarkably successful with both staff and children developing these partnerships. The project has developed many offshoots; for instance, we are at present developing a joint art presentation between the three schools and a fourth Russian school and have ambitions to have part of this collaboration on view on the net. This will involve the staff in the use of hardware not before used, such as scanners and all sorts of multimedia presentations.

As well as the email links, two of the partner schools have set up web pages: these are the Swedish school and ourselves. In order to set up our own website, work was exchanged using email on the children's dreams for the world and the children of both schools visited each other's work on the web and exchanged comments. At Christmas, Christmas cards designed by the children using paintbrush software were sent to the Scandinavian schools using email links and we have ambitions to form a schools' art gallery in cyber space by scanning our joint art work and linking our sites. Many links have been established between the schools through overland mail between individual children and we would like these penpals to develop the relationship through email links which are to be encouraged through the setting up of an email club. This has been made possible by the school acquiring a new mail server which allows for multiple addresses at the same site. In this way we hope that much more interactive projects will develop between the schools.

Linda Bear is entering a new cycle as she is now on a second round of the schools, as well as having been on holiday with one of the teachers to the United States from which she reported back in diary form by email. We have plans to broaden her horizons and she may be making a trip to Australia in the near future and who knows she may gain a Koala buddy while there. We also want to diversify the curriculum content of the project so that, as well as a strong language component, we develop areas such as history, geography, art and music. We have already made a start with the art as regards the art exchange and the exchange of Christmas cards. In geography Linda's journal has a contribution to make and in music we have already begun to exchange by tape the children's music and are looking for ways to do this over the net.

The project has also been characterised by the fact that we have been able to involve children of all ages in the different projects right through from the early years to the Year 6 juniors and that this has been made possible by a strong staff commitment and ensuring that the project is seen as something that supports National Curriculum development and does not take away precious teaching time from it.

European Waterways project

Another European project underway involving extensive use of ICT is the European Waterways project. This involves a focus on trade travel and leisure. Children and staff function transnationally as partners between France, Sweden, England and with the Czech Republic as a sleeping partner. The project is developing the curriculum in several areas including language, science, music and dance and geography. ICT has been used to exchange emails, and audio and visual tapes have been exchanged of children's productions and musical compositions. The children's language and research skills have been enhanced through the use of the internet. All partner schools prioritise involvement with the wider business and higher education organisations. University and teacher education commitment is assured. The harbour and river authorities have also promised their support. All the schools involved in the project teach one or more European languages and Hermitage School has been facilitated in this by the acquisition of a French Lingua assistant. The project itself has been funded primarily by Socrates, Comenius action 1.

The Renata project

Among email and internet links that have been established are the links to the Renata project involving the boat *Renata* which is sailing around the world and maintaining email links and answering the children's questions.

The further aims of the project are to achieve collective agreement on monitoring, evaluation and dissemination between the schools. The schools will also develop and exchange teaching materials.

We are currently working to establish a Communication Centre at the school which will incorporate high-quality publishing and communication facilities and this will obviously facilitate development of the project.

Networks within the European Schools Project

The European Schools Project (ESP)[10] is a group which you can join and which has been meeting and communicating regularly for several years. One of the characteristics of ESP projects is the idea of Teletrips, which are virtual visits to European countries. The ESP teachers attempt to solve the problem of languages across Europe by linking schools which can communicate in the second language of both. So a German school might link with a French one and communicate in English most of the time. This means that both sets of pupils are practising their second language skills and that neither group has the advantage of their home language. As more British primary schools begin to teach a foreign language, this might be a good way for children to practise their emerging language skills. Of course, not all ESP projects fall into this pattern; for example, the one below, originating in one of the newer European countries, Slovakia, uses English language and is open to a number of different participants, rather than the one-to-one partnership of a Teletrip. Virtual field trips are also ways in which schools are using the web for projects.[11]

Activity 13.4 Evaluating international networks

As you read the extract below from this ESP project proposal, there are a few issues which you might examine. Are there other points would which arise from participation in it?

A project for children and teachers

There are very many such projects now available through websites for schools,[12] but this one seems very carefully planned and takes an interesting personal approach through messages to both teachers and children. Is this an advantage or would it be better just to address teachers and then let them introduce the network to their own pupils?

Timescale

The timescale is quite tightly controlled, but this might be a problem in international networks, since there are often problems over which participants have little control. Networks actually work better if there is some flexibility in the timetable arrangements, rather than a very tight schedule.

continued

English as an additional language

Since the organisers of this project are considering the needs of children with English as a foreign language, it might be interesting for a British teacher to focus some of the activities on children in the class who speak English as an additional language (EAL). Although many international writing projects are intended to support the needs of non-English speakers, it is less frequent that they also support EAL children in English-speaking schools.

ESP project proposal

Name of project: WRITE ME YOUR STORY (a project suitable for primary school students)
Name of co-ordinating school: A university in Slovakia
Age group of class: 5 – 15
Language of communication: English
Countries of priority: any country
Period of project: October – December

Project description:

Dear teachers,
You will learn the details in an enclosed letter addressed to your students and in a schedule. If you find this proposal interesting, please subscribe for the 'WRITE ME YOUR STORY' project at the email address given above. The student teachers of the co-ordinating Presov University will collect the selected stories and drawings, and produce a project website. It would be wonderful if you could involve your colleagues teaching younger children, and help them to participate as well. We believe that together we will give the children involved a chance to write, draw, translate and read having a nice reason for all these tasks – to listen and to be heard.

Dear children,
This is a call for your stories that happened to you a long time ago, recently or even this morning. You can write about yourself, your families, or your friends. The stories might be funny, sad, exciting or just describing simple events of everyday life. What is most important, children in other countries will learn more about you and you will learn more about them. The stories will be written in English.

continued

Schedule

Week 1

Subscribing for the project and providing the essential information about your school and class.

Week 2

Forming project teams. You will learn the address of your partner. (This will depend on the number of participants. The teams might be formed by 2–3 classes or groups from different countries.

Week 3

Sending the first greeting to other classes forming your team. Write and translate stories to English. Draw illustrations and/or take photographs. Email collections of your stories to the other classes of your team. Send illustrations by regular mail.

Week 4

Read the stories of your partner with your students, and choose 3–5 that they like most. Email 'winning' stories to Slovakia, and if they are accompanied with drawings, snail mail them to Slovakia too.

Week 5

Students at the co-ordinating centre will create a web page of 'WRITE ME YOUR STORY' project. If we succeed in raising money, a collection of stories will be published and distributed to all the participants.

Activity 13.5 Learning outcomes in network projects

Compare the aims of the network in the 'ESP project proposal' with the list of objectives from another similar one – an American project initiated by AT&T – which follows. Which aims and learning outcomes might be more appropriate for a British primary school? Would it depend on the age and experience of the children in the class and

continued

whether they had already participated in networks and projects? The aim below of 'improving English proficiency and writing skills' would need considerable adaptation to make it into a series of appropriate learning outcomes, specific enough for you to be able to assess these.

Objectives from an American project initiated by AT&T

Participants (students and teachers) will learn to:

- communicate via open chat forums;
- plan, design and create web pages;
- program in HTML;
- publish websites using FTP;
- collaborate and communicate across cultures;
- improve English proficiency and writing skills;
- delegate and carry out tasks and make group decisions.

Although the skills and attitudes encountered by the children in both projects might be similar, the emphasis in the Slovakia one is much more on the human/social reasons for global communication, rather than on the technical skills associated with this. Teachers will often have different reasons for using ICT in their classes; this may depend on the prior experiences of the teacher, as well as those of the children, on the age of the learners, on the syllabus or programme of study prescriptions, the time of year, etc.

International or North American projects and networks

One of the problems which may arise is that teachers and pupils want to join a project which appears to be global in nature, only to find that it really only focuses on North America – the extract below falls into that category, with original documentation requiring registration which demanded city, state and zip codes. It is not clear anywhere in the extensive documentation whether this is open to participants outside the USA. Even the inclusion of time zones, actually refers to USA time zones, rather than global ones. It can be disconcerting to enter a project like this, where everything is pre-ordained and timetabled, only to find that you have wasted your time and that there are few learning benefits for your own pupils. However, the project is very well organised and has plenty of supporting ideas and suggestions for teachers, so it could easily be adapted without too much teacher time being spent on its organisation.

Project name: geogame: geography game

Purpose: Learn geography terms, learn how to read and interpret maps, increase awareness of geographical and cultural diversity

Subjects: Geography, social studies, writing

Grade level: Open to all grade levels.
(Most appropriate for 4th to 9th grade)

Summary: Each participating class completes a questionnaire about their own location, including information about latitude, typical weather, land formations, nearest river, time zone, points of interest, for whom/what famous, direction from capital, and population.

   The co-ordinator collects responses from all the participating sites, scrambles the information, and returns the data to participants as puzzles for the classes to solve.

   Students, with help from maps, atlases, and other reference materials, match the description of each location (based on the questionnaire) with the name of the corresponding city.

   At the conclusion of the project, the co-ordinator will email the correct answers. The 'winning' classes are those with the most correct solutions to the game.

   While you are waiting, gather a few materials for the class so that students can break up into small groups to begin the process of matching locations up with descriptions. (Large United States map showing time zones and latitudes, set of encyclopedias for individual state maps and maps of other countries, AAA road maps, Rand McNally Road Atlas, Almanac, etc.)

The project proposal above has some interesting ideas, including the competitive aspects, which are not so common in networked initiatives, where co-operative work tends to be favoured. However, it does seem to assume that all the participants will be from the USA, rather than other countries. Perhaps, if it was not open to participants from outside the USA, the ideas it contains would be useful to teachers thinking of organising a geography project. You could extend the activities to include more about the human populations of the various places included, such as the special foods eaten, the festivals or national holidays celebrated. Other geographical or scientific data might be collected and compared, such as times of sunrise and sunset, which could be correlated to the data about latitude, longitude and time zones.

Summary

In this chapter you have seen a number of models for networks involving primary schools. We began with a very brief discussion of ways of physically networking schools, and the wider networks which link computers world-wide into the internet. We then looked at some examples of projects which teachers have organised, along with the intended learning outcomes for children. Networks as learning organisations were described in a range of contexts, some of which involved only a few teachers and children, others were much more ambitious. Some networks required extra funding to make them operate, such as those which rely on European grants, like Comenius. Networks can be effective ways of teaching and learning in many curriculum areas – some networks focus more on ICT skills as their learning outcomes, while others may be more concerned with personal and social aspects of learning; others still may focus on specific parts of the curriculum, such as writing and literacy. The technology behind networks is not usually the important factor in networks for primary schools, but rather the opportunities this technology gives for enriching the curriculum, motivating children and teachers and providing a learning environment which is appropriate in the new millennium.

Notes

1 The Commonwealth governments have set up CENSE [http://www.col.org/cense] and at the European level, governments have set up the European School Net [http://www.eun.org].
2 TeachernetUK is an organisation of teachers and other educators:
   • developing an independent online professional community where teachers and all educators can talk openly about educational issues and share ideas and resources;
   • providing a paper-based magazine as well as a web-based magazine focused on how we can use ICT to support professional development;
   • lobbying government about teachers' concerns about ICT e.g., training and equipment issues for staff and schools;
   • working with industry to develop online profiling which uses new technology to enable a teacher to be kept up to date in areas of their own interest – without them having to trawl the web looking for such materials.
3 MirandaNet is a project which links industry and education as partners in a variety of action research activities in schools of all types. Independent (public) schools work alongside state and special needs teachers to provide a well-resourced environment where learning is enhanced through ICT. Teachers mainly use portable computers and online communications in their work and the projects often involve international partners in the Czech Republic, Chile, and other places.
4 There is an electronic translation option on AltaVista's front page which can be of some help translating websites in other languages or emails: http://www.altavista.com; or go straight to the page on: http://babelfish.altavista.com/cgi-bin/translate?
5 IECC is International Educational Cross-cultural Communication, an international group which supports links and networks at school, further and higher

education levels. Although the focus is on cultural exchanges, in fact many of the projects do deal with curriculum subjects.

6 The European School Net is an organisation set up to help co-ordinate networks and projects in schools across Europe. The website containing further information is at *http://www.eun.org*

7 The British Council Montage site is one which helps schools to join projects and find partners *http://www.bc.org.au/montage*

8 A Listserv is the name for a technical program which supports a group email system. The most popular Listserv organiser in the UK, dealing with academic issues including education, is called Mailbase. Further information about it can be found at *http://www.mailbase.ac.uk*

9 Ros Keep was the manager of a project in Britain which aimed at exploring the advantages of electronic networks in education. She edited the final report of the project as well as regular newsletter during its running. There were up to eleven groups of teachers working on local and national, as well as international, networks with a variety of curricular interests including English language, social inclusion, environmental studies and modern foreign languages.

10 Instructions for joining the European Schools Project (ESP) are available on the website on *http://www.kuleuven.ac.be/soi/esp/fullidxc.htm*

11 Virtual field trips can be found on *http://www.teleport.com/~eotic/index.html* and *http://www.field-guides.com*

12 See, for example, the IECC website at *http://www.iecc.edu*

References and further reading

Harasim, L., Hiltz, S.R., Teles, L. and Turoff, M. (1995) *Learning Networks: A Field Guide to Teaching and Learning Online*, Cambridge, MA: MIT Press.

Keep, R. (ed.) (1990) *Communique: Summary of the Final Report of the Communications Collaborative Project*, Coventry: NCET.

Chapter 14

Linking Home and School Use

*Marilyn Leask and Norbert Pachler
with Ray Barker and Glen Franklin*

Introduction

Open access and flexible approaches to learning are increasingly being provided by colleges and universities and are supported by government policies. The foundation of the University for Industry in the UK in the late 1990s demonstrates the commitment at government level to support lifelong learning in the community.

Primary schools in particular are well placed to play a key role in developing the access of their local community to a wide range of lifelong learning opportunities. In this chapter, Ray Barker describes how workshops for parents were developed in the Docklands in London (see Wolfendale and Bastiani (in press) for more details) so that parents learnt the skills which they needed to support their children working on homework projects using portable computers. Internet access, which in time all primary schools will have, potentially allows the benefits of a range of ICT to be available to the communities served by the primary schools.

In this chapter a number of ideas for developing home–school links are discussed. Clearly there are issues of equity when a school starts to move towards using ICT to communicate with parents. These need to be addressed and each school will need to devise solutions to suit their community needs.

Objectives

By the end of this chapter you will have been introduced to ideas about:

- developing a school website to aid home–school communication;
- advice to parents on ICT issues;
- using ICT for homework – including examples of ways in which parents, school and pupils have worked together using portable computers.

Developing the school web site

School websites which are open to the public have a number of functions and purposes, some of which are outlined below. As they show the public face of the school and so fulfil a publicity and marketing function, they need to be updated regularly. This can be an expensive and time-consuming task if it becomes a sole responsibility of a member of staff.

The functions and purpose of the school website

The school website can perform a number of functions:

- publicity: for recruitment of pupils or sponsors
- information: for pupils, parents, governors, student teachers, potential parents
  - about the curriculum
  - about policies
  - about extra curricular activities
  - about homework and resources for learning
  - about school events
  - about the history of the school
  - contact details.

In addition, the site can be used for communication with parents and the local community – with visitors to the site being actively invited to contribute and with parents and members of the local community playing an active role in designing, maintaining and developing the website.

Finding resources to maintain the website

Some schools build the updating of the website into governor or parent support groups or the work of the IT club. If updating the site is built into the curriculum activities of a particular year group then the activity can have clear educational purposes attached to it. For example, each year group can be provided with the opportunities to develop their skills, knowledge, understanding and attitudes about ICT in a systematic way through activities encompassing reading and writing through research across the year groups to find out relevant information for inclusion in the school website. Where the website has a section for parents, the work of updating the section could include collecting data about homework schedules and sporting schedules as well as school trips and meetings to which parents are invited.

Thus the process of working with pupils in creating a school website can involve a number of traditional educational purposes. In addition the children will develop technical skills through this exercise, such as the use of digital cameras, digital video cameras, scanners, as well as computer soft-ware, the construction of web pages, ways in which to search the internet, questions of design and marketing, and their communication skills. Similarly pupils may improve these skills through developing a school's intranet (a network private to the school with similar features to the internet) (see Chapter 13 on networks).

In considering the content of the school's website, the question of the level of interactivity to be provided has to be decided. There has to be a reason for anyone to return to the site for a second visit. Providing interactivity and regular updating of key aspects of the site is therefore to be planned for. Some schools will provide an email link to the school and provide curricu-lum materials which can be downloaded; for example, by parents.

The need for an email policy

As teachers gain their own email addresses at work, a school will wish to develop a policy about parent–teacher contact. Where numbers of pupils are small, this may not be problematic, though teachers should be wary of sending emails without considering that they have the same status as formal letters from the school. Where parents are separated, the separated parent may wish to keep better contact with the child's progress through contact with the teacher and the school website. Before schools offer parents open access to teachers via email, the implications for teacher time should be carefully considered. Some teachers recommend that email messages between teachers and parents be treated as a formal communication from the school. This means that procedures followed for the sending of formal letters between home and school should be applied. These may include a requirement for clearance from the headteacher and record keeping through central filing.

Ethical issues

A school may decide to have only part of the website public with other areas being accessed only by those who have passwords. There are ethical issues related to the publication of material on the public site. Pupils' names, photographs and contact details should be kept private. For this reason, the school intranet may provide the major electronic work area for staff and pupils. The public open access site of the school would then be differ-ently managed. How communication with parents is managed in this situation is a school decision.

Copyright issues need to be given due consideration and disclaimers should be added where appropriate. BECTA give guidance on copyright issues.[1] Schools must also consider their obligations under the Data Protection Act.[2]

Activity14.1 Evaluating the school's website

Does the school in which you are teaching have a website? View this or one from a similar school and consider its purposes and functions. Who is the intended audience: parents, prospective parents, pupils, other members of the community, Ofsted? Who are the majority of users of the site? How are children and members of the wider community involved? Review your ideas about the functions and purposes of these websites against the options in 'The functions and purpose of the website' (p. 231) and 'Extract from Sutton on Sea Primary School website' (below).

The construction of a website

Sutton on Sea Primary School in Lincolnshire provides useful guidance on school website building. This is set out below.

Extract from Sutton on sea Primary School website

Hints and tips for building a web-site:
REMEMBER YOUR AUDIENCE
Provide something of interest for children, teachers, parents and the local community
Invite them to give comments and suggestions
When appropriate, write in a one-to-one style
Make them feel welcome
MAKE IT FUN!
Think carefully about colour schemes
Provide plenty of content for kids – remember that they come in all ages!
Stay away from the site just being an electronic school brochure – most visitors haven't time to wade through pages of text. Unless you are presenting something new, brochures are perhaps better left to traditional methods
Provide humour: Most 'surfers' use the internet as a leisure activity – it should be pleasurable
UPDATE REGULARLY
Allocate and share responsibilities for different parts of the site around the school

continued

Keep news new and don't be afraid to use the Delete button on out-of-date pages
Your site WILL grow – plan for expansion from the start
GIVE SOMETHING FOR FREE
Something to print & use. Postcards of your town by Snail Mail on request
A free to enter competition
KEEP IT FAST
Limit the number and size of graphics on any one page
Don't make pages too long – it's hard mouse work scrolling! Break a long page into 2 or 3 smaller ones and link them.
Make navigation and links easy to follow – text links are simple, fast and obvious
PROMOTE YOUR SITE
Register with the internet search engines
Add your web and email address to school notepaper
Make links to other school sites and ask them to link back to you
Notify education newsgroups and mailing lists (*http://www.sutton. lincs.sch.uk/tes/article/hintstips.html*)

You may have heard of HTML. This is the programming language which is used to construct web pages. However, there are a number of software packages which allow you to construct web pages in much the same way that you produce any word processed document so that you do not need to know HTML. Also some modern PCs allow you to save text or documents as HTML files. Demonstration copies of these are often available free of charge.[3] Software which is being used for educational purposes is often available at a substantial discount. It is also possible to download pages from the internet using software designed for the purpose. Webwhacker software is available as a free trial.[4]

When you have produced your web pages, they will need to be sent (uploaded) to a computer set up for this purpose (a server). If your school is part of a wider grouping of schools, for example, an LEA, then it is possible that you will be allowed to have space on the LEA intranet service. Alternatively the company providing the internet service for your school will be able to advise you about the availability of server space.

In recent months, a number of internet service providers have started to offer services free of charge, including the hosting of websites. A list of these can be obtained from the website supporting the secondary version of this book.[5]

Advice to parents on ICT issues

Schools need to be able to respond to parents' queries about appropriate software, hardware and ways of supporting their children's learning using ICT. In many cases, schools will be able to draw on advice from a local authority team and, through them, to the shared body of knowledge about good practice developed by teachers in the local area. In other cases, schools have established relationships with independent advisers. In some areas, what were LEA services for advice and support in ICT are now offered independently and parents themselves may be able to take advantage of bulk purchases organised by such centres.

The work pupils do at home using ICT should complement not replace what is done at school, therefore, recommendations to parents about useful CD-ROMs should take that into account. Schools and teachers need to ensure that those pupils who have not got access to computers at home are not disadvantaged. Alternative supplementary and complementary materials to computer work should also be suggested. Where parents are able to provide access to computers and the internet at home, schools may wish to encourage parents to work with pupils on structured activities around carefully selected sites for various curriculum areas. There are a number of emerging online resources for parents which you may find useful to explore (see section 'Useful website resources for parents' at end of chapter).

Where pupils are accessing the internet from home, then parents may be interested in having the guidelines about use set out in 'Extract from Sutton on Sea Primary School website' (p. 233–4) and 'Safety guidelines' (below).

Advising parents: internet use

As far as work with ICT within school is concerned, the adoption of an acceptable use policy such as the one suggested by the National Association for Co-ordinators and Teachers of IT, ACITT[6] seems imperative. Guidelines for ICT use outside school are starting to become available. Stephen Heppell at ULTRALAB, a research unit of Anglia Polytechnic University, offers some useful advice, available on the *Schools OnLine* web-pages.[7]

Safety guidelines for students, teachers and parents

The internet reaches out across the whole world and has come of age as a communication medium. This is exciting but also means that the full spectrum of individuals that make our world interesting and occasionally dangerous are also 'out there' on the internet too. Common sense rules that work in the rest of our lives also work on

continued

the internet. Common sense is valuable in any context, including this one.

- Never give out identifying information – your home address, phone number, school – in a public messaging area like chat or user groups.
- People at the other end of an email are not always what they seem. Someone claiming to be 'she' and 14 could be 'he' and 40. This may not matter but think carefully before giving personal information out, or developing a relationship.
- If you come across messages that are deliberately provocative, obscene, racist, illegal, pornographic, threatening or that simply make you feel uncomfortable, do not respond to them. In doing so you would be opening a dialogue with the person who posted the message.
- If you receive messages that are harassing or otherwise disturbing, talk about it with people you trust and forward the message(s) to your service provider with a note about your concerns.
- Just because it comes out of a computer does not mean it is true! Be sceptical of information over the net until you have identified its source. Seemingly credible stories can be invented and circulated for many reasons (for example political advantage).
- Any offer that is 'too good to be true' is probably neither 'too good' nor 'true'!
- Put computers in social areas. Our own (and our friends') social rules and habits are a good check of our behaviours. In schools don't place monitors facing the wall, in homes get computers out of the bedroom. It will be worth the move for the discussion around the screen that will result.
- Never, ever, ever arrange to meet as a result of an electronic contact unless parents and/or teachers are aware of what is happening. If you do meet, make sure the first meetings are in a public place in the presence of friends, parents or adults that they know.
- Don't panic! There is simply so much that is good and useful and exciting on the net; working together on projects and tasks will always be less likely to cause problems than just browsing around endlessly.
- Talking about what we all discover and exploring each other's discoveries will all help to build constructive use of time.

Also, parents could be in touch with relevant organisations such as the Parent Information Network (PIN),[8] an independent national support membership organisation with the aim of helping parents support children using computers. There is a lot of useful material on their site. Another useful information source might be the quarterly magazine *PC Home*, which features articles on educational issues as well as information on hardware and software.[9]

ULTRALAB, Anglia Polytechnic University's learning technology research centre, produces a number of useful guides.[10]

Of interest is, of course, also BECTA's *Information sheet on parents and IT*[11] which gives an introduction to how ICT can be used to support children's learning and some advice for parents *vis-à-vis* computer use. BECTA stresses, for instance, that computer literacy and ICT capability in children goes beyond requisite technical skills and encompasses knowledge about when and when not to use ICT and an ability to reflect on personal ICT use. An appreciation of some of the ethical issues surrounding ICT use are also deemed to be of importance and the role of parents in all these contexts is pointed out.

BECTA's advice about safeguarding appropriate computer use in the home is shown below.

Advice to parents

- Keep the computer in a communal area of your home, such as the living room.
- Take an interest in what children are doing with the computer.
- Ask children to show you how it works and explain how they use computers in school.
- If a modem is being used, control the activity by monitoring times used and numbers dialled.
- Advise children to take care whenever they are online reminding them never to give out any personal information about themselves – particularly full names, addresses, phone numbers, or financial information.
- Ask children to avoid responding to anyone who leaves obnoxious, sexual or menacing email and report all electronic harassment and/or abuse to their parents.
- Make sure that computing and video games are only two activities amongst many that children enjoy.

Homework and ICT

In the case study which follows, the school provided computers for every pupil. Equity of access is a particular problem for teachers who wish to use ICT in setting homework: schools overcome these issues by providing access in the library area, in lunchtime and after-school clubs, and in homework clubs. Pachler identifies a number of ways in which homework can be used to 'supplement, extend and/or differentiate what happens in the classroom and it can reinforce or consolidate work carried out in school' (1999: 240). He goes on to point out that 'Pupils can benefit from the attention given to them by "significant others", e.g., their parents/guardians at home or ICT/homework club supervisors in school, as well as make use of reference material which might not be available during the lesson' (1999: 241). Many teachers also cite the BBC *Bitesize Revision* material[12] as being helpful.

Schools may wish to consider the implications of the findings of a survey commissioned by *HomeCampus*, an old online learning service from BT. The findings stated that the use of computers at home seems to increase fathers' involvement with their children's school-related work:

> 16 per cent of dads with home computers were involved with their children's home learning, compared with just 9 per cent of fathers relying on traditional homework resources. Computers and the internet provide men with the opportunity and incentive to interact more with their children, BT suggests.
>
> (*The Guardian*, January 13, 1998)

The following case study shows how in one project teachers ran workshops for parents so that they were able to support their children who were using portable computers at home for homework.

Case study: working with parents and very small portable computers – developing home/school links

In this section Ray Barker and Glen Franklin describe the work with parents undertaken in the National Literacy Association's Docklands Learning Acceleration Project.

This Project, as described earlier, in association with the London Docklands Development Corporation, worked with over six hundred 8 and 9 year-olds, aiming to raise standards and expectations of children's literacy through using a range of multimedia and portable technology, as well as more traditional methods. The Project team worked alongside teachers and children in the classroom, initiating activities and developing work for home and school.

The Project used small hand-held portable computers (Acorn Pocket Books similar to Psion Organisers – hand-held and about 14cm × 8cm) to develop literacy skills and to involve the families and the local community.

The portable computers were introduced into the Project as a way of allowing children and their parents and carers access to ICT in a portable format. The London Docklands Development Corporation had a focus, not only to work with schools, but also to contribute to the lives of Docklands residents: enriching their literacy skills and perhaps improving job prospects in the area. The Project looked to provide links between work at home and in school, setting up a home/school literacy partnership with a technological focus. Teachers set up contracts with parents, so that the children took a portable computer home on a regular basis, with a class topic to research or homework to finish.

It became clear that, although most parents welcomed and supported this initiative, some had little experience of working with ICT and felt apprehensive about this new approach. We were aware that we could get into the situation of a parent being unable to support the child through lack of confidence (like being unable to help with maths homework!) which could damage the partnership process. Although the children were being trained in school so that they could be the 'expert' at home, the parents needed to be aware of the operating procedures if they were going to be an active partner in the homework activity.

Aims

As part of the Project, the team decided to initiate workshops for the parents and carers of the children in our target group in order to:

- provide parents with initial word processing skills using the computers;
- assist parents by providing practical activities which could be carried out at home with their children using the computers;
- support parents in their understanding of the whole process of writing, through from drafting to publication, and the role they can play in supporting their children in this process.

Proposed outcomes

At the end of the workshops, it was hoped that there would be positive outcomes for both the parents involved and the schools who were hosting the workshops.

For the parents:

- a certificate of accreditation from the NLA;
- practical structured activities for working at home with children;

- increased understanding of literacy teaching methods;
- established links with schools.

For the schools:

- increased parental involvement and interest;
- benefits for learning – home/school work will be given a higher profile.

The workshops had a double focus: it was hoped that parents would extend their own ICT skills, whilst at the same time gaining knowledge and understanding of the learning process. Consequently the learning outcomes were as follows.

In word-processing, to:

- identify the elements of hardware and software required to produce a finished product using the computers;
- understand the necessary computer terminology to complete the tasks required;
- input text, using Spell Check and Thesaurus facilities;
- understand and complete the process of downloading and printing from the Pocket Books to a desktop (Acorn or PC) computer;
- begin to explore formatting, importing of graphics and changing fonts on the desktop computer as appropriate to task;
- understand and use the basic principles of file management, memory space and interacting between one or more programs.

In supporting their child's progress, to:

- produce simple activities, games and books, related to a specific language aspect to support their own child at home;
- complete a writing task from an original idea through the drafting and editing procedures to a final presentation;
- begin to understand some of the processes used by schools in the teaching of literacy.

A certificate of Accreditation from the National Literacy Association would be presented to course participants who completed the above activities.

The workshop sessions

The workshops were held over four weeks for one afternoon a week. The sessions were structured in the following way:

- Initial introductions on the first day.

- Feedback from previous sessions – sharing the homework activities.
- Introducing one new area of word processing each week stressing the educational links.
- Provide opportunities to practise this and to devise an activity to try at home.

The host school loaned the portable computers for each afternoon, although the Project provided replacement batteries, which was greatly appreciated by the school!

It was important to the success of the workshops that the Project team staffed and ran the workshop sessions, so no school staff time was required. We needed this to be beneficial to the school and not to cause organisational disruption in an already busy day. However, communication between school and the Project team was crucial if the teachers were to build on the success of the workshops.

When the workshops were completed, there was a special presentation ceremony, when the Headteacher helped the children to present the certificates to their parents.

Was it successful?

In almost all the schools, parents who attended the workshops continued to come into school and work alongside children using the portable computers. Also, interestingly, they continued to develop ICT skills, moving into wider word-processing and data-handling applications. One parent went on to enrol on a full-time technical course.

As parents gained in confidence using the technology, they became more interested in the literacy and language work in the school, and provided positive support and encouragement both to their own children and to others in the class. Barriers between home and school had been broken down and a positive working partnership established.

The majority of the parents who attended the workshops were women. Initially tentative about their ability with ICT, they gained in confidence and increased their skills base. This also provided a positive role model for the girls in the class who were reticent about their own ability on computers.

Parents' enthusiasm for the technology has led to more interest being shown and thus has increased the children's motivation. Everyone is learning together.

Links with other parents in the school were made, developing a network of school support which has continued to grow after the Project intervention has ceased.

The workshops have contributed towards engendering positive and supportive attitudes to the acquisition of literacy, and played an important role in the success of the Docklands Learning Acceleration Project.

Activity 14.2 Using small hand-held computers to develop literacy

If you wish to replicate the project Ray and Glen describe in your own school, find out the likely cost to your school of these small portable computers. Do not get fixated on the problems with choosing and buying lots of equipment – the computer is only a tool used to help pupils achieve learning outcomes more effectively. Ray and Glen recommend that you start with enough of the computers for one group; for example, approximately six pupils. Start small with a pilot project focusing on a specific aspect of literacy and then develop the project from there, learning from your mistakes in the pilot. Consider whether there are ways of funding the purchase of these through school activities or community links. If your school is prepared to support development in this area, draw up a plan for action to take the ideas forward. Headings for an action plan are provided in Table 14.1 to give you a planning framework.

Case study: parents and children's writing stories with portable computers

The aims of The National Literacy Association's Docklands Learning Acceleration Project are described earlier (p. 238). The Project used Acorn Pocket Book computers (similar to Psion Organiser that is, hand-held) to develop story writing and to involve the families at home.

At the start of the Project the stories written by the children tended to be in the present tense and the first person, with little development of text and limited vocabulary. Also, the children did not see the need for redrafting. They had written it by hand once; they thought they had finished!

The Project provided class sets of Acorn Pocket Books. These offered great opportunities for differentiation in the classroom. For example, less able children began by taking the text of familiar story books and using the edit facilities to change characters, adjectives and events. This provided scaffolding. The children did not have to create stories out of thin air. The computer helped them to see how stories are constructed.

The more able children used the Pocket Book for their first draft. This first attempt tended to be of the '– and then I did –' variety, but the drafting process can become more complex depending on the child.

Using the Pocket Book, it was easy to break the original piece into manageable chunks and ask 'What happened next?' Putting in line breaks

Table 14.1 Hand-held computers project action plan

What exact curriculum focus do you wish to develop through the use of the computers	What actions have to be taken for you to be able to do this*	Who may be able to provide the support and resources or what activities could provide resources (e.g., sponsored event)	Timescale	Deadline for completion	Criteria for successful achievement of your goal

* Answering this question will provide a list of actions. Answer the questions in the following columns for each action. Consider financial resources, training of staff, involvement of parents, designing of an appropriate curriculum task, establishing a group of teachers to work together and so on.

and paragraphs, enabled the children to see the need for further clarification and information in their story. Once the work had been through one or two redrafts on the portable computers, the story was printed out from the PC and the children used pen and paper to continue editing their work. Seeing their work in print looked more real to them and they were able to see the story in a format similar to how the final piece would look. Once the last draft was complete the children were then able to go back to the PC and complete their story for presentation. At this stage children began to decide on the appropriate software to produce their final piece. The Pocket Book was definitely a means to an end!

Using the portable computers meant children were more in control of their own writing. Children who were having great difficulty with writing now felt that they could write well. The Pocket Book provided access to a range of tools which, as children gained confidence in the operating procedures, they could utilise as required. There is a level of ICT capability the children need to reach (they need to be able to use the software on the computer, this is very, very basic word processing, spreadsheet and database software), but once this is established they can forge ahead. For example, they can use the Spell program to experiment and have fun with words.

In order to involve parents in the writing process, once children had completed an initial draft, they took their Pocket Book home and worked on the editing with their parents. The exciting part is that when you send the Portable computers out, you just do not know what is going to come back! In the past, sometimes sending written drafts home was not popular with children or parents. It often seemed to cause arguments: spelling and handwriting were such obvious concerns for parents that they focused on the child's errors more than supporting the content of the work. There had not been enough guidance given to parents about how to help. Now, using the Pocket Book, there seemed to be more awareness of drafting procedures. Editing became a more sharing and productive activity. There have been positive outcomes using spell checkers. The spell check shows words that are wrong, but it also tells children words they have got right! This has been a great boost to children who are beginning to succeed as writers.

Pieces of work returned to school were produced with obvious support from home, in families where literacy does not usually have a high status. Parental support can be such a boost to children's self-esteem!

The Project team gave guidance and suggested activities to parents, showing how to use the spell check positively with their children by looking at the options the check provides and comparing the child's attempt with the correct spelling: 'see how close you were!'

There had to be careful preparation before the Portable computers were sent home. Teachers needed to spend time getting to know the Pocket Book for themselves, becoming familiar with the technology and what it would do. Training sessions were provided by the Project team. Also, the children needed to be familiar with using the operating procedures. It was important to have a focus: the children had to see that the Pocket Book was an appropriate tool for the task. Too much, too quickly served only to confuse. They needed to be secure in the operations if they were to be in the role of 'expert' at home.

Once the children were confident, the parents were contacted and invited to sign a contract agreeing to be responsible for the computer whilst it was at home and to ensure that their child would be escorted to and from school on the days the Pocket Book was coming home.

Management issues, such as maintenance of batteries, became easier as the children developed in confidence and technical proficiency. Schools organised rotas for homework activities, asking families to identify which days were more suitable. Organising the days in this way gave teachers space and time to respond to the work completed at home. It was essential that the homework was integrated back into the school work as immediately as possible, so that children felt their teacher was valuing the input.

Parents responded positively to becoming involved with the homework activities. The main reason for such a positive response was the enthusiasm of the children. Once they saw the value they were able to tell their parents 'Look I've got this and I want to use it!' The Project ran accredited Pocket Book Workshops for parents which were very successful.

Parents sometimes expressed concern about 'real' writing, meaning handwriting. Teachers ensured that there was a balance of activities in the classroom and continually emphasised that the Pocket Book is a tool which is useful for specific tasks – it was not the only method for writing schools used!

The children in the Docklands Project developed as writers. They saw ICT as a route to becoming 'real writers' – actively creative rather than simply scribes. These children now have a different approach to language. Their story writing is slower and more reflective. Teachers are seeing development in quality as opposed to quantity: it is not a case any more of extremely long ramblings. Often pieces are shorter, but with witty word play, a range of descriptive language and evidence of choices made. The Pocket Book offers a framing of text for the more reluctant writer. It looks more self-contained and not as daunting as a large, blank A4 sheet!

Using word processing has also made conferencing between teacher and child much easier, as the work is clearer in print. In some cases, children can read this back more confidently than they can read their own handwriting. It also helps them to spot punctuation and spelling errors.

The outcomes show the children are more technically capable. They can select appropriate tools for their task. They are sharing their work productively with their families. They are able to produce writing of quality and are proud to say 'I wrote that!'

Activity 14.3 Strategies for involving parents

Consider the strategies used in the Docklands project to involve parents. How would you go about this in your school?

Summary

Each school finds itself in a unique position with respect to the ways in which ICT can be used to link home and school use for their local community. In this chapter, the intention has been to introduce issues which schools may wish to consider in using ICT in this way and to highlight some existing practice which many schools will be able to adopt. Issues of equity of access were highlighted in the introduction and it is acknowledged that a variety of approaches may be appropriate for schools as they manage a situation where some children and parents are more computer literate than many of the staff and yet at the same time, there are children and parents in their school community who have virtually no access to computers.

Notes

1 BECTA guidance on copyright issues on the web is available on *http://www. becta.org.uk/info-sheets/copyright.html*

2 Information about the Data Protection Act can be found on *http://www. open.gov.uk/dpr/dprhome.htm*

3 Sites such as the Tucows site on *http://tucows.cableinet.net/* or on *http://www. datafellows.com* offer the opportunity to download software for use on a trial basis. Some software is also free to use without restriction. For an example of software designed for children to use together in the construction of a website try Web Workshop from Tag Developments Ltd, 25 Pelham Road, Gravesend, Kent DA11 OHU.

4 Try *http://www.bluesquirrel.com/products/whacker.html* for a demonstration version. These take some time to download if you are using a modem. The following pack which includes an instruction guide plus the software is very easy to use: *Educators' Guide to Webwhacker* available from Logotron, 124 Cambridge Science Park, Milton Road, Cambridge CB4 4ZS, tel: 01223 425558 fax: 01223 425 349.

5 The website for *Learning to Teach with ICT in the Secondary School* list many free ISPs. It is available on *http://www.ioe.ac.uk/lie/ict*

6 Advice to parents on an acceptable use policy is suggested by the National Association for Co-ordinators and Teachers of IT, ACITT see *http://www.acitt. org.uk/aup.html*

7 The *Schools OnLine* web-pages are available at *http://sol.ultralab.anglia.ac. uk/pages/schools_online/*

8 Parent Information Network (PIN) can be found on *Parent Information Network (PIN): http://www.pin-parents.com*

9 PC Home is available on *http://www.idg.co.uk/pchome/*

10 ULTRALAB, Anglia Polytechnic University's learning technology research centre, provides *Safety guidelines for students, teachers and parents* by Stephen Heppell at *http://sol.ultralab.anglia.ac.uk/pages/schools_online/userSupport/Safety_ advice/* and ULTRALAB at *http://www.ultralab.anglia.ac.uk*

11 BECTA's *Information Sheet on Parents and IT* is available from *http://www.becta. org.uk/info-sheets/parents.html*

12 The BBC *Bitesize Revision* material is available at: *http://db.bbc.co.uk/education-bitesize/pkg_main.p_home*

References and Further Reading

Pachler, N. (1999) 'Linking school with home use', in Leask, M. and Pachler, N. *Learning to Teach using ICT*, London: Routledge.

Wolfendale, S. and Bastiani, J. (in press) *The Contribution of Parents to School Effectiveness*, London: David Fulton.

Useful website resources for parents

Sites providing resources for parents include the following:

Anglia Campus by British Telecom and Anglia Multimedia
http://www.angliacampus.com

GCSE Bitesize revision by the BBC
http://db.bbc.co.uk/education-bitesize/pkg_main.p_home

Information sheet on: Parents and IT by BECTA
http://www.becta.org.uk/info-sheets/parents.html

Learning Station by the BBC
http://www.bbc.co.uk/education/schools/index.html

Parent Information Network (PIN)
http://www.pin-parents.com

PC Home
http://www.idg.co.uk/pchome/

Safety guidelines for Students, Teachers And Parents by Stephen Heppell
http://sol.ultralab.anglia.ac.uk/pages/schools_online/userSupport/Safety_advice/

ULTRALAB
http://www.ultralab.anglia.ac.uk

Argosphere
http://www.argosphere.net

BBC Education: Parents (Primary focus)
http://www.bbc.co.uk/education/parents/

Education Online Home Education Pages
http://www.educate.co.uk/homelinks.htm

Education Otherwise
http://www.netlink.co.uk/users/e_o/mindex.htm

The Exploratorium
http://www.exploratorium.edu

IT for all
http://www.ITforall.org.uk

Appendix

Initial Teacher Training National Curriculum for the Use of Information and Communications Technology in Subject Teaching

Introduction

IMPORTANT

This curriculum is different from those for primary and secondary English, mathematics and science because it does not relate to a particular subject. It is concerned with the ways in which Information and Communications Technology (ICT) can be used effectively in the teaching of other subjects in the pupils' National Curriculum.

ICT is more than just another teaching tool. Its potential for improving the quality and standards of pupils' education is significant. Equally, its potential is considerable for supporting teachers, both in their everyday classroom role, for example by reducing the time occupied by the administration associated with it, and in their continuing training and development. It covers the wide range of ICT now available, e.g. computers, the Internet, CD-ROM and other software, television and radio, video, cameras and other equipment. While it is recognised that many teachers will also be responsible for developing pupils' IT capability using ICT, that is not the focus of this document.

The requirements will come into effect from September 1998. The final year of undergraduate courses will be exempt from this requirement for 1998/99 only.

For primary trainees, this curriculum applies to training in the core subjects (English, mathematics and science) and their specialist subject(s). For secondary trainees, this curriculum applies to training in their specialist subject(s).

The curriculum aims, in particular, to equip every newly qualified teacher with the knowledge, skills and understanding to make sound decisions about when, when not, and how to use ICT effectively in teaching particular subjects. Although this curriculum applies to all trainees, the knowledge, understanding and skills required will often differ between subjects or phases.

Some examples are given in the document to illustrate particular points, but it is the responsibility of the ITT provider to ensure that the ways trainees are taught to use ICT are firmly rooted within the relevant subject and phase, rather than teaching how to use ICT generically or as an end in itself. In order to support providers in this, the TTA proposes to produce separate exemplification, by subject and phase, which can be used in conjunction with this document.

With the introduction of the National Grid for Learning, it becomes even more important for newly qualified teachers (NQTs) to be confident and competent in using ICT effectively in their teaching. The ITT curriculum will also form the basis of the Lottery-funded training for serving teachers in the use of ICT.

Providers of ITT must ensure that only those trainees who have shown that they have the knowledge, understanding and skills to use ICT effectively in teaching subject(s) are judged to have successfully completed an ITT course leading to Qualified Teacher Status (QTS). Detailed requirements of what trainees must demonstrate they know, understand, and can do before being awarded QTS are set in the *Standards for the Award of Qualified Teacher Status (Annex A)*.

The National Curriculum for the use of ICT in subject teaching should therefore be read alongside the relevant ITT National Curriculum, where applicable, and the *Standards for the Award of Qualified Teacher Status (Annex A)*.

Every attempt has been made to 'future-proof' the content of this document, but ICT is changing rapidly and it will be necessary to keep the curriculum under close review. In order to make the requirements of the ICT curriculum clear to a wide readership, the use of jargon and technical language has been avoided, but the correct terminology has been used where appropriate.

The curriculum is in two sections.

Section A   Effective teaching and assessment methods
This section sets out the teaching and assessment methods which, as part of all courses, all trainees must be taught and be able to use. This curriculum focuses on teaching and assessment methods which have a particular relevance to the use of ICT in subject teaching. Trainees must be given opportunities to practise, in taught sessions and in the classroom, those methods and skills described in this section.

Section B   Trainees' knowledge and understanding of and competence with information and communications technology
This section sets out the knowledge and understanding of, and competence with, ICT which trainees need to support effective reaching. Providers of ITT must audit trainees' knowledge and understanding of the ICT specified in paragraphs 12–19.

Where gaps in trainees' knowledge are identified, providers must make arrangements to ensure that trainees gain that knowledge during the course and that, *by the end of the course*, they are competent in using their knowledge of ICT in their teaching. ITT providers will decide how best to teach the content of Section B. While some of the content may require direct teaching, some could be taught alongside aspects of Section A.

The ITT National Curriculum for ICT does not attempt to cover everything that needs to be taught to trainee teachers if they are to use ICT effectively in their teaching. It is expected that providers of ITT will include in their courses other aspects of ICT, which are not specified in this curriculum, in relation to particular subjects.

This document specifies a *curriculum*. It is not a course model. All ITT courses must include the content specified, but it is for providers to decide how and where the various aspects should be included. For example, although this curriculum is set out in separate sections, there is no expectation that providers will teach these discretely. Indeed, it is expected that many providers will integrate aspects of the sections when designing courses. Similarly there is no intention to impose on providers of ITT the way in which the curriculum should be delivered and assessed, nor to specify the materials or activities which should be used to support the training. Providers should use this curriculum as the basis for devising courses which are coherent, intellectually stimulating and professionally challenging.

Initial teacher training is the first stage in the professional preparation of teachers and this curriculum provides the foundation of knowledge, understanding and skills which will enable every NQT to use ICT effectively in their first teaching post. Providers may, if they wish, go beyond the minimum standard specified in this document. They should, however, guard against over-interpretation of the content if the curriculum is to remain manageable, e.g. in Section B, the content listed in paragraph 12 should be interpreted at a level appropriate for a general ICT user and not at a level which would be required by a network or system manager. The content specified should therefore be interpreted at a level which supports effective teaching by a newly qualified teacher in their first post.

The TTA Career Entry Profile will enable a summary of each NQT's strengths and priorities for development during the induction year to be conveyed from initial teacher training to his or her first teaching post. During their induction year, NQTs will have the opportunity to consolidate and build on what they have learned in initial training. It is expected that, throughout their careers, teachers will continue to improve their teaching skills, and keep up to date with ICT and its application to subject pedagogy, so that they can teach rigorously and in a way which communicates their enthusiasm for the subject to pupils, in order to stimulate pupils' intellectual curiosity and to maintain and raise standards of attainment.

Throughout the document, the examples are non-statutory. The numbers and letters throughout the curriculum are for reference purposes only, and do not necessarily indicate a particular teaching sequence or hierarchy of knowledge, skills and understanding.

A   Effective teaching and assessment methods

1   Trainees must be taught how to decide when the use of ICT is beneficial to achieve teaching objectives in the subject and phase, and when the use of ICT would be less effective or inappropriate. In making these decisions, trainees must be taught how to take account of the functions of ICT and the ways that these can be used by teachers in achieving subject teaching and learning objectives. This includes:

   a   how the speed and automatic functions of ICT can enable teachers to demonstrate, explore or explain aspects of their teaching, and pupils' learning, more effectively;

   b   how the capacity and range of ICT can enable teachers and pupils to gain access to historical, recent or immediate information;

   c   how the provisional nature of information stored, processed and presented using ICT allows work to be changed easily;

   d   how the interactive way in which information is stored, processed and presented can enable teachers and pupils to:

      i   explore prepared or constructed models and simulations, where relevant to the subject and phase;

      ii   communicate with other people, locally and over distances, easily and effectively;

      iii search for and compare information from different sources;

      iv   present information in ways which are accessible in different forms for different audiences.

Trainees should be taught what the implications of these functions are for achieving teaching objectives in the relevant subjects(s), e.g. in mathematics and science, the use of a calculator or a spreadsheet may remove the tedium of repetitive calculations and enable pupils to focus their attention on an emerging numerical pattern or the relationship between successive readings. However, trainees must be made aware when pupils' skills in mental or written calculation are not being developed and therefore the activity may not suit the particular teaching objectives in hand.

2   Trainees must be taught how to use ICT most effectively in relation to subject-related objectives, including:

a   using ICT because it is the most effective way to achieve teaching and learning objectives, not simply to motivate pupils or as a reward or sanction for good or poor work or behaviour;

b   avoiding the use of ICT for simple or routine tasks which would be better accomplished by other means;

c   knowing that, where ICT is to be used, appropriate preparation of equipment, content and methodology is required;

d   avoiding giving the impression that the quality of presentation is of overriding importance and supersedes the importance of content;

e   structuring pupils' work to focus on relevant aspects and to maximise use of time and resource, e.g. teaching pupils to refine searches rather than allowing pupils to search freely on the Internet or on CD-ROM;

f   having high expectations of the outcomes of pupils' work with ICT, including:

　　i   expecting pupils to use ICT to answer valid questions appropriate to the subject matter being taught;

　　ii   when appropriate, requiring pupils to save work, and evaluate and improve it;

g   making explicit the links between:

　　i   the ICT application and the subject matter it is being used to teach;

　　ii   ICT and its impact on everyday applications.

3   For these aspects of lessons where ICT is to be used, trainees must be taught to identify in their planning:

a   the way(s) in which ICT will be used to meet teaching and learning objectives in the subject;

b   key questions to ask and opportunities for teacher intervention in order to stimulate and direct pupils' learning;

c   the way(s) in which pupils' progress will be assessed and recorded;

d   criteria to ensure that judgements about pupils' attainment and progress in the subject are not masked because ICT has been used;

e   any impact of the use of ICT on the organisation and conduct of the subject lesson and how this is to be managed;

f   how the ICT used is appropriate to the particular subject-related objectives in hand and to pupils' capabilities, taking account of the fact that some pupils may already be very competent, e.g. because of home access or through participation in extra-curricular ICT activities, and some may need additional support.

4   Trainees must be taught the most effective organisation of classroom ICT resources to meet learning objectives in the subject, including how to:

a   use ICT with the whole class or a group for introducing or reviewing a topic and ensuring that all pupils cover the key conceptual features of the topic, e.g. through the use of a single screen or display;

b   organise individuals, pairs or groups of children working with ICT to ensure that each participant is engaged, that collaborative effort is balanced, and that teacher intervention and reporting back by pupils takes place where appropriate;

c   make ICT resources available to pupils for research or other purposes which may arise either spontaneously during lessons or as part of planned activity, ensuring that the resource is used profitably to achieve subject-related objectives;

d   position resources for ease of use, to minimise distraction, and with due regard to health and safety;

e   ensure that work done using ICT is linked to work away from the screen, allowing ICT to support teaching rather than dominate activities, e.g. providing sufficient desk/floor space around the hardware to enable the ICT to be used with other materials; providing space to write as well as input from the keyboard; positioning ICT so that pupils are able to sit facing the teacher when required.

5 Trainees must be taught to recognise the specific contribution that ICT can make to teaching pupils with special educational needs in mainstream classrooms based upon the need to:

a   provide access to the curriculum in a manner appropriate to pupils' needs;

b   provide subject-specific support.

6 Trainees must be taught how to choose and use the most suitable ICT to meet teaching objectives, by reviewing a range of generic and subject-specific software critically, including how to:

a   assess its potential for helping to meet teaching objectives;

b   judge its suitability for the age of pupils, their stage of development, and their prior experiences, taking account of language, social and cultural background;

c   evaluate the success of its use in relation to teaching objectives.

7 Trainees must be taught how to contribute to the development and consolidation of pupils' ICT capability within the context of the subject being taught through:

a   explicit discussion and, where necessary, teaching of the ICT skills and applications which are used in the subject;

b   using ICT terminology accurately and appropriately, and explaining to pupils any ICT terminology which arises from the application of ICT to the subject;

    c   using ICT in ways which provide models of good practice for pupils, and insisting that pupils employ correct procedures when using applications.

8   In order to understand how to monitor, evaluate and assess their teaching and pupils' learning in the subject when using ICT, and to evaluate the contribution that ICT has made to the teaching of their subject, trainees must be taught:

    a   how to monitor pupils' progress by:

        i   being clear about teaching objectives and the use of ICT in achieving them;

        ii   observing and intervening in pupils' ICT-based activities to monitor and support their progression towards the identified objectives;

        iii   asking key questions which require pupils to reflect on the appropriateness of their use of ICT;

    b   how to recognise standards of attainment in the subject when ICT resources are used, including:

        i   recognising how access to computer functions might change teacher expectation of pupil achievements, e.g. automatic spell-checking, image-making, graphical representation;

        ii   identifying criteria by which pupils can show what they have learnt as a result of using ICT-based resources from the Internet or CD-ROM, and insisting that pupils acknowledge the reference sources used in their work, e.g. requiring pupils to interpret and present the information gained from a CD-ROM for a specific purpose rather than simply printing off information;

        iii   how to determine the achievement of individuals when the 'product' is the result of a collaborative effort, through observation, record keeping, teacher intervention and pupil–teacher dialogue;

        iv   how to ensure that assessment of ICT-based work reflects pupils' learning and the quality of their work within the subject(s) rather than just the quality of presentation or the complexity of the technology used;

    c   how to use formative, diagnostic and summative methods of assessing pupils' progress in the subject where ICT has been used, including how to set up ICT activities with targeted objectives for assessment and make provision in those activities for all pupils to demonstrate achievement, conceptual understanding and learning through the use of ICT.

9   In addition, trainees on courses providing for pupils aged 3–8 and 3–11 must be taught the importance of introducing pupils in nursery and

reception classes to the use of ICT and to recognise the contribution that ICT can make to this age group, including how to:

a   encourage pupils to become familiar with ICT and positive users of it;

b   ensure that all pupils have opportunities to use ICT, and that their experience takes account of any home use or other previous experience of ICT;

c   identify and teach the skills necessary for handling input devices effectively, e.g. switches, mouse, keyboard;

d   use ICT to support the development of language and literacy, through the use of programs which develop reading and writing, e.g. to reinforce letter/sound correspondence, and encourage pupils to engage with stories, songs and rhymes presented on the screen, as well as through the use of high quality educational broadcasts;

e   use ICT to support the development of numeracy through the use of computer programs and robots which develop and reinforce the use of mathematical language, and the recognition and exploration of numbers, simple mental operations and patterns;

f   use ICT to support pupils' creative development through the use of computer programs which encourage them to explore and experiment with pattern, shape, pictures, sound and colour;

g   encourage pupils working collaboratively with ICT to share responsibilities for making decisions and reaching conclusions, e.g. as they progress through a simple computer adventure game.

10 Opportunities to practise
Trainees must be given opportunities to practise, in taught sessions and in the classroom, those methods and skills described above.

B   Trainees' knowledge and understanding of, and competence with, Information and Communications Technology

Knowledge, understanding and skills in using ICT in subject teaching

Trainees enter initial teacher training with a variety of experiences in ICT. For many, their own knowledge and understanding of ICT may not be sufficient to ensure that they understand how to use ICT in ways which support good teaching, as set out in the QTS standards, including, for example, good pace, challenge, questioning and high expectations of pupils. It may also not be sufficient to ensure that they feel confident about, and are competent in using, ICT to secure progress in pupils' learning within the phase and in the subject(s) they are training to teach. It is likely that most trainees will be familiar with more traditional forms of ICT, e.g. television, video, tape-recorders, and will have experienced their use in education. The content of Section B, therefore, gives greater emphasis to computer-related ICT because it is new, and because trainees' knowledge, understanding and skills in this area may vary considerably from what is required.

Audit

Providers should audit trainees' knowledge, understanding and skills in ICT against the relevant ICT content set out in paragraphs 12 to 19 below. Where gaps in trainees' ICT knowledge, understanding and skills are identified, providers must make arrangements, for example through supported self-study, to ensure that trainees gain the relevant knowledge and understanding during the course and that, *by the end of the course*, trainees are competent in using the ICT specified within the relevant phase and subject(s).

11 In relation to the ICT content set out in paragraphs 12 to 19, trainees must be given opportunities to:
    a   evaluate a range of information and communication technologies, and the content associated with them, e.g. television and radio, video, computers, the Internet, cameras and other equipment, justifying the selection and use of ICT in relation to aspects of their planning, teaching, assessment and class management, including for personal professional use, e.g. in downloading on-line materials for teaching or writing reports;
    b   understand and use correctly the specialist terms associated with the ICT used in the subject which are necessary to enable them to be precise in their explanations to pupils, to discuss ICT in relation to the subject at a professional level, and to read inspection and classroom-focused research evidence with understanding.

Several of the following sections have been divided into two columns. The left-hand column specifies the knowledge and understanding of ICT which all trainees are required to demonstrate by the end of their course. The relevance of different aspects of the specified content will depend on the subjects and ages of the pupils being taught, and providers should pay particular attention to those aspects which are most relevant in each case. The right-hand column has been included to indicate the level of knowledge and understanding required and to give it relevance to teaching in different subjects. The TTA will provide, separately, more detailed subject-specific exemplification which can be used in conjunction with this document.

12 Trainees must demonstrate that they are competent in those areas of ICT which support pedagogy in every subject, including that they:

a   can employ common ICT tools for their own and pupils' benefit, e.g. word processing, e-mail, presentation software, data handling and can use a range of ICT resources, at the level of general users (rather than as network or system managers), including;

i   the common user interfaces, using menus, selecting and swapping between applications, cutting, pasting and copying files, and cutting, copying and pasting data within and between applications;

ii   successfully connecting and setting up ICT equipment, including input devices, e.g. a mouse, touch screen, overlay keyboard, microphone and output devices e.g. printers, screens and loudspeakers;

e.g. connecting a printer to a computer with the correct driver; connecting an overlay keyboard and ensuring that it works;

iii loading and running software;

e.g. CD-ROM;

iv   file management;

e.g. copying, deleting, naming and renaming files;

v   seeking and using operating information, including from on-line help facilities and user guides;

vi   coping with everyday problems and undertaking simple, routine maintenance, with due consideration to health and safety;

e.g. including checking the power is on; checking for loose connections; managing and replacing consumables; good practice in avoiding viruses;

vii understanding the importance of passwords and the general security of equipment and access to it.

b   know and understand the characteristics of information, including:

i   that information must be

e.g. drawing information from

evaluated in terms of its accuracy, validity, reliability, plausibility, bias;

ii   that information takes up memory and that there are implications when saving and compressing files;

iii   that information has to be stored somewhere;

iv   that ICT systems can present static information or changing information;

v   that information can be directly and dynamically linked between applications;

vi   that applications and information can be shared with other people at remote locations.

a CD. ROM (encyclopaedia or newspaper collection);

e.g. a colour image contains more information than its black and white equivalent and can be saved in different ways to increase the amount of available memory;

e.g. in memory, on disc, on a local server, on the Internet; static information e.g. a picture on the screen or a page of text; changing information, e.g. simulations, control programmes;

e.g. changes to numbers in a spreadsheet can link directly to changes in a word processed report; a video clip can be linked to a button on a multimedia application; a picture or text may be linked to on-line information on a network or the Internet;

e.g. for a collaborative project between pupils or teachers in the same or different locations.

13   Trainees must demonstrate in relation to the subject and age(s) of pupils to be taught that they:

a   know how to use ICT to find things out, including, as appropriate for the subjects and the age of pupils to be taught:

i   identifying sources of information and discriminating between them;

e.g. disk, CD-ROM, Internet; up-to-date information from a weather station; low status sources on the Internet with no editorial scrutiny; CD-ROM information which has been through some editorial scrutiny but may be out of date;

ii   planning and putting together a search strategy, including framing useful questions, widening and narrowing down searches;

iii   how to search for information, including using key words and strings and logical operators, such as AND, OR and NOT, indexes and directories;

e.g. translating enquiries expressed in ordinary language into forms required by the system;

iv   collecting and structuring data and storing it for later retrieval, interpretation and correction;

v   interpreting what is retrieved;

e.g. in searching a database or employing an Internet search engine;

vi   considering validity, reliability and reasonableness of outcomes;

e.g. knowing the probable outcome of a calculation rather than just relying on the calculator;

b   know how to use ICT to try things out, make things happen and understand how they happen as appropriate for the subject(s) and the age of pupils to be taught:

i   exploring alternatives;

e.g. changing the variables in a spreadsheet or a simulation;

ii   modelling relationships;

e.g. exploring how changes in variables such as weather and market forces might influence the crop rotation cycle planned by a farmer;

iii   considering cause and effect

e.g. in text editing and presentation; determining the effect of increases in the cost of raw materials when costing production on a spreadsheet; designing a weekly diet to meet nutritional requirements; programming a simple model using LOGO;

iv   predicting patterns and rules, recognising patterns, and hypothesising;

e.g. hypothesising about a rule that underpins a pattern; predicting and simulating; evaluating outcomes e.g.

v knowing how to give instructions

e.g. knowing the importance of the grammar and syntax of instructions in ICT;

graphical outcomes, exploration of colour, shape and form, exploration of sound;

vi sequencing actions;

e.g. moving floor turtles or robots; following a sequence of actions to produce a result;

vii defining conditions e.g. 'if this happens, do that . . .';

e.g. programming feedback into a control device or putting conditions into a spreadsheet formula;

vii understanding how feedback works and the difference between things that do and do not rely on feedback;

e.g. an automatic window opener on a greenhouse; an appliance that will not work until the lid is closed, such as a dishwasher;

c know how to use ICT to communicate and exchange ideas as appropriate to the subject(s) and the age of pupils to be taught:

i presenting ideas, including: identification of audience and purpose; deciding the best means with which to communicate;

e.g. text, numbers, images, sounds or a combination; selecting the appropriate technology to produce the material; adapting the material to ensure that it achieves what it set out to do;

ii exchanging ideas, including identifying the most appropriate medium, and information.

e.g. fax, e-mail or a conferencing system, taking into account the number of people involved, urgency and cost-effectiveness.

14 Trainees must demonstrate that they know those features of ICT which can be used, separately or together, to support teaching and learning in subjects, including:

a speed and automatic functions – the function of ICT which enables routine tasks to be completed and repeated quickly, allowing the user to concentrate on thinking and on tasks such as analysing and looking for patterns within data, asking questions and looking for answers, and explaining and presenting results, as appropriate to the subject(s) and age of pupils being taught, including how ICT can be used to:

i   measure events at long or short time intervals in order to compress or expand events which would normally take very short or long periods of time, and illustrate them to pupils at speeds appropriate to their pace of learning;

e.g. measuring and recording the reducing height of a bouncing ball using freeze-frame video; or measuring and recording the changes in temperature and pressure throughout a weather front; performing rapidly repeating calculations in a spreadsheet to illustrate patterns of numbers; illustrating changes in the distribution of working populations;

ii measure and record events which might otherwise be impossible to gather within a classroom environment;

e.g. collecting data on the movement of people around a school over the period of a week; recording weather data from the passage of a weather front;

iii explore sequences of actions and link the sensing of events with the control of actions;

e.g. building and controlling a working lift or programming the movement of a buggy;

b   capacity and range – the function of ICT, as appropriate to the subject(s) and age of pupils to be taught, to access and to handle large amounts of information; change timescales, or remove barriers of distance; give teachers and pupils access to and control over situations which would normally be outside their everyday experience, including:

i   the range of forms in which ICT can present information;

e.g. voice, text, images, sounds or video;

ii the range of possible appropriate ICT sources, including local sources such as CD-ROM, and remote databases such as the Internet and the National Grid for Learning;

iii how to judge the accuracy of the information and the credibility of its source;

e.g. discussing the fact that anyone can set up a website and there is no quality control over its content;

iv how ICT can be used to gain access to expertise outside the classroom, the school and the local community through communications with experts;

c provisionality – the function of ICT which allows changes to be made easily and enables alternatives to be explored readily, and as appropriate to the subject(s) and age of pupils to be taught:

i how to make best use of the ability to make rapid changes, including how to create texts, designs and models which may be explored and improved in the light of evaluation;

e.g. word-processing, computer-aided design and manufacture, spreadsheet models, animations, sound or video presentations;

ii how to judge when and when not to encourage exploration and change using ICT;

iii how saving work at different stages enables a record to be kept of the development of ideas;

e.g. whether the clarity and accuracy of pupils' writing might be improved through drafting and redrafting;

d interactivity – the function of ICT which enables rapid and dynamic feedback and response, as appropriate to the subject(s) and age of pupils to be taught, including how to determine the most appropriate media to use.

e.g. the changing values in a spreadsheet or the feedback provided from simulation or measurements of factors in an experiment; the responses to queries of an Internet search engine.

15 Trainees must demonstrate that they are aware of the potential of ICT to enable them to prepare and present their teaching more effectively, taking account of:

a the intended audience, including matching and adapting work to subject matter and objectives, pupils' prior attainment, reading ability or special educational needs; recognising the efficiency with which such adaptations can be made using ICT;

b   the most appropriate forms of presentation to meet teaching objectives, e.g. illustrating or explaining using: text; sound; still or moving pictures; live video links; illustrations, graphics or animations; numbers, graphs or charts, separately or in combination.

16   Trainees must demonstrate that they:

a   know and understand the ICT requirements of the pupils' National Curriculum in relation to the phase(s) and subject(s) to be taught;

b   are familiar with the standards as set out in the pupils' National Curriculum for IT, relevant to the phase for which they are training to teach, and know the level of IT capability they should expect of pupils when applying ICT in the subject(s).

17   Trainees must demonstrate that they know how each of the following is relevant to the specialist subject and phase for which they are training:

a   generic procedures and tools, including

    i   understanding the key features and functions used within the subject;

       e.g. word-processors, graphics and desk-top publishing packages, spreadsheets, databases, multimedia and web page authoring tools;

    ii   using ICT to prepare material for pupil use;

       e.g. the use of a word-processing package to create templates to help pupils to write in a modern foreign language; setting up a spreadsheet to help pupils explore relationships and patterns; preparing a video or music sequence;

b   reference resources, including;

    i   how to search reference resources;

       e.g. reference CD-ROMs and World Wide Web sites on the Internet;

    ii   how to incorporate the use of reference resources into teaching;

c   the ICT specific to the subject;

       e.g. graphics packages and scanners in art; computer-aided design (CAD) software and computer-controlled equipment in Design and Technology; sequencing software and midi keyboards in music; dynamic geometry software in mathematics;

d the major teaching programs or 'courseware' to ensure that material is matched to the pupils' competences;

i where content and activities are presented in sequence to teach specific topics;

e.g. multimedia distance learning activities; a series of educational television programmes;

ii where teaching activities are combined with assessment tasks and tests.

e.g. integrated learning systems (ILS); distance learning packages.

18 Trainees must demonstrate that they are aware of:
   a the current health and safety legislation relating to the use of computers, and can identify potential hazards and minimise risks;
   b legal considerations including those related to:
      i keeping personal information on computers, as set out in the Data Protection Act;
      ii copyright legislation relating to text, images and sounds and that relating to copying software;
      iii material which is illegal in this country;
   c ethical issues including:
      i access to illegal and/or unsuitable material through the Internet:
      ii acknowledging sources;
      iii data confidentiality;
      iv the ways in which users of information sources can be (and are) monitored;
      v material which may be socially or morally unacceptable.

19 Trainees must demonstrate that they know how to use ICT to improve their own professional efficiency and to reduce administrative and bureaucratic burdens, including:
   a using ICT to aid administration, record-keeping, reporting and transfer of information;
   b knowing about current classroom-focused research and inspection evidence about the application of ICT to teaching their specialist subject(s), and where it can be found;
   c knowing how to use ICT to join in professional discussions and to locate and access teaching plans, material and other sources of help and support, including through the National Grid for Learning;
   d knowing how ICT can support them in their continuing professional development.

Index